Modal Testing:
Theory and Practice

MECHANICAL ENGINEERING RESEARCH STUDIES

ENGINEERING DYNAMICS SERIES

Series Editor: **Dr. J. B. Roberts,** *University of Sussex, England*

1. Feedback Design of Systems with Significant Uncertainty
    M. J. Ashworth

2. Modal Testing: Theory and Practice
    D. J. Ewins

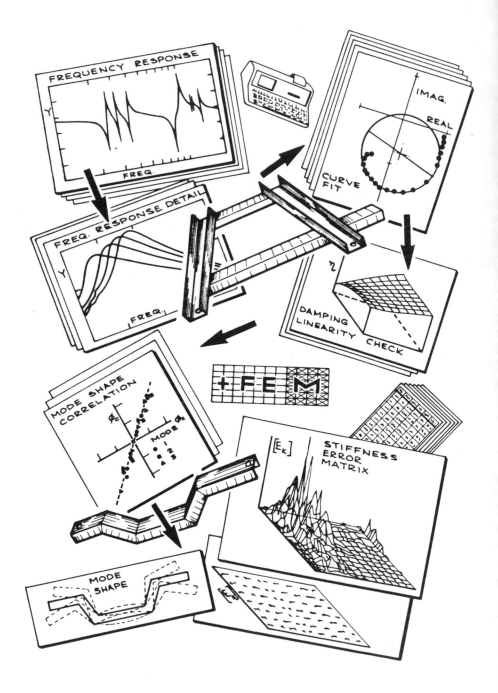

Modal Testing:
Theory and Practice

D. J. Ewins
Professor of Vibration Engineering,
Imperial College of Science and Technology,
London, England

RESEARCH STUDIES PRESS LTD.
Letchworth, Hertfordshire, England

BRÜEL & KJÆR

RESEARCH STUDIES PRESS LTD.
58B Station Road, Letchworth, Herts. SG6 3BE, England

Copyright © 1986, by Research Studies Press Ltd.

First published by Research Studies Press Ltd. in 1984.
Reprinted 1985.

Reprinted with amendments by Research Studies Press
Ltd. for Brüel & Kjær, 1986.

ISBN 0 86380 036 X

Printed in Great Britain

Preface

This book attempts to provide a reasonably detailed coverage of the technology of modal testing. This is not a new subject although many of the most powerful techniques have only recently been developed and the potential of the method only recently recognised. Modal testing is, in effect, the process of constructing a mathematical model to describe the vibration properties of a structure based on test data, rather than a conventional theoretical analysis. As such, it has applications throughout the entire field of engineering.

The subject matter in the book is presented in a particular order, and that for a particular reason. In order to take the maximum advantage of the methods of modal testing, it is essential that an appropriate level of expertise be reached not only in measurement and (data) analysis methods, but also in the theoretical basis upon which the technique is founded. To this end, the reader is encouraged to make a detailed study or review of the theory in Chapter 2 before proceeding to the more practical aspects of the measurement process in Chapter 3. Even here, however, a relatively high level of theoretical competence is expected in order to understand properly the implications and limitations of the different types of measurement method — sine, random and transient excitations and the like.

In Chapter 4, the modal analysis methods used to process the measured data are described, ranging from the basic and relatively simple to the more advanced, computer-dependent. The analysis phase continues into Chapter 5 where the overall modelling process is outlined, treating different levels of complexity of model which are appropriate to the different applications. Then, in Chapter 6, examples are given of some of the many uses to which the product of a modal test may be put, a list which will undoubtedly grow in the next few years.

The opening chapter is rather more general, and serves both as an Introduction to the text and also as an Overview of the subject. As such, it provides an introduction to the rest of the work for the serious student but also presents a condensation of the whole subject for readers who wish to be apprised of the general activities and capabilities of a modal testing facility but who lack the opportunity of the extensive 'hands-on' experience which is essential for mastery of the subject. (In the short course upon which the book is based, the Overview is intended not only for those who will attend the whole course but also for their managers who can only spare a few hours!)

Acknowledgments

It is inevitable that many people contribute to such a work such as this and I should like to acknowledge the support and assistance I have received from several friends and colleagues.

I must record first my gratitude to Professor Peter Grootenhuis with whom I have had the pleasure and privilege of studying and working for some 20 years. His support and encouragement both launched and sustained me in the work which has culminated in this book. The text has developed alongside a series of short courses on Modal Testing, which I have given together with my colleague at Imperial College, David Robb. I am most grateful for his helpful comments on the book and for his many practical contributions. Other university colleagues, both in London and elsewhere, have kindly provided illustrations and, on many occasions, stimulating discussion on all aspects of the subject and I must also acknowledge the very significant contributions provided by several generations of students whose researches have resulted in many of the examples cited in the book. Likewise, many colleagues in industry have provided me with opportunities to work on real-life problems, adding relevance to our research, and have permitted the use of examples from some of these for illustrations here. Without the cooperation of all of these people, there would have been no book.

The actual preparation of the text has been a major undertaking and I am indebted to my secretary, Lavinia Micklem, who has cheerfully produced draft after draft of the manuscript until the publication deadline forced me to abandon further 'improvements'. Scrutiny of each draft brought to light a number of mistakes in the text: I hope that the most recent and concentrated efforts of Frank Lacey, the publishers and myself have succeeded in reducing these to a tolerable number, although I suspect one or two still remain! The illustrations were drawn from many sources but the majority have been prepared by Judi Parkes and Ron Potter, and for their efficient and careful efforts I am most grateful.

Lastly, I must pay tribute to the understanding and support of my family who have patiently watched the date for my 'finishing' the book slip through several of the best months of 1984.

D J Ewins
London, September 1984

Postscript This special reprint appears almost exactly one year after the first edition and I have taken the opportunity to correct a number of errors in the text which survived the initial proof reading stages. I have also made a number of other minor modifications, many in response to some very helpful comments by the first generation of readers. To those who have taken the trouble to bring these various points to my attention I am indeed most grateful.

London, September 1985

ix

Contents

CHAPTER 1
Overview

1.1 INTRODUCTION TO MODAL TESTING

The experimental study of structural vibration has always provided a major contribution to our efforts to understand and to control the many vibration phenomena encountered in practice. Since the very early days of awareness of vibrations, experimental observations have been made for the two major objectives of (a) determining the nature and extent of vibration response levels and (b) verifying theoretical models and predictions. Today, structural vibration problems present a major hazard and design limitation for a very wide range of engineering products. First, there are a number of structures, from turbine blades to suspension bridges, for which structural integrity is of paramount concern, and for which a thorough and precise knowledge of the dynamic characteristics is essential. Then, there is an even wider set of components or assemblies for which vibration is directly related to performance, either by virtue of causing temporary malfunction during excessive motion or by creating disturbance or discomfort, including that of noise. For all these examples, it is important that the vibration levels encountered in service or operation be anticipated and brought under satisfactory control.

The two vibration measurement objectives indicated above represent two corresponding types of test. The first is one where vibration forces or, more usually, responses are measured during 'operation' of the machine or structure under study, while the second is a test where the structure or component is vibrated with a known excitation, often out of its normal service environment. This second type of test is generally made under much more closely-controlled conditions than the former and consequently yields more accurate and detailed information. This type of test – including both the data acquisition and its subsequent analysis – is nowadays called 'Modal Testing' and is the subject of the following text. While we shall be defining the specific quantities and parameters used as we proceed, it is perhaps appropriate to state clearly at this point just what we mean by the name 'Modal Testing'. It is used here to encompass "the processes involved in testing components or structures with the objective of obtaining a mathematical description of their dynamic or vibration behaviour". The form of the 'mathematical description' or model varies considerably from one application to the next: it can be an estimate of natural frequency and damping factor in one case and a full mass-spring-dashpot model for the next.

Although the name is relatively new, the principles of modal testing were laid down many years ago. These have evolved through various phases when descriptions such as 'Resonance Testing' and 'Mechanical Impedance Methods' were used to describe the general area of activity. One of the more important milestones in the development of the subject was provided by the paper in 1947 by Kennedy and Pancu [1]*. The methods described there found application in the accurate determination of natural frequencies and damping levels in aircraft structures and were not out-dated for many years, until the rapid advance of measurement and analysis techniques in the 1960s. This activity paved the way for more precise measurements and thus more powerful applications. A paper by Bishop and Gladwell in 1963 [2] described the state of the theory of resonance testing which, at that time, was considerably in advance of its practical implementation. Another work of the same period but from a totally different viewpoint was the book by Salter [3] in which a relatively non-analytical approach to the interpretation of measured data was proposed. Whilst more demanding of the user than today's computer-assisted automation of the same tasks, Salter's approach rewarded with a considerable physical insight into the vibration of the structure thus studied. However, by 1970 there had been major advances in transducers, electronics and digital analysers and the current techniques of modal testing were established. There are a great many papers which relate to this period, as workers made further advances and applications, and a bibliography of several hundred such references now exists [4], [5]. The following pages set out to bring together the major features of all aspects of the subject to provide a comprehensive guide to both the theory and the practice of modal testing.

One final word by way of introduction: this subject (like many others but perhaps more than most) has generated a wealth of jargon, not all of it consistent! We have adopted a particular notation and terminology throughout this work but in order to facilitate 'translation' for compatibility with other references, and in particular the manuals of various analysis equipment and software in widespread use, the alternative names will be indicated as the various parameters are introduced.

1.2 APPLICATIONS OF MODAL TESTING

Before embarking on both summarised and detailed descriptions of the many aspects of the subject, it is important that we raise the question of why modal tests are undertaken. There are many applications to which the results from a modal test may be put and several of these are, in

* References are listed in Pages 252-254

fact, quite powerful. However, it is important to remember that no single test or analysis procedure is 'best' for all cases and so it is very important that a clear objective is defined before any test is undertaken so that the optimum methods or techniques may be used. This process is best dealt with by considering in some detail the following questions: what is the desired outcome from the study of which the modal test is a part? and, in what form are the results required in order to be of maximum use?

First then, it is appropriate to review the major application areas in current use. In all cases, it is true to say that a modal test is undertaken in order to obtain a mathematical model of the structure but it is in the subsequent use of that model that the differences arise.

(A) Perhaps the single most commonly used application is the measurement of vibration modes in order to compare these with corresponding data produced by a finite element or other theoretical model. This application is often born out of a need or desire to validate the theoretical model prior to its use for predicting response levels to complex excitations, such as shock, or other further stages of analysis. It is generally felt that corroboration of the major modes of vibration by tests can provide reassurance of the basic validity of the model which may then be put to further use. For this specific application, all that we require from the test are: (i) accurate estimates of natural frequencies and (ii) descriptions of the mode shapes using just sufficient detail and accuracy to permit their identification and correlation with those from the theoretical model. At this stage, accurate mode shape data are not essential. It is generally not possible to 'predict' the damping in each mode of vibration from a theoretical model and so there is nothing with which to compare measurements of modal damping from the tests. However, such information is useful as it can be incorporated into the theoretical model, albeit as an approximation, prior to that being called upon to predict specific response levels (which are often significantly influenced by the damping).

(B) Many cases of experiment – theory comparison stop at the stage of obtaining a set of results by each route and simply comparing them. Sometimes, an attempt will be made to adjust or correct the theoretical model in order to bring its modal properties closer into line with the measured results, but this is usually done using a trial-and-error aproach.

A logical evolution of the procedure outlined above is the correlation, rather than the comparison, of experimental and theoretical results. By this is meant a process whereby the two sets of data are combined, quantitatively, in order to identify specifically the causes of the discrepancies between predicted and measured properties. Such an application is clearly more powerful than its less ambitious forerunner but, equally, will be more demanding in terms of the accuracy required in the data taken from the modal test. Specifically, a much more precise description of the mode shape data (the 'eigenvectors') is required than is generally necessary to depict or describe the general shape in pictorial form.

(C)   The next application area to be reviewed is that of using a modal test in order to produce a mathematical model of a component which may then be used to incorporate that component into a structural assembly. This is often referred to as a 'substructuring process' and is widely used in theoretical analysis of complex structures.   Here again, it is a fully quantitative model that is sought – with accurate data required for natural frequencies, modal dampings and mode shapes – and now has the added constraint that <u>all</u> modes must be included simultaneously.   It is not sufficient to confine the model to certain individual modes – as may be done for the previous comparisons or correlations – since out-of-range modes will influence the structure's dynamic behaviour in a given frequency range of interest for the complete assembly.   Also, it is not possible to ignore certain modes which exist in the range of interest but which may present some difficulties for measurement or analysis.   This application is altogether more demanding than the previous ones and is often underestimated, and so inappropriately tackled, with the result that the   results do not match up to expectations.

(D)   There is a variant of the previous application which is becoming of considerable interest and potential and that is to the generation of a model which may be used for predicting the effects of modifications to the original structure, as tested.   Theoretically, this falls into the same class of process as substructuring and has the same requirements of data accuracy and quantity.   However, sometimes the modification procedure involves relatively minor changes to the original, in order to fine-tune a structure's dynamics, and this situation can relax the data requirements somewhat.

One particular consideration which applies to both this and the previous case concerns the need for information about rotational motion, i.e. moments (as well as forces) and rotational displacements (as well as translational ones).   These are automatically included in theoretical analyses but are generally ignored in experimentally-based studies for the simple reason that they are so much more difficult to measure. Nevertheless, they are generally an essential feature in coupling or modification applications.

(E)   A different application for the model produced by a modal test is that of force determination.   There are a number of situations where knowledge of the dynamic forces causing vibration is required but where direct measurement of these forces is not practical.   For these cases, one solution is offered by a process whereby measurements of the response caused by the forces are combined with a mathematical description of the transfer functions of the structure in order to deduce the forces.   This process can be very sensitive to the accuracy of the model used for the structure and so it is often essential that the model itself be derived from measurements; in other words, via a modal test.

(F) Lastly, in our review of applications it is appropriate to note that whereas the normal procedure is (a) to measure, (b) to analyse the measured data and then (c) to derive a mathematical model of the structure, there are some cases where this is not the optimum procedure. The last step, (c), is usually taken in order to reduce a vast quantity of actual measurements to a small and efficient data set usually referred to as the 'modal model'. This reduction process has an additional benefit of eliminating small inconsistencies which will inevitably occur in measured data. However, it is sometimes found that the smoothing and averaging procedures involved in this step reduce the validity of the model and in applications where the subsequent analysis is very sensitive to the accuracy of the input data, this can present a problem. Examples of this problem may be found particularly in (E), force determination, and in (C), subsystem coupling. The solution adopted is to generate a model of the test structure using 'raw' measured data – unsmoothed and relatively unprocessed – which, in turn, may well demand additional measurements being made, and additional care to ensure the necessary accuracy.

1.3 PHILOSOPHY OF MODAL TESTING

One of the major requirements of the subject of modal testing is a thorough integration of three components:

(i)   the theoretical basis of vibration;
(ii)   accurate measurement of vibration and
(iii)   realistic and detailed data analysis

There has in the past been a tendency to regard these as three different specialist areas, with individual experts in each. However, the subject we are exploring now demands a high level of understanding and competence in all three and cannot achieve its full potential without the proper and judicious mixture of the necessary components.

For example: when taking measurements of excitation and response levels, a full knowledge of how the measured data are to be processed can be essential if the correct decisions are to be made as to the quality and suitability of that data. Again, a thorough understanding of the various forms and trends adopted by plots of frequency response functions for complex structures can prevent the wasted effort of analysing incorrect measurements: there are many features of these plots that can be assessed very rapidly by the eyes of someone who understands the theoretical basis of them.

Throughout this work, we shall repeat and re-emphasise the need for this integration of theoretical and experimental skills. Indeed, the route chosen to develop and to explain the details of the subject takes us first through an extensive review of the necessary theoretical foundation of structural vibration. This theory is regarded as a necessary prerequisite to the subsequent studies of measurement techniques, signal processing and data analysis.

With an appreciation of both the basis of the theory (and if not with all the detail straight away, then at least with an awareness that many such details do exist), we can then turn our attention to the practical side; to the excitation of the test structure and to the measurement of both the input and response levels during the controlled testing conditions of mobility measurements. Already, here, there is a bewildering choice of test methods – harmonic, random, transient excitations, for example – vying for choice as the 'best' method in each application. If the experimenter is not to be left at the mercy of the sophisticated digital analysis equipment now widely available, he must fully acquaint himself with the methods, limitations and implications of the various techniques now widely used in this measurement phase.

Next, we consider the 'Analysis' stage where the measured data (invariably, frequency response functions or mobilities) are subjected to a range of curve-fitting procedures in an attempt to find the mathematical model which provides the closest description of the actually-observed behaviour. There are many approaches, or algorithms, for this phase and, as is usually the case, no single one is ideal for all problems. Thus, an appreciation of the alternatives is a necessary requirement for the experimenter wishing to make optimum use of his time and resources.

Generally, though not always, an analysis is conducted on each measured curve individually. If this is the case, then there is a further step in the process which we refer to as 'Modelling'. This is the final stage where all the measured and processed data are combined to yield the most compact and efficient description of the end result – a mathematical model of the test structure – that is practicable.

This last phase, like the earlier ones, involves some type of averaging as the means by which a large quantity of measured data are reduced to a (relatively) small mathematical model. This is an operation which must be used with some care. The averaging process is a valid and valuable technique provided that the data thus treated contain random variations: data with systematic trends, such as are caused by non-linearities, should not be averaged in the same way. We shall discuss this problem later on.

Thus we have attempted to describe the underlying philosophy of our approach to modal testing and are now in a position to review the highlights of the three main phases: theory, measurement and analysis in order to provide a brief overview of the entire subject.

1.4   SUMMARY OF THEORY

In this and the following two sections an overview of the various aspects of the subject will be presented. This will highlight the key features of each area of activity and is included for a number of reasons. First, it provides the serious student with a non-detailed review of the different subjects to be dealt with, enabling him to see the context of each without being distracted by the minutiae, and thus acts as a useful introduction to the full study. Secondly, it provides him with a breakdown of the subject into identifiable topics which are then useful as milestones for the process of acquiring a comprehensive ability and understanding of the techniques. Lastly, it also serves to provide the non-specialist or manager with an explanation of the subject, trying to remove some of the mystery and folklore which may have developed.

We begin with the theoretical basis of the subject since, as has already been emphasised, a good grasp of this aspect is an essential prerequisite for successful modal testing.

It is very important that a clear distinction is made between the free vibration and the forced vibration analyses, these usually being two successive stages in a full vibration analysis. As usual with vibration studies, we start with the single degree-of-freedom (SDOF) system and use this familiar model to introduce the general notation and analysis procedures which are later extended to the more general multi degree-of-freedom (MDOF) systems. For the SDOF system, a free vibration analysis yields its natural frequency and damping factor while a particular type of forced response analysis, assuming a harmonic excitation, leads to the definition of the frequency response function – such as mobility, the ratio of velocity response to force input. These two types of result are referred to as 'modal properties' and 'frequency response characteristics' respectively and they constitute the basis of all our studies. Before leaving the SDOF model, it is appropriate to consider the form which a plot of the mobility (or other type of frequency response function) takes. Three alternative ways of plotting such information are shown in Fig. 1.1 and, as will be discussed later, it is always helpful to select the format which is best suited to the particular application to hand.

Next we consider the more general class of systems with more than one degree-of-freedom. For these, it is customary that the spatial properties – the values of the mass, stiffness and damper elements which make up the model – be expressed as matrices. Those used throughout this work are [M], the mass matrix, [K], the stiffness matrix, [C], the viscous damping matrix and [H], the structural or hysteretic damping matrix. The first phase (of three) in the vibration analysis of such systems is that of setting up the governing equations of motion which, in effect, means determining the elements of the above matrices. (This is a process which does exist for the SDOF system but is often trivial.) The second phase is that of performing a free-vibration analysis using the equations of motion. This analysis produces first a set of N natural frequencies and damping factors (N being the number of degrees of freedom, or equations of motion) and secondly a matching set of 'shape' vectors, each one of these being associated with a specific natural frequency and damping factor. The complete free-vibration solution is conveniently contained in two matrices, $\lceil \lambda^2 \rfloor$ and $[\Phi]$, which are again referred to as the 'modal properties' or, sometimes, as the eigenvalue (natural frequency and damping) and eigenvector (mode shape) matrices. One element from the diagonal matrix (λ^2_r) contains both the natural

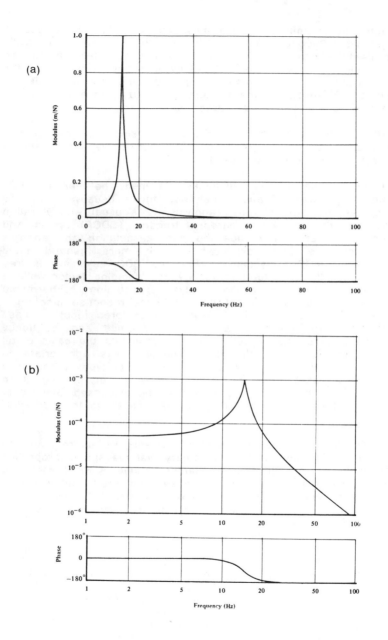

Fig 1.1   Alternative Formats for Display of Frequency Response
Function of a Single-Degree-of-Freedom System
(a)   Linear
(b)   Logarithmic

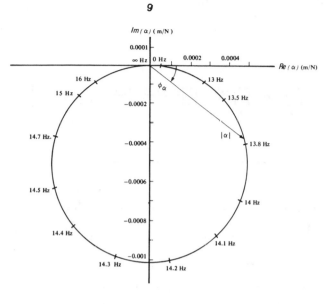

Fig 1. 1   (c)   Nyquist Plot

frequency <u>and</u> the damping factor for the rth normal mode of vibration of the system while the corresponding column from the full eigenvector matrix, $\{\phi\}_r$, describes the shape (the relative displacements of all parts of the system) of that same mode of vibration. There are many detailed variations to this general picture, depending upon the type and distribution of damping, but all cases can be described in the same general way.

The third and final phase of theoretical analysis is the forced response analysis, and in particular that for harmonic (or sinusoidal) excitation. By solving the equations of motion when harmonic forcing is applied, we are able to describe the complete solution by a single matrix, known as the 'mobility matrix' [Y(ω)], although unlike the previous two matrix descriptions, the elements of this matrix are not constants but are frequency-dependent, each element being itself a frequency response (or mobility) function. Thus, element $Y_{jk}(\omega)$ represents the harmonic response in one of the coordinates, x_j, caused by a single harmonic force applied at a different coordinate, f_k. Both these harmonic quantities are described using complex algebra to accommodate the magnitude <u>and</u> phase information, as also is $Y_{jk}(\omega)$.

The particular relevance of these specific response characteristics is the fact that they are the quantities which we are most likely to be able to measure in practice. It is, of course, possible to describe each individual frequency response function in terms of the various mass, stiffness and damping elements of the system but the relevant expressions

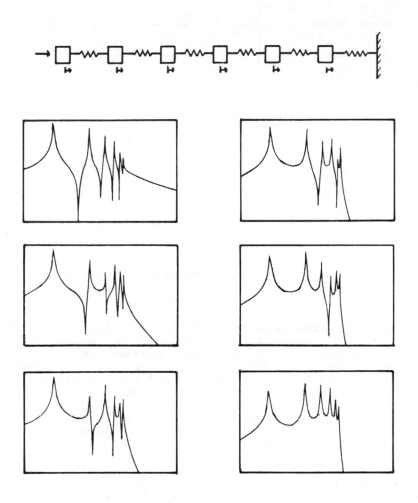

Fig 1.2   Typical FRF Plots for a Multi-Degree-of-Freedom System
System (a) Bode Plots

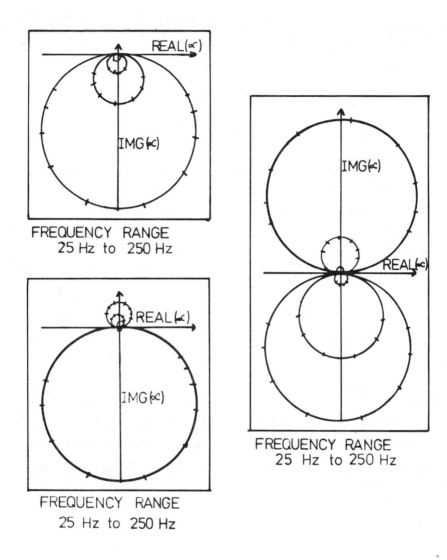

FREQUENCY RANGE
25 Hz to 250 Hz

FREQUENCY RANGE
25 Hz to 250 Hz

FREQUENCY RANGE
25 Hz to 250 Hz

Fig 1. 2   (b) Nyquist Plots of Receptance

can be drastically simplified if we use the modal properties instead of the spatial properties and it is possible to write a general expression for <u>any</u> mobility function, $Y_{jk}(\omega)$ as:

$$Y_{jk}(\omega) = \frac{\dot{x}_j}{f_k} = i\omega \sum_{r=1}^{N} \frac{({}_r\phi_j)({}_r\phi_k)}{\lambda_r^2 - \omega^2} \tag{1.1}$$

where λ_r^2 is the eigenvalue of the rth mode (its natural frequency and damping factor combined;

$_r\phi_j$ is the jth element of the rth eigenvector $\{\phi\}_r$ (ie, the relative displacement at that point during vibration in the rth mode);

N is the number of degrees of freedom (or modes)

This single expression is the foundation of modal testing: it shows a direct connection between the modal properties of a system and its response characteristics. From a purely theoretical viewpoint it provides an efficient means of predicting response (by performing a free vibration analysis first) while from a more practical standpoint, it suggests that there may be means of determining modal properties from mobilities which are amenable to direct measurement. Here again, it is appropriate to consider the form which a plot of such an expression as (1.1) will take, and some examples are shown in Fig 1.2 which can be deduced entirely from the equation itself, using different values for the modal properties or coefficients in the expression.

Thus we find that by making a thorough study of the theory of structural vibration, we are able to 'predict' what we might expect to find if we make mobility–type measurements on actual hardware. Indeed, we shall see later how these predictions can be quite detailed, to the point where it is possible to comment on the likely quality of measured data.

We have outlined above the major aspects of the 'theoretical route' of vibration analysis. There are also a number of topics which need to be covered dealing with aspects of signal processing, non–harmonic response characteristics and non–linear behaviour, but these may be regarded as additional details which may be required in particular cases while the above–mentioned items are fundamental and central to <u>any</u> application of modal testing.

1.5   SUMMARY OF MEASUREMENT METHODS

In the previous section, we reviewed the major features of the appropriate theory and these all led up to the frequency response characteristics. Thus the main measurement techniques which must be devised and developed are those which will permit us to make direct measurements of the various mobility properties of the test structure.

In this review, we shall concentrate on the basic measurement system used for single-point excitation, the type of test best suited to mobility measurement, the main items of which are shown in Figure 1.3. Essentially, there are three aspects of the measurement process which demand particular attention in order to ensure the acquisition of the high-quality data which are required for the next stage – data analysis. These are:

(i)   the mechanical aspects of supporting and (correctly) exciting the structure;

(ii)   the correct transduction of the quantities to be measured – force input and motion response; and

(iii)   the signal processing which is appropriate to the type of test used.

In the first category, we encounter questions as to how the testpiece should be suspended, or supported, and how it should be driven. Usually, one of three options is chosen for the support: <u>free</u>, or unrestrained, (which usually means suspended on very soft springs); <u>grounded</u>, which requires its rigid clamping at certain points; or <u>in situ</u>, where the testpiece is connected to some other structure or component which presents a non-rigid attachment. The choice itself will often be decided by various factors. Amongst these may be a desire to correlate the test results with theory and in this case it should be remembered that free boundaries are much easier to simulate in the test condition than are clamped, or grounded ones. Also, if tests are being made on one component which forms part of an assembly, these may well be required for the free-free condition.

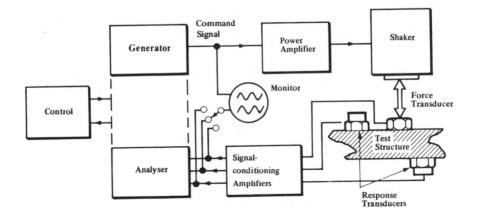

Fig 1.3   Basic Components of Measurement System

The mechanics of the excitation are achieved either by connecting a vibration generator, or shaker, or by using some form of transient input, such as a hammer blow or sudden release from a deformed position. Both approaches have advantages and disadvantages and it can be very important to choose the best one in each case.

Transducers are very important elements in the system as it is essential that accurate measurements be made both of the input to the structure and of its response. Nowadays, piezoelectric transducers are widely used to detect both force and acceleration and the major problems associated with them are to ensure that they interfere with the test structure as little as possible and that their performance is adequate for the ranges of frequency and amplitude of the test. Incorrect transducer selection can give rise to very large errors in the measured data upon which all the subsequent analysis is based.

The mobility parameters to be measured can be obtained directly by applying a harmonic excitation and then measuring the resulting harmonic response. This type of test is often referred to as 'sinewave testing' and it requires the attachment to the structure of a shaker. The frequency range is covered either by stepping from one frequency to the next, or by slowly sweeping the frequency continuously, in both cases allowing quasi-steady conditions to be attained. Alternative excitation procedures are now widely used. Periodic, pseudo-random or random excitation signals often replace the sine-wave approach and are made practical by the existence of complex signal-processing analysers which are capable of resolving the frequency content of both input and response signals, using Fourier analysis, and thereby deducing the mobility parameters required. A further extension of this development is possible using impulsive or transient excitations which may be applied without connecting a shaker to the structure. All of these latter possibilities offer shorter testing times but great care must be exercised in their use as there are many steps at which errors may be incurred by incorrect application. Once again, a sound understanding of the theoretical basis − this time of signal processing − is necessary to ensure successful use of these advanced techniques.

As was the case with the theoretical review, the measurement process also contains many detailed features which will be described below. Here, we have just outlined the central and most important topics to be considered. One final observation which must be made is that in modal testing applications of vibration measurements, perhaps more than many others, accuracy of the measured data is of paramount importance. This is so because these data are generally to be submitted to a range of analysis procedures, outlined in the next section, in order to extract the results eventually sought. Some of these analysis processes are themselves quite complex and can seldom be regarded as insensitive to the accuracy of the input data. By way of a note of caution, Fig 1.4 shows the extent of variations which may be obtained by using different measurement techniques on a particular test structure [6].

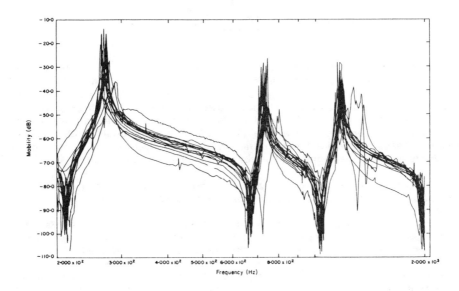

Fig 1.4   *Various Measurements on Standard Testpiece*

1.6   SUMMARY OF ANALYSIS

The third skill required for modal testing is concerned with the analysis of the measured mobility data. This is quite separate from the signal processing which may be necessary to convert raw measurements into frequency responses. It is a procedure whereby the measured mobilities are analysed in such a way as to find a theoretical model which most closely resembles the behaviour of the actual testpiece. This process itself falls into two stages: first, to identify the appropriate type of model and second, to determine the appropriate parameters of the chosen model. Most of the effort goes into this second stage, which is widely referred to as 'experimental modal analysis'.

We have seen from our review of the theoretical aspects that we can 'predict' or, better, 'anticipate' the form of the mobility plots for a multi-degree-of-freedom system and we have also seen that these may be directly related to the modal properties of that system. The great majority of the modal analysis effort involves matching or curve-fitting an expression such as equation (1.1) above to the measured mobility functions and thereby finding the appropriate modal parameters.

A completely general curve-fitting approach is possible but generally inefficient. Mathematically, we can take an equation of the form

$$Y(\omega) = i\omega \sum_{r=1}^{N} \frac{A_r}{\lambda_r^2 - \omega^2} \qquad (1.2)$$

and curve-fit a set of measured values $Y_m(\omega_1)$, $Y_m(\omega_2)$ .... etc. to this expression so that we obtain estimates for the coefficients A_1, A_2, ..., λ_1^2, λ_2^2 .... etc. These coefficients are, of course, closely related to the modal properties of the system. However, although such approaches are made, they are inefficient and neither exploit the particular properties of resonant systems nor take due account of the unequal quality of the various measured points in the data set $Y_m(\omega_1)$, $Y_m(\omega_2)$ .... etc, both of which can have a significant influence on the overall process.

Thus there is no single modal analysis method but rather a selection, each being the most appropriate in differing conditions.

The most widespread and one of the most useful approaches is that known as the 'Single-Degree-of-Freedom Curve-Fit' or, often, the 'Circle Fit' procedure. This method uses the fact that at frequencies close to a natural frequency, the mobility can often be approximated to that of a single-degree-of-freedom system plus a constant offset term (which approximately accounts for the other modes). This assumption allows us to use the circular nature of a modulus/phase polar plot (the Nyquist plot) of the frequency response function of a SDOF system (see Fig 1.1(c)) by curve-fitting a circle to just a few measured data points, as illustrated in Fig 1.5. This process can be repeated for each resonance individually until the whole curve has been analysed. At this stage, a theoretical regeneration of the mobility function is possible using the set of coefficients extracted, as illustrated in Fig 1.6.

The method can be used for many of the cases encountered in practice but it becomes inadequate and inaccurate when the structure has modes which are 'close', a condition which is identified by the lack of an obviously-circular section on the Nyquist plot. Under these conditions it becomes necessary to use a more complex process which accepts the simultaneous influence of more than one mode. These latter methods are referred to as 'MDOF Curve-fits' and are naturally more complicated and require more computation time but, provided the data are accurate, they have the capability of producing more accurate estimates for the modal properties (or at least for the coefficients in equation(1.2)).

In this subject, again, there are many detailed refinements but the analysis process is always essentially the same: that of finding – by curve-fitting – a set of modal properties which best match the response characteristics of the tested structure. Some of the more detailed considerations include: compensating for slightly non-linear behaviour; simultaneously analysing more then one mobility function and curve-fitting to actual time histories (rather than the processed frequency response functions).

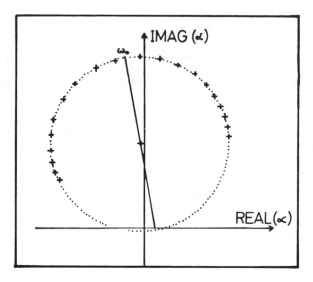

Fig 1.5   Curve-Fit to Resonant Data

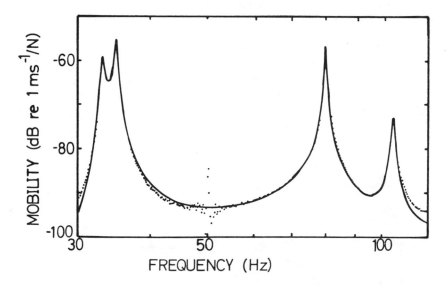

Fig 1.6   Regeneration of Mobility Curve From Circle-Fit Data

1.7 REVIEW OF TEST PROCEDURE

Having now outlined the major features of the three necessary ingredients for modal testing, it is appropriate to end this introduction with a brief review of just how these facilities are drawn together to conduct a modal test.

The overall objective of the test is to determine a set of modal properties for a structure. These consist of natural frequencies, damping factors and mode shapes. The procedure consists of three steps:

(i)   measure an appropriate set of mobilities;

(ii)   analyse these using appropriate curve-fitting procedures; and

(iii)   combine the results of the curve-fits to construct the required model.

Using our knowledge of the theoretical relationship between mobility functions and modal properties, it is possible to show that an 'appropriate' set of mobilities to measure consists of just one row or one column in the mobility matrix, $[Y(\omega)]$. In practice, this either means exciting the structure at one point and measuring responses at all points or measuring the response in one direction at one point while the excitation is applied separately at each point in all directions in turn. (This last option is most conveniently achieved using a hammer or other non-contacting excitation device.)

In practice, this relatively simple procedure will be embellished by various detailed additions, but the general method is always as described here.

CHAPTER 2
Theoretical Basis

2.0 INTRODUCTION

It has already been emphasised that the theoretical foundations of modal testing are of paramount importance to its successful implementation. Thus it is appropriate that this first chapter deals with the various aspects of theory which are used at the different stages of modal analysis and testing.

The majority of this chapter (Sections 2.1 to 2.8) deals with an analysis of the basic vibration properties of the general linear structure, as these form the basis of experimental modal analysis. Later sections extend the theory somewhat to take account of the different ways in which such properties can be measured (2.9) and some of the more complex features which may be encountered (2.10). There are some topics of which knowledge is assumed in the main text but for which a review is provided in the Appendices in case the current usage is unfamiliar.

Before embarking on the detailed analysis, it is appropriate to put the different stages into context and this can be done by showing what will be called the 'theoretical route' for vibration analysis (Fig. 2.1). This illustrates the three phases through which a typical vibration analysis progresses. Generally, we start with a description of the structure's physical characteristics, usually in terms of its *mass, stiffness* and *damping* properties, and this is referred to as the SPATIAL MODEL.

Then it is customary to perform an analytical modal analysis of the spatial model which leads to a description of the structure's behaviour as a set of vibration modes; the MODAL MODEL. This model is defined as a set of *natural frequencies* with corresponding *vibration mode shapes* and *modal damping factors*. It is important to remember that this solution always describes the various ways in which the structure is capable of vibrating naturally, i.e. without any external forcing or excitation, and so these are called the 'normal' or 'natural' modes of the structure.

The third stage is generally that in which we have the greatest interest, namely the analysis of exactly how the structure will vibrate under given

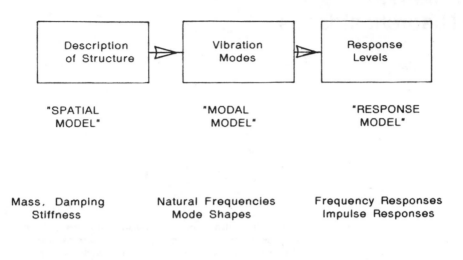

Fig 2.1   Theoretical Route to Vibration Analysis

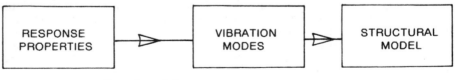

Experimental
Modal Analysis

Fig 2.2   Experimental Route to Vibration Analysis

excitation conditions and, especially, with what amplitudes. Clearly, this will depend not only upon the structure's inherent properties but also on the nature and magnitude of the imposed excitation and so there will be innumerable solutions of this type. However, it is convenient to present an analysis of the structure's response to a 'standard' excitation (from which the solution for any particular case can be constructed) and to describe this as the RESPONSE MODEL. The standard excitation chosen throughout this work will be that of a unit-amplitude sinusoidal force applied to each point on the structure individually, and at every frequency within a specified range. Thus our response model will consist of a set of *frequency response functions* (FRFs) which must be defined over the applicable range of frequency.

Throughout the following analysis we shall be focusing on these three stages and types of model – SPATIAL, MODAL and RESPONSE – and it is essential to understand fully their interdependence as it is upon this characteristic that the principles of modal testing are founded. As indicated in Fig. 2.1, it is possible to proceed from the spatial model through to a response analysis. It is also possible to undertake an analysis in the reverse direction – i.e. from a description of the response properties (such as measured frequency response functions) we can deduce modal properties and, in the limit, the spatial properties. This is the 'experimental route' to vibration analysis which is shown in Fig. 2.2 and will be discussed in detail in Chapter 5.

2.1 SINGLE-DEGREE-OF-FREEDOM (SDOF) SYSTEM THEORY

Although very few practical structures could realistically be modelled by a single-degree-of-freedom (SDOF) system, the properties of such a system are very important because those for a more complex multi-degree-of-freedom (MDOF) system can always be represented as the linear superposition of a number of SDOF characteristics.

Throughout this chapter we shall describe three classes of system model:

(a) undamped
(b) viscously damped
(c) hysteretically (or structurally) damped

and we shall also make extensive use of complex algebra to describe the time-varying quantities of displacement, force etc. (Appendix 1 gives some notes on the use of complex algebra for harmonic quantities).

The basic model for the SDOF system is shown in Fig. 2.3 where $f(t)$ and $x(t)$ are general time-varying force and displacement response quantities. The spatial model consists of a mass (m) and a spring (k) plus (when damped) either a viscous dashpot (c) or hysteretic damper (h).

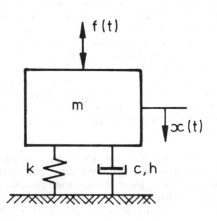

Fig 2.3   *Single–Degree–of–Freedom (SDOF) System*

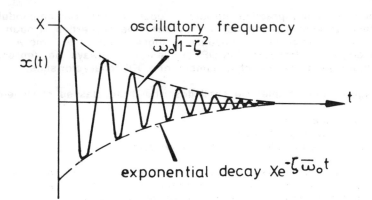

Fig 2.4   *Free–Vibration Characteristic of Damped SDOF System*

2.1.1   Undamped

As stated, the spatial model consists of m and k

For the modal model, we consider the properties of the system with no external forcing, i.e. $f(t) = 0$ and for this case the governing equation of motion is:

$$m\ddot{x} + kx = 0 \qquad (2.1)$$

The trial solution, $x(t) = xe^{i\omega t}$ leads to the requirement that $(k - \omega^2 m) = 0$.

Hence the modal model consists of a single solution (mode of vibration) with a natural frequency $\bar{\omega}_0$ given by $(k/m)^{1/2}$.

Now, turning to a frequency response analysis, we consider an excitation of the form:

$$f(t) = fe^{i\omega t}$$

and assume a solution of the form

$$x(t) = xe^{i\omega t}$$

where x and f are complex to accommodate both the amplitude and phase information (see Appendix 1).   Now the equation of motion is

$$(k - \omega^2 m)xe^{i\omega t} = fe^{i\omega t} \qquad (2.2)$$

from which we extract the required response model in the form of a frequency response function (FRF):

$$\boxed{\frac{x}{f} = \frac{1}{k - \omega^2 m} = \alpha(\omega) \text{ , the system "Receptance"}} \qquad (2.3)$$

Note that this function, along with other versions of the FRF, is independent of the excitation.

2.1.2   Viscous Damping

If we add a viscous dashpot c, the equation of motion for free vibration becomes

$$m\ddot{x} + c\dot{x} + kx = 0 \qquad (2.4)$$

and we must now use a more general trial solution:

$$x(t) = xe^{st} \qquad \text{(where s is complex, rather than imaginary, as before)}$$

with which we obtain the condition:

$$(m \, s^2 + cs + k) = 0 \qquad (2.5)$$

This in turn leads to $s_{1,2} = - \dfrac{c}{2m} \pm \dfrac{\sqrt{c^2 - 4km}}{2m}$

$$(2.6)$$

$$= -\bar{\omega}_0 \zeta \pm i\bar{\omega}_0\sqrt{1 - \zeta^2}$$

where $\bar{\omega}_0^2 = (k/m)$; $\zeta = c/c_0 = (c/2\sqrt{km})$

which implies a modal solution of the form:

$$x(t) = x \, e^{-\bar{\omega}_0\zeta t} \, e^{i(\bar{\omega}_0\sqrt{1-\zeta^2})t} = x \, e^{-at} \, e^{i\omega_0't}$$

which is a single mode of vibration with a complex natural frequency having two parts:

- the imaginary or oscillatory part: a frequency of $\omega_0' = (\bar{\omega}_0\sqrt{1 - \zeta^2})$,

- the real, or decay part, a damping rate of $a(= \zeta\bar{\omega}_0)$

The physical significance of these two parts of the modal model is illustrated in the typical free response plot, shown in Fig 2.4.

Lastly, we consider the forced response when $f(t) = f \, e^{i\omega t}$ and, as before, we assume $x(t) = xe^{i\omega t}$. Here, the equation of motion:

$$(-\omega^2 m + i\omega c + k)x \, e^{i\omega t} = f \, e^{i\omega t} \qquad (2.7)$$

gives a receptance FRF of the form

$$\boxed{\alpha(\omega) = \frac{1}{(k - \omega^2 m) + i(\omega c)}} \qquad (2.8)$$

which is now complex, containing both magnitude and phase information.

Note that

$$|\alpha(\omega)| = \frac{|x|}{|f|} = \frac{1}{\sqrt{(k - \omega^2 m)^2 + (\omega c)^2}}$$

and $\angle\alpha(\omega) = \angle x - \angle f = tg^{-1}(-\omega c/(k - \omega^2 m)) = -\theta_\alpha$

2.1.3 Structural Damping

Close inspection of the behaviour of real structures suggests that the viscous damping model used above is not very representative when applied to MDOF systems. There appears to be a frequency-dependence exhibited by real structures which is not described by the standard viscous dashpot and what is required, apparently, is a damper whose rate varies inversely with frequency: i.e. $c = (b/\omega)$.

An alternative damping model is provided by the hysteretic or structural damper which has not only the advantage mentioned above, but also provides a much simpler analysis for MDOF systems, as shown below (in 2.5). However, it presents difficulties to a rigorous free vibration analysis and attention is generally focused on the forced response analysis. In this case we can write an equation of motion

$$(-\omega^2 m + k + i\ h)\ x\ e^{i\omega t} = f\ e^{i\omega t} \qquad (2.9)$$

giving
$$\frac{x}{f} = \alpha(\omega) = \frac{1}{(k - \omega^2 m) + i(h)} \qquad (2.10)$$

or
$$\boxed{\alpha(\omega) = \frac{1/k}{(1 - (\omega/\bar{\omega}_o)^2 + i\eta)}} \qquad (2.11)$$

where η is the *structural damping loss factor.*

The similarities between the FRF expressions for the different cases are evident from equations (2.3) (2.8) and (2.10)

2.2 PRESENTATION AND PROPERTIES OF FRF DATA FOR SDOF SYSTEM

Having developed expressions for the basic receptance frequency response function of the SDOF system, we now turn our attention to the various ways of presenting or displaying these data. We shall first discuss variations in the basic form of the FRF and then go on to explore different ways of presenting the properties graphically. Finally we shall examine some useful geometric properties of the resulting plots.

2.2.1 Alternative Forms of FRF

So far we have defined our receptance frequency response function $\alpha(\omega)$ as the ratio between a harmonic displacement response and the harmonic force. This ratio is complex as there is both an amplitude ratio ($\alpha(\omega)$) and a phase angle between the two sinusoids (θ_α).

We could equally have selected the response velocity $v(t)$ $(= \dot{x}(t))$ as the 'output' quantity and defined an alternative frequency response function – *Mobility* – as

$$\boxed{Y(\omega) = \frac{v e^{i\omega t}}{f e^{i\omega t}} = \frac{v}{f}} \qquad (2.12)$$

However, when considering sinusoidal vibration we have a simple relationship between displacement and velocity (and thus between receptance and mobility) because:

$$x(t) = xe^{i\omega t}$$

and
$$v(t) = \dot{x}(t) = i\omega xe^{i\omega t}$$

So, $Y(\omega) = \dfrac{v}{f} = i\omega \dfrac{x}{f} = i\omega\alpha(\omega)$ (2.13)

Thus $|Y(\omega)| = \omega |\alpha(\omega)|$

and $\theta_Y = \theta_\alpha - 90°$

so that mobility is closely related to receptance. Similarly, we could use acceleration ($a(t) = \ddot{x}(t)$) as our response parameter (since it is customary to measure acceleration in tests) so we could define a third FRF parameter – *Inertance* or *Accelerance* – as

$$A(\omega) = \frac{a}{f} = -\omega^2\alpha(\omega)$$ (2.14)

These represent the main formats of FRF although there exist yet more possibilities by defining the functions in an inverse way, namely as:

$$\left(\frac{force}{displacement}\right):\quad \textit{"Dynamic Stiffness"};$$

$$\left(\frac{force}{velocity}\right):\quad \textit{"Mechanical Impedance"};$$

or
$$\left(\frac{force}{acceleration}\right):\quad \textit{"Apparent Mass"}.$$

However, these latter formats are discouraged, except in special cases, as they can lead to considerable confusion and error if improperly used in MDOF systems.

Table 2.1 gives details of all 6 of the FRF parameters and of the names and symbols variously used for them.

2.2.2 Graphical Display of FRF data

There is an overriding complication to plotting FRF data which derives from the fact that they are complex and thus there are three quantities – frequency plus 2 parts of the complex function – and these cannot be fully displayed on a standard x-y graph. Because of this, any such simple

Response Parameter R	Standard R/F	Inverse F/R
DISPLACEMENT	RECEPTANCE ADMITTANCE DYNAMIC COMPLIANCE DYNAMIC FLEXIBILITY	DYNAMIC STIFFNESS
VELOCITY	MOBILITY	MECHANICAL IMPEDANCE
ACCELERATION	INERTANCE ACCELERANCE	APPARENT MASS

Table 2.1   Definitions of Frequency Response Functions

plot can only show two of the three quantities and so there are different possibilities available. all of which are used from time to time.

The three most common forms of presentation are:

(i)   Modulus (of FRF) vs Frequency
         and Phase vs Frequency   (the Bode type of plot.
                                    consisting of 2 graphs)

(ii)   Real Part (of FRF) vs Frequency
         and Imaginary Part vs Frequency   (2 plots) ; and

(iii)   Real Part vs Imaginary Part   (Nyquist plot: a single graph
          which does not explicitly contain frequency information).

We shall now examine the use of these types of graphical display and identify the particular advantages or features of each.

(i) A classical FRF plot is shown in Fig. 2.5(a) for the receptance of a typical SDOF system without damping.   Corresponding plots for the mobility and inertance of the same system are shown in Figs. 2.5(b) and (c) respectively.

One of the problems with these FRF properties. as with much vibration data. is the relatively wide range of values which must be

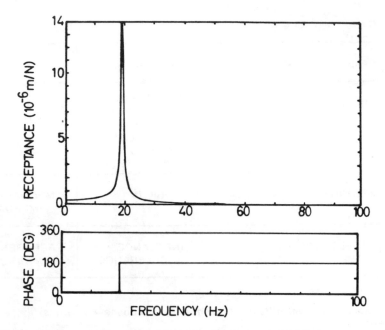

Fig 2.5(a)   Receptance Plot for Undamped SDOF System

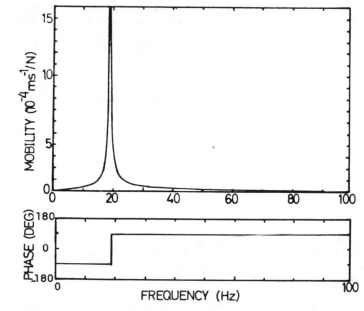

Fig 2.5(b)   Mobility Plot for Undamped SDOF System

encompassed no matter which type of FRF is used. In order to cope with this problem, it is often appropriate to make use of logarithmic scales and the three functions specified above have been replotted in Fig. 2.6(a), (b) and (c) using logarithmic scales for all frequency and modulus axes. The result is something of a transformation in that each plot can now be divided into three regimes:

- a low-frequency straight-line characteristic;
- a high-frequency straight-line characteristic, and
- the resonant region with its abrupt magnitude and phase variations.

It is helpful and instructive to superimpose on these log-log plots a grid of lines which show the relevant FRF characteristics separately of simple mass elements and simple spring elements. Table 2.2 shows the corresponding expressions for α_m, α_k, Y_m, etc. and from this it is possible to see that mass and stiffness properties will always appear as straight lines on log (modulus) vs log (frequency) plots, as shown in Fig. 2.7. These have in fact been included in Fig. 2.6 but their significance can be further appreciated by reference to Fig. 2.7 which shows the mobility modulus plots for 2 different systems. By referring to and interpolating between the mass- and stiffness-lines drawn on the plot, we can deduce that system (a) consists of a mass of 1 kg with a spring stiffness of 2.5 kN/m while system (b) has corresponding values of 0.8 kg and 120 kN/m respectively.

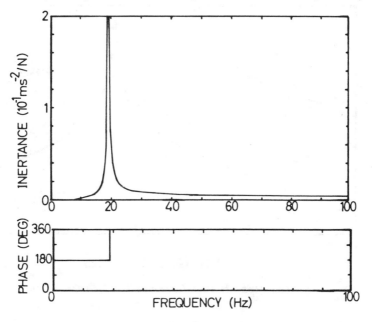

Fig 2.5(c)   Inertance (or Accelerance) Plot for Undamped SDOF System

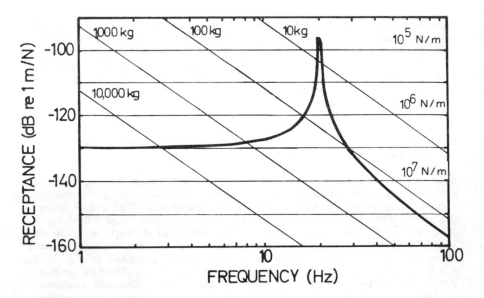

Fig 2.6(a)   Log-Log Receptance Plot for Undamped SDOF System

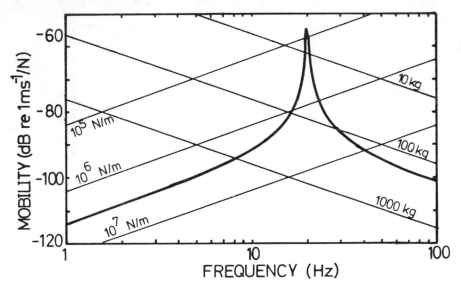

Fig 2.6(b)   Log-Log Mobility Plot for Undamped SDOF System

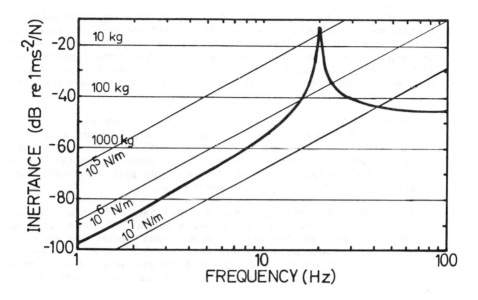

Fig 2.6(c)   Log-Log Inertance Plot for Undamped SDOF System

FRF PARAMETER	MASS	STIFFNESS
RECEPTANCE $\alpha(\omega)$ $\log\|\alpha(\omega)\|$	$-1/\omega^2 m$ $-\log(m)-2\log(\omega)$	$1/k$ $-\log(k)$
MOBILITY $Y(\omega)$ $\log\|Y(\omega)\|$	$-i/\omega m$ $-\log(m)-\log(\omega)$	$i\omega/k$ $\log(\omega)-\log(k)$
INERTANCE $A(\omega)$ $\log\|A(\omega)\|$	$1/m$ $-\log(m)$	$-\omega^2/k$ $2\log(\omega)-\log(k)$

Table 2.2   Frequency Responses of Mass and Stiffness Elements

This basic style of displaying FRF data applies to all types of system, whether damped or not, while the other forms are only applicable to damped systems and then tend to be sensitive to the type of damping. Fig. 2.8 shows the basic example system plotted for different levels of viscous damping with a zoomed detail of the narrow band around resonance which is the only region that the damping has any influence on the FRF plot.

(II) Companion plots for Real Part *vs* Frequency and Imaginary Part *vs* Frequency are shown in Fig. 2.9 for the SDOF system with light viscous damping. All three forms of the FRF are shown and from these we can see how the phase change through the resonance region is characterised by a sign change in one part accompanied by a peak (max or min) value in the other part.

It should be noted here that the use of logarithmic scales is not feasible in this case primarily because it is necessary to accommodate both positive and negative values (unlike the modulus plots) and this would be impossible with logarithmic axes. Partly for this reason, and others which become clearer when dealing with MDOF systems, this format of display is not so widely used as the others.

(III) The Nyquist or Argand plane plot, however, is widely used and is a very effective way of displaying the important resonance region in some detail.

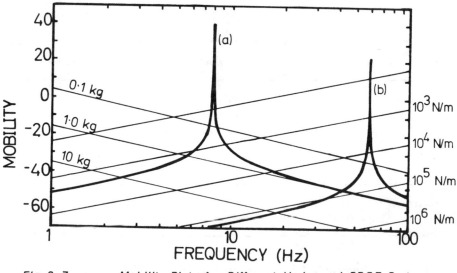

Fig 2.7   *Mobility Plots for Different Undamped SDOF Systems*

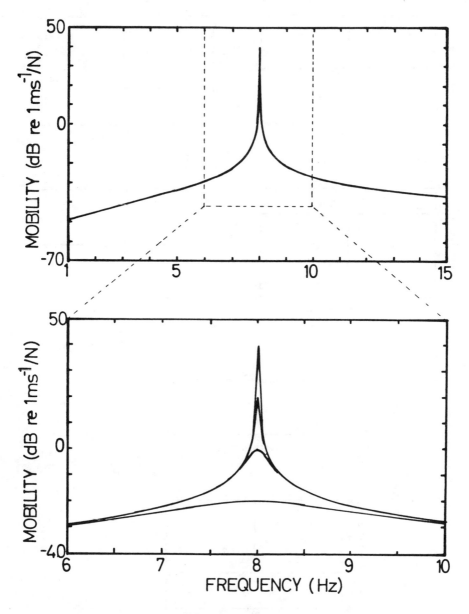

Fig 2.8   *Resonance Detail of Mobility Plot for Damped SDOF System*

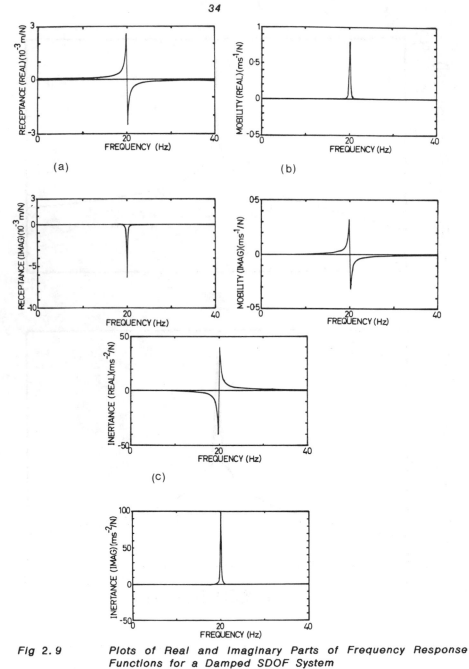

Fig 2.9   Plots of Real and Imaginary Parts of Frequency Response
            Functions for a Damped SDOF System
            (a)   Receptance
            (b)   Mobility
            (c)   Inertance

Fig. 2.10 shows Nyquist-type FRF plots corresponding to the viscously-damped SDOF system previously illustrated in Figs. 2.8 and 2.9. As this style of presentation consists of only a single graph, the missing information (in this case, frequency) must be added by identifying the values of frequency corresponding to particular points on the curve. This is usually done by indicating specific points on the curve at regular increments of frequency. In the examples shown, only those frequency points closest to resonance are clearly identifiable because those away from this area are very close together. Indeed, it is this feature — of distorting the plot so as to focus on the resonance area — that makes the Nyquist plot so attractive for modal testing applications.

It is clear from the graphs in Fig. 2.10, and also from the companion set in Fig. 2.11 for hysteretic damping, that each takes the approximate shape of a circle. In fact, as will be shown below, within each set one is an exact circle (marked by *), while the others only approximate to this shape. For viscous damping, it is the *mobility* Y(ω) which traces out an exact circle while for hysteretic damping, it is the *receptance* ($\alpha(\omega)$) which does so. In the other cases, the degree of distortion from a circular locus depends heavily on the amount of damping present — becoming negligible as the damping decreases.

2.2.3 Properties of SDOF FRF Plots

Lastly we shall examine some of the basic geometric properties of the various plots we have introduced for the FRF properties of the SDOF system, or oscillator.

We shall consider three specific plots:

(i)   Log mobility modulus versus frequency
(ii)   Nyquist mobility for viscous damping
(iii) Nyquist receptance for hysteretic damping.

It may be observed from Figs. 2.6(b), 2.7 and 2.8, and elsewhere, that for light damping (typically less than 1%) the mobility FRF plot exhibits a degree of symmetry about a vertical line passing through the resonance frequency. As was pointed out by Salter, the basic form of this plot can be constructed quite accurately using the reference values indicated on Fig. 2.12.

Turning to the Nyquist plots, we shall show that the two particular cases referred to above, namely:

-    mobility for a viscously-damped system, and
-    receptance for a hysteretically-damped system

both trace out exact circles as frequency ω sweeps from 0 to ∞.

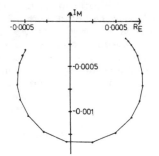

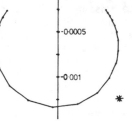

(a)

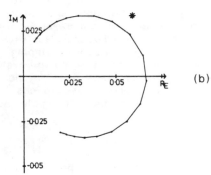

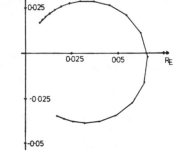

(b)

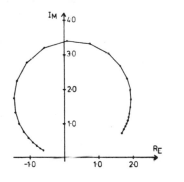

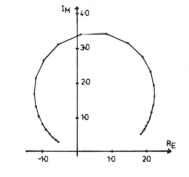

(c)

Fig 2.10 Nyquist Plots for SDOF
System with Viscous
Damping
   (a)   Receptance
   (b)   Mobility*
   (c)   Inertance

Fig 2.11   Nyquist Plots for
SDOF System with
Structural Damping
   (a)   Receptance*
   (b)   Mobility
   (c)   Inertance

Take first the viscous damping case. From equations (2.8) and (2.13) we have that the mobility is

$$Y(\omega) = i\omega\alpha(\omega) = \frac{i\omega}{k-\omega^2 m + i\omega c} = \frac{\omega^2 c + i\omega(k-\omega^2 m)}{(k-\omega^2 m)^2 + (\omega c)^2} \qquad (2.15)$$

So, $\quad Re(Y) = \dfrac{\omega^2 c}{(k - \omega^2 m)^2 + (\omega c)^2} \quad ; \quad Im(Y) = \dfrac{\omega(k - \omega^2 m)}{(k - \omega^2 m)^2 + (\omega c)^2}$

Let $\quad U = \left(Re(Y) - \dfrac{1}{2c} \right)$ and $\quad V = \Big(Im(Y) \Big)$

Then $\quad U^2 + V^2 = \dfrac{((k - \omega^2 m)^2 + (\omega c)^2)^2}{4c^2 \left((k - \omega^2 m)^2 + (\omega c)^2 \right)^2} = \left(\dfrac{1}{2c} \right)^2 \qquad (2.16)$

Hence, a plot of Re $(Y(\omega))$ vs Im $(Y(\omega))$ for $\omega = 0 \to \infty$ will trace out a circle of radius $1/2c$ and with its centre at (Re = $1/2c$, Im =0), as illustrated clearly in Fig. 2.10(b).

For the hysteretic damping case we have, from equation (2.10), a slightly different expression for the FRF:

$$\alpha(\omega) = \frac{1}{(k - \omega^2 m) + ih} = \frac{(k - \omega^2 m) - i(h)}{(k - \omega^2 m)^2 + (h)^2} \qquad (2.17)$$

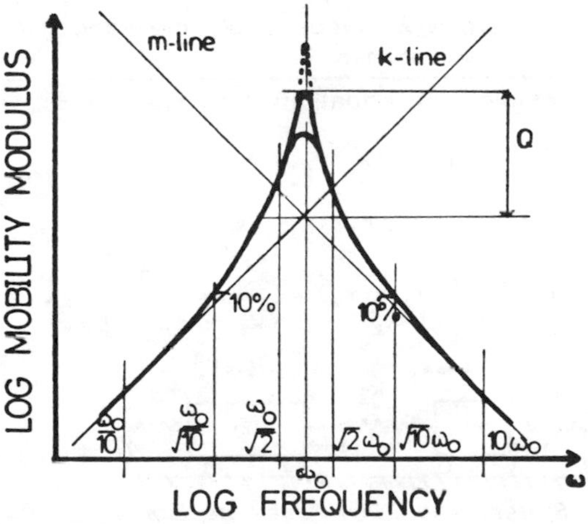

Fig 2.12   *Geometric Properties of SDOF Mobility Curve*

so that $Re(\alpha) = \dfrac{k - \omega^2 m}{(k - \omega^2 m)^2 + (h)^2}$; $Im(\alpha) = \dfrac{h}{(k - \omega^2 m)^2 + (h^2)}$

Although not the same expressions as those above for viscous damping, it is possible to see that

$$\left(Re \right)^2 + \left(Im + \frac{1}{2h} \right)^2 = \left(\frac{1}{2h} \right)^2 \qquad (2.18)$$

demonstrating that a Nyquist plot of receptance for a hysteretically-damped SDOF system will form a circle of radius (1/2h) and centre at (0, - 1/2h) as illustrated in Fig. 2.11(a).

2.3 UNDAMPED MULTI-DEGREE-OF-FREEDOM (MDOF) SYSTEM

Throughout much of the next 6 sections, we shall be discussing the general multi-degree-of-freedom (MDOF) system, which might have 2 degrees of freedom, or 20 or 200, and in doing so we shall be referring to 'matrices' and 'vectors' of data in a rather abstract and general way. In order to help visualise what some of these generalities mean, a specific 2DOF system, shown in Fig. 2.13, will be used although the general expressions and solutions will apply to the whole range of MDOF systems.

For an undamped MDOF system, with N degrees of freedom, the governing equations of motion can be written in matrix form as

$$[M]\, \{\ddot{x}(t)\} + [K]\, \{x(t)\} = \{f(t)\} \qquad (2.19)$$

where [M] and [K] are N x N mass and stiffness matrices respectively and

$\{x(t)\}$ and $\{f(t)\}$ are N x 1 vectors of time-varying displacements and forces

For our 2DOF example, the equations become

$$m_1\, \ddot{x}_1 + (k_1 + k_2)x_1 - (k_2)x_2 = f_1$$

$$m_2\, \ddot{x}_2 + (k_2 + k_3)x_2 - (k_2)x_1 = f_2$$

or

$$\begin{bmatrix} m_1 & 0 \\ 0 & m_2 \end{bmatrix} \begin{Bmatrix} \ddot{x}_1 \\ \ddot{x}_2 \end{Bmatrix} + \begin{bmatrix} (k_1 + k_2) & (-k_2) \\ (-k_2) & (k_2 + k_3) \end{bmatrix} \begin{Bmatrix} x_1 \\ x_2 \end{Bmatrix} = \begin{Bmatrix} f_1 \\ f_2 \end{Bmatrix}$$

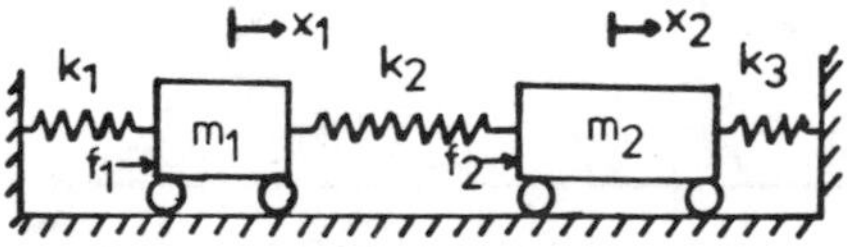

Fig 2.13   System with 2DOF Used as Example
$m_1 = 1\ kg$ $m_2 = 1\ kg$ $k_1 = k_3 = 0.4\ MN/m$
$k_2 = 0.8\ MN/m$

or, using the data given in Fig 2.13:

$$M = \begin{bmatrix} 1 & 0 \\ 0 & 1 \end{bmatrix} \text{(kg)} ; \quad K = \begin{bmatrix} 1.2 & -0.8 \\ -0.8 & 1.2 \end{bmatrix} \text{(MN/m)}$$

We shall consider first the free vibration solution (in order to determine the normal or natural modal properties) by taking

$$\{f(t)\} = \{0\}$$

In this case we shall assume that a solution exists of the form

$$\{x(t)\} = \{x\}e^{i\omega t}$$

where $\{x\}$ is an N x 1 vector of time-independent amplitudes for which case it is clear that $\{\ddot{x}\} = -\omega^2\{x\}e^{i\omega t}$

(NOTE that this assumes that the whole system is capable of vibrating at a single frequency, ω.)

Substitution of this condition and trial solution into the equation of motion (2.19), leads to

$$([K] - \omega^2[M]) \{x\} e^{i\omega t} = \{0\} \tag{2.20}$$

for which the only non-trivial solution is

$$\det|[K] - \omega^2[M]| = 0 \tag{2.21}$$

or: $d_{2N}\omega^{2N} + d_{2N-2}\omega^{2N-2} + \ldots d_0 = 0$

from which condition can be found N values of ω^2: ($\bar{\omega}_1^2$, $\bar{\omega}_2^2$ ... $\bar{\omega}_r^2$ ... $\bar{\omega}_N^2$), the undamped system's natural frequencies.

Substituting any one of these back into (2.20) yields a corresponding set of relative values for $\{x\}$, i.e. $\{\psi\}_r$, the so-called mode shape corresponding to that natural frequency.

The complete solution can be expressed in two NxN matrices – the eigenmatrices – as

$$\begin{bmatrix} \ddots & & \\ & \bar{\omega}_r^2 & \\ & & \ddots \end{bmatrix} , \quad \begin{bmatrix} \Psi \end{bmatrix}$$

where $\bar{\omega}_r^2$ is the rth eigenvalue, or natural frequency squared, and $\{\psi\}_r$ is a description of the corresponding mode shape.

Various numerical procedures are available which take the system matrices [M] and [K] (the SPATIAL MODEL), and convert them to the two eigenmatrices $\lceil \bar{\omega}_r^2 \rfloor$ and [Ψ] (which constitute the MODAL MODEL).

It is very important to realise at this stage that one of these two matrices – the eigenvalue matrix – is unique, while the other – the eigenvector matrix – is not. Whereas the natural frequencies are fixed quantities, the mode shapes are subject to an indeterminate scaling factor which does not affect the <u>shape</u> of the vibration mode, only its amplitude. Thus, a mode shape vector of

$$\begin{Bmatrix} 1 \\ 2 \\ 1 \\ 0 \\ \cdot \end{Bmatrix}$$ shows exactly the same vibration mode as $$\begin{Bmatrix} 3 \\ 6 \\ 3 \\ 0 \\ \cdot \end{Bmatrix}$$

and so on.

What determines how the eigenvectors are scaled, or "normalised" is largely governed by the numerical procedures followed by the eigensolution. This topic will be discussed in more detail below.

For our 2DOF example, we find that equation (2.21) becomes

$$\det \begin{vmatrix} (k_1 + k_2 - \omega^2 m_1) & (-k_2) \\ (-k_2) & (k_2 + k_3 - \omega^2 m_2) \end{vmatrix}$$

$$= \omega^4 (m_1 m_2) - \omega^2 ((m_1 + m_2)k_2 = 0 \\ + m_1 k_3 + m_2 k_1) \\ + k_1 k_2 + k_1 k_3 + k_2 k_3$$

Numerically

$$\omega^4 - \omega^2 (2.4 \times 10^6) + (0.8 \times 10^{12}) = 0$$

This condition leads to $\bar{\omega}_1^2 = 4 \times 10^5 (r/s)^2$ and $\bar{\omega}_2^2 = 2 \times 10^6 (r/s)^2$

Substituting either value of ω into the equation of motion, gives

$$(k_1 + k_2 - \bar{\omega}_r^2 m_1)_r X_1 = (k_2)_r X_2$$

or

$$\{\psi\}_r = \begin{Bmatrix} r\psi_1 \\ r\psi_2 \end{Bmatrix} \equiv \begin{Bmatrix} rX_1/X_0 \\ rX_2/X_0 \end{Bmatrix}$$

Numerically, we have a solution

$$\lceil \bar{\omega}_r^2 \rfloor = \begin{bmatrix} 4 \times 10^5 & 0 \\ 0 & 2 \times 10^6 \end{bmatrix} ; [\Psi] = \begin{bmatrix} 1 & 1 \\ 1 & -1 \end{bmatrix}$$

Before proceeding with the next phase – the response analysis – it is worthwhile to examine some of the properties of the modal model as these greatly influence the subsequent analysis.

The modal model possesses some very important properties – known as the ORTHOGONALITY properties – which, concisely stated, are as follows:

$$[\Psi]^T \ [M] \ [\Psi] \ = \ \lceil m_r \rfloor$$

$$[\Psi]^T \ [K] \ [\Psi] \ = \ \lceil k_r \rfloor \qquad (2.22)$$

from which: $\lceil \bar{\omega}_r^2 \rfloor = \lceil m_r \rfloor^{-1} \lceil k_r \rfloor$ where m_r and k_r are often referred to as the *modal* or *generalised mass* and *stiffness* of mode r. Now, because the eigenvector matrix is subject to an arbitrary scaling factor, the values of m_r and k_r are not unique and so it is inadvisable to refer to "the" generalised mass or stiffness of a particular mode. Many eigenvalue extraction routines scale each vector so that its largest element has unit magnitude (1.0), but this is not universal. In any event, what is found is that the ratio of (k_r/m_r) <u>is</u> unique and is equal to the eigenvalue – $(\bar{\omega}_r^2)$. Among the many scaling or normalisation processes, there is one which has most relevance to modal testing and that is *mass–normalisation*. The mass–normalised eigenvectors are written as $[\Phi]$ and have the particular property that

$$\left[\ \Phi \ \right]^T \ \left[\ M \ \right] \ \left[\ \Phi \ \right] = \left[\ I \ \right]$$

and thus
$$\left[\ \Phi \ \right]^T \ \left[\ K \ \right] \ \left[\ \Phi \ \right] = \left[\ \bar{\omega}_r^2 \ \right] \qquad (2.23)$$

The relationship between the mass–normalised mode shape for mode r, $\{\phi\}_r$, and its more general form, $\{\psi\}_r$, is, simply:

$$\{\phi\}_r = \frac{1}{\sqrt{m_r}} \ \{\psi\}_r \qquad (2.24)$$

or $\quad [\Phi] = [\psi] \lceil m_r \rfloor^{-1/2}$

A proof of the orthogonality properties is as follows. The equation of motion may be written

$$([K] - \bar{\omega}^2 \ [M]) \ \{x\} e^{i\omega t} = \{0\} \qquad (2.25)$$

For a particular mode, we have

$$([K] - \bar{\omega}_r^2 \ [M]) \ \{\psi\}_r = \{0\} \qquad (2.26)$$

Premultiply by a different eigenvector, transposed:

$$\{\psi\}_s^T ([K] - \bar{\omega}_r^2 [M]) \ \{\psi\}_r = 0 \qquad (2.27)$$

We can also write

$$([K] - \bar{\omega}_s^2 [M]) \ \{\psi\}_s = \{0\} \qquad (2.28)$$

which we can transpose, and postmultiply by $\{\psi\}_r$, to give

$$\{\psi\}_s^T \ ([K]^T - \bar{\omega}_s^2 [M]^T) \ \{\psi\}_r = 0 \qquad (2.29)$$

But, since [M] and [K] are symmetric, they are identical to their transposes and equations (2.27) and (2.29) can be combined to give

$$(\bar{\omega}_r{}^2 - \bar{\omega}_s{}^2)\{\psi\}_s{}^T [M]\{\psi\}_r = 0 \qquad (2.30)$$

which, if $\bar{\omega}_r \neq \bar{\omega}_s$, can only be satisfied if

$$\{\psi\}_s{}^T[M]\{\psi\}_r = 0; \qquad r \neq s \qquad (2.31)$$

Together with either (2.27) or (2.29), this means also that

$$\{\psi\}_s{}^T[K]\{\psi\}_r = 0; \qquad r \neq s \qquad (2.32)$$

For the special cases where $r = s$, equations (2.31) and (2.32) do not apply, but it is clear from (2.27) that

$$(\{\psi\}_r{}^T[K]\{\psi\}_r) = \bar{\omega}_r{}^2(\{\psi\}_r{}^T[M]\{\psi\}_r) \qquad (2.33)$$

so that $\{\psi\}_r{}^T[M]\{\psi\}_r = m_r$ and $\{\psi\}_r{}^T[K]\{\psi\}_r = k_r$

and $\bar{\omega}_r{}^2 = k_r/m_r$

Putting together all the possible combinations of r and s leads to the full matrix equation (2.22) above.

For our 2DOF example, the numerical results give eigenvectors which are clearly plausible. If we use them to calculate the generalised mass and stiffness, we obtain

$$\begin{bmatrix} 1 & 1 \\ 1 & -1 \end{bmatrix}\begin{bmatrix} 1 & 0 \\ 0 & 1 \end{bmatrix}\begin{bmatrix} 1 & 1 \\ 1 & -1 \end{bmatrix} = \begin{bmatrix} 2 & 0 \\ 0 & 2 \end{bmatrix} = \lceil m_r \rfloor$$

$$\begin{bmatrix} 1 & 1 \\ 1 & -1 \end{bmatrix}\begin{bmatrix} 1.2 & -0.8 \\ -0.8 & 1.2 \end{bmatrix}\begin{bmatrix} 1 & 1 \\ 1 & -1 \end{bmatrix}10^6 = \begin{bmatrix} 0.8 & 0 \\ 0 & 4 \end{bmatrix}10^6 = \lceil k_r \rfloor$$

clearly $\lceil m_r \rfloor^{-1}\lceil k_r \rfloor = \begin{bmatrix} 0.4 & 0 \\ 0 & 2.0 \end{bmatrix}10^6 = \lceil \omega_r{}^2 \rfloor$

To obtain the mass normalised version of these eigenvectors, we must calculate

$$[\Phi] = \begin{bmatrix} 1 & 1 \\ 1 & -1 \end{bmatrix}\lceil m_r \rfloor^{-1/2} = \begin{bmatrix} 0.707 & 0.707 \\ 0.707 & -0.707 \end{bmatrix}$$

Turning now to a response analysis, we shall consider the case where the structure is excited sinusoidally by a set of forces all at the same frequency, ω, but with various amplitudes and phases. Then

$$\{f(t)\} = \{f\}\, e^{i\omega t}$$

and, as before, we shall assume a solution exists of the form

$$\{x(t)\} = \{x\}\, e^{i\omega t}$$

where $\{f\}$ and $\{x\}$ are Nx1 vectors of time-independent complex amplitudes.

The equation of motion then becomes

$$([K] - \omega^2[M])\{x\}e^{i\omega t} = \{f\}e^{i\omega t} \qquad (2.34)$$

or, rearranging to solve for the unknown responses,

$$\{x\} = ([K] - \omega^2[M])^{-1}\{f\} \qquad (2.35a)$$

which may be written

$$\{x\} = [\alpha(\omega)]\{f\} \qquad (2.35b)$$

where $[\alpha(\omega)]$ is the NxN receptance matrix for the system and constitutes its RESPONSE MODEL. The general element in the FRF matrix, $\alpha_{jk}(\omega)$, is defined as follows:

$$\alpha_{jk}(\omega) = \left(\frac{x_j}{f_k}\right) \quad f_m = 0; \; m = 1,N \; ; \neq k \qquad (2.36)$$

and as such represents an individual receptance expression very similar to that defined earlier for the SDOF system.

It is clearly possible for us to determine values for the elements of $[\alpha(\omega)]$ at any frequency of interest simply by substituting the appropriate values into (2.35). However, this involves the inversion of a system matrix at each frequency and this has several disadvantages, namely:

- it becomes costly for large-order systems (large N);
- it is inefficient if only a few of the individual FRF expressions are required;
- it provides no insight into the form of the various FRF properties.

For these, and other, reasons an alternative means of deriving the various FRF parameters is used which makes use of the modal properties for the system.

Returning to (2.35) we can write

$$([K] - \omega^2[M]) = [\alpha(\omega)]^{-1} \qquad (2.37)$$

Premultiply both sides by $[\Phi]^T$ and postmultiply both sides by $[\Phi]$ to obtain

$$[\Phi]^T([K] - \omega^2[M])[\Phi] = [\Phi]^T[\alpha(\omega)]^{-1}[\Phi]$$

or $\quad \diagdown (\overline{\omega}_r^2 - \omega^2) \diagdown = [\Phi]^T[\alpha(\omega)]^{-1}[\Phi] \qquad (2.38)$

which gives

$$[\alpha(\omega)] = [\Phi] \diagdown (\overline{\omega}_r^2 - \omega^2) \diagdown^{-1}[\Phi]^T \qquad (2.39)$$

It is clear from this equation that the receptance matrix $[\alpha(\omega)]$ is symmetric and this will be recognised as the principle of reciprocity which applies to many structural characteristics. Its implications in this situation are that:

$$\alpha_{jk} = (x_j/f_k) = \alpha_{kj} = (x_k/f_j)$$

Equation (2.39) permits us to compute any individual FRF parameter, $\alpha_{jk}(\omega)$ using the following formula

$$\alpha_{jk}(\omega) = \sum_{r=1}^{N} \frac{(_r\phi_j)(_r\phi_k)}{\bar{\omega}_r^2 - \omega^2} = \sum_{r=1}^{N} \frac{(_r\psi_i)(_r\psi_k)}{m_r(\bar{\omega}_r^2 - \omega^2)} \qquad (2.40)$$

or:

$$\alpha_{jk}(\omega) = \sum_{r=1}^{N} \frac{_rA_{jk}}{\bar{\omega}_r^2 - \omega^2}$$

which is very much simpler and more informative than by means of the direct inverse, eq. (2.35a). Here we introduce a new parameter, $_rA_{jk}$, which we shall refer to as a MODAL CONSTANT: in this case, that for mode r for this specific receptance linking coordinates j and k. (Note that other presentations of the theory sometimes refer to the modal constant as a 'RESIDUE' together with the use of 'POLE' instead of our natural frequency.) The above is a most important result and is in fact the central relationship upon which the whole subject is based. From the general equation (2.35a), the typical individual FRF element $\alpha_{jk}(\omega)$, defined in (2.36), would be expected to have the form of a ratio of two polynomials:

$$\alpha_{jk}(\omega) = \frac{b_0 + b_1\omega^2 + b_2\omega^4 + \dots b_{N-1}\omega^{2N-2}}{d_0 + d_1\omega^2 + d_2\omega^4 + \dots d_N \omega^{2N}} \qquad (2.41)$$

and in such a format it would be difficult to visualise the nature of the function, $\alpha_{jk}(\omega)$. However, it is clear that an expression such as (2.41) can also be rewritten as

$$\alpha_{jk}(\omega) = B \frac{(\Omega_1^2 - \omega^2)(\Omega_r^2 - \omega^2) \dots (\Omega_{(N-1)}^2 - \omega^2)}{(\bar{\omega}_1^2 - \omega^2)(\bar{\omega}_2^2 - \omega^2) \dots (\bar{\omega}_N^2 - \omega^2)} \qquad (2.42)$$

and by inspection of the form of (2.35a) it is also clear that the factors in the denominator, $\bar{\omega}_1^2$, $\bar{\omega}_2^2$ etc. are indeed the natural frequencies of the system, $\bar{\omega}_r^2$ (this is because the denominator is necessarily formed by the $det|[K]-\omega^2[M]|$.)

All this means that a forbidding expression such as (2.41) can be expected to be reducible to a partial fractions series form, such as

$$\alpha_{jk}(\omega) = \sum_{r=1}^{N} \frac{_rA_{jk}}{\bar{\omega}_r^2 - \omega^2} \qquad (2.43)$$

Thus, the solution we obtain through equations (2.37) to (2.40) is not unexpected, but its significance lies in the very simple and convenient formula it provides for the coefficients, $_rA_{jk}$, in the series form.

We can observe some of the above relationships through our 2DOF example. The forced vibration equations of motion give

$$(k_1 + k_2 - \omega^2 m_1) x_1 + (-k_2) x_2 = f_1$$

$$(-k_2) x_1 + (k_2 + k_3 - \omega^2 m_2) x_2 = f_2$$

which, in turn, give (for example):

$$\left(\frac{x_1}{f_1}\right)_{f_2=0} = \frac{k_2 + k_3 - \omega^2 m_2}{\omega^4 m_1 m_2 - \omega^2 ((m_1 + m_2)k_2 + m_1 k_3 + m_2 k_1) + (k_1 k_2 + k_2 k_3 + k_1 k_3)}$$

or, numerically, $\quad = \dfrac{(1.2 \times 10^6 - \omega^2)}{(0.8 \times 10^{12} - 2.4 \times 10^6 \omega^2 + \omega^4)}$

Now, if we use the modal summation formula (2.40) together with the results obtained earlier, we can write

$$\alpha_{11} = \left(\frac{x_1}{f_1}\right) = \frac{(_1\phi_1)^2}{\bar{\omega}_1{}^2 - \omega^2} + \frac{(_2\phi_1)^2}{\bar{\omega}_2{}^2 - \omega^2}$$

or numerically, $\quad = \dfrac{0.5}{0.4 \times 10^6 - \omega^2} + \dfrac{0.5}{2 \times 10^6 - \omega^2}$

which is equal to $(1.2 \times 10^6 - \omega^2)/(0.8 \times 10^{12} - 2.4 \times 10^6 \omega^2 + \omega^4)$, as above.

The above characteristics of both the modal and response models of an undamped MDOF system form the basis of the corresponding data for the more general, damped, cases.

The following sections will examine the effects on these models of adding various types of damping, while a discussion of the presentation of MDOF frequency response data is given in 2.7.

2.4 PROPORTIONAL DAMPING

In approaching the more general case of damped systems, it is convenient to consider first a special type of damping which has the advantage of being particularly easy to analyse. This type of damping is usually referred to as 'proportional' damping (for reasons which will be clear later) although this is a somewhat restrictive title. The particular advantage of using a proportional damping model in the analysis of structures is that the modes of such a structure are almost identical to those of the undamped version of the model. Specifically, the mode shapes *are* identical and the natural frequencies are very similar to those of the simpler system also. In effect, it is possible to derive the modal properties of a proportionally damped system by analysing in full the undamped version and then making a correction for the presence of the damping. While this procedure is often used in the theoretical analysis of structures, it should be noted that it is only valid in the case of this special type or distribution of damping, which may not generally apply to the real structures studied in modal tests.

If we return to the general equation of motion for a MDOF system, equation (2.19), and add a viscous damping matrix [C] we obtain:

$$[M]\{\ddot{x}\} + [C]\{\dot{x}\} + [K]\{x\} = \{f\} \qquad (2.44)$$

which is not so amenable to the type of solution followed in Section 2.3. A general solution will be presented in the next section, but here we shall examine the properties of this equation for the case where the damping matrix is directly proportional to the stiffness matrix; i.e.

$$[C] = \beta[K] \qquad (2.45)$$

(NOTE It is important to note that this is not the only type of proportional damping – see below)

In this case, it is clear that if we pre- and post-multiply the damping matrix by the eigenvector matrix for the undamped system [Ψ], in just the same way as was done in equation (2.22) for the mass and stiffness matrices, then we shall find:

$$[Ψ]^T[C][Ψ] = \beta \lceil k_r \rfloor = \lceil c_r \rfloor \qquad (2.46)$$

where the diagonal elements c_r represent the generalised damping of the various modes of the system. The fact that this matrix is also diagonal means that the undamped system mode shapes are also those of the damped system, and this is a particular feature of this type of damping. This statement can easily be demonstrated by taking the general equation of motion above (2.44) and, for the case of no excitation, pre- and post-multiplying the whole equation by the eigenvector matrix, [Ψ]. We shall then find:

$$\lceil m_r \rfloor \{\ddot{p}\} + \lceil c_r \rfloor \{\dot{p}\} + \lceil k_r \rfloor \{p\} = \{0\}; \quad \{p\} = [Ψ]^{-1}\{x\} \qquad (2.47)$$

from which the rth individual equation is:

$$m_r \ddot{p}_r + c_r \dot{p}_r + k_r p_r = 0 \qquad (2.48)$$

which is clearly that of a single-degree-of-freedom system, or of a single mode of the system. This mode has a complex natural frequency with an oscillatory part of

$$\omega_r' = \bar{\omega}_r\sqrt{1 - \zeta_r^2} \; ; \; \bar{\omega}_r^2 = \frac{k_r}{m_r} \; ; \; \zeta_r = \frac{c_r}{2\sqrt{k_r m_r}} = \frac{1}{2}\beta\bar{\omega}_r$$

and a decay part of

$$a_r = \zeta_r\bar{\omega}_r = \frac{\beta}{2}$$

(using the notation introduced above for the SDOF analysis).

These characteristics carry over to the forced response analysis in which a simple extension of the steps detailed between equations (2.34) and (2.40) leads to the definition for the general receptance FRF as:

$$[\alpha(\omega)] = [K + i\omega C - \omega^2 M]^{-1}$$

or

$$\alpha_{jk}(\omega) = \sum_{r=1}^{N} \frac{(_r\psi_j)(_r\psi_k)}{(k_r - \omega^2 m_r) + i(\omega c_r)} \qquad (2.49)$$

which has a very similar form to that for the undamped system except that now it becomes complex in the denominator as a result of the inclusion of damping.

General Forms of Proportional Damping

It may be seen from the above that other distributions of damping will bring about the same type of result and these are collectively included in the classification 'proportional damping'. In particular, if the damping matrix is proportional to the mass matrix, then exactly the same type of result ensues and, indeed, the usual definition of proportional damping is that the damping matrix [C] should be of the form:

$$[C] = \beta[K] + \gamma[M] \qquad (2.50)$$

In this case, the damped system will have eigenvalues and eigenvectors as follows:

$$\omega_r' = \bar{\omega}_r\sqrt{1-\zeta_r^2} \; ; \quad \zeta_r = \beta\bar{\omega}_r/2 + \gamma/2\bar{\omega}_r$$

and $[\psi^{damped}] = [\psi^{undamped}]$

Distributions of damping of the type described above are generally found to be plausible from a practical standpoint: the actual damping mechanisms are usually to be found in parallel with stiffness elements (for internal material or hysteresis damping) or with mass elements (for friction damping). There is a more general definition of the condition required for the damped system to possess the same mode shapes as its undamped counterpart, and that is:

$$([M]^{-1} [K])([M]^{-1} [C]) = ([M]^{-1} [C])([M]^{-1} [K]) \qquad (2.51)$$

although it is more difficult to make a direct physical interpretation of its form.

Finally, it can be noted that an identical treatment can be made of a MDOF system with hysteretic damping, producing the same essential results. If the general system equations of motion are expressed as:

$$[M] \{\ddot{x}\} + ([K+iH]) \{x\} = \{f\} \qquad (2.52)$$

and the hysteretic damping matrix $[H]$ is 'proportional', typically:

$$[H] = \beta[K] + \gamma[M] \qquad (2.53)$$

then we find that the mode shapes for the damped system are again identical to those of the undamped system and that the eigenvalues take the complex form:

$$\lambda_r^2 = \bar{\omega}_r^2 (1+i\eta_r) \; ; \; \bar{\omega}_r^2 = k_r/m_r \; ; \; \eta_r = \beta + \gamma/\bar{\omega}_r^2 \qquad (2.54)$$

Also, the general FRF expression is written:

$$\alpha_{jk}(\omega) = \sum_{r=1}^{N} \frac{{}_r\psi_j \; {}_r\psi_k}{(k_r - \omega^2 m_r) + i\eta_r k_r} \qquad (2.55)$$

2.5 STRUCTURAL DAMPING – GENERAL CASE

The analysis in the previous section for proportionally-damped systems gives some insight into the characteristics of this more general description of practical structures. However, as was stated there, the case of proportional damping is a particular one which, although often justified in a theoretical analysis because it is realistic and also because of a lack of any more accurate model, does not apply to all cases. In our studies here, it is very important that we consider the most general case if we are to be able to interpret and analyse correctly the data we observe on real structures. These, after all, know nothing of our predilection for assuming proportionality. Thus, we consider in the next two sections the properties of systems with general damping elements, first of the structural or hysteretic type, then viscous.

We start by writing the general equation of motion for a MDOF system with hysteretic damping and harmonic excitation (as it is this that we are working towards):

$$[M]\ \ddot{(x)} + [K]\ (x) + i[H]\ (x) = (f)e^{i\omega t} \tag{2.56}$$

Now, consider first the case where there is no excitation and assume a solution of the form:

$$(x) = (x)e^{i\lambda t} \tag{2.57}$$

Substituted into (2.56), this trial solution leads to a complex eigenproblem whose solution is in the form of two matrices (as for the earlier undamped case), containing the eigenvalues and eigenvectors. In this case, however, these matrices are both complex, meaning that each natural frequency and each mode shape is described in terms of complex quantities. We choose to write the rth eigenvalue as

$$\lambda_r^2 = \omega_r^2(1+i\eta_r) \tag{2.58}$$

where ω_r is the natural frequency and η_r is the damping loss factor for that mode. It is important to note that the natural frequency ω_r is not (necessarily) equal to the natural frequency of the undamped system, $\bar{\omega}_r$, as was the case for proportional damping, although the two values will generally be very close in practice.

The complex mode shapes are at first more difficult to interpret but in fact what we find is that the amplitude of each coordinate has both a magnitude and a phase angle. This is only very slightly different from the undamped case as there we effectively have a magnitude at each point plus a phase angle which is either $0°$ or $180°$, both of which can be completely described using real numbers. What the inclusion of general damping effects does is to generalise this particular feature of the mode shape data.

This eigensolution can be seen to possess the same type of orthogonality properties as those demonstrated earlier for the undamped system and may be defined by the equations:

$$[\Psi]^T[M][\Psi] = \lceil m_r \rfloor$$

$$[\Psi]^T [K+iH] [\Psi] = \lceil k_r \rfloor \tag{2.59}$$

Again, the generalised mass and stiffness parameters (now complex) depend upon the normalisation of the mode shape vectors for their magnitudes but always obey the relationship:

$$\lambda_r^2 = k_r/m_r \tag{2.60}$$

and here again we may define a set of mass-normalised eigenvectors as:

$$(\phi)_r = (m_r)^{-1/2} (\psi)_r \tag{2.61}$$

NUMERICAL EXAMPLES WITH STRUCTURAL DAMPING

Some further numerical examples are included to illustrate the characteristics of more general damped systems, based on the following 3DOF model:

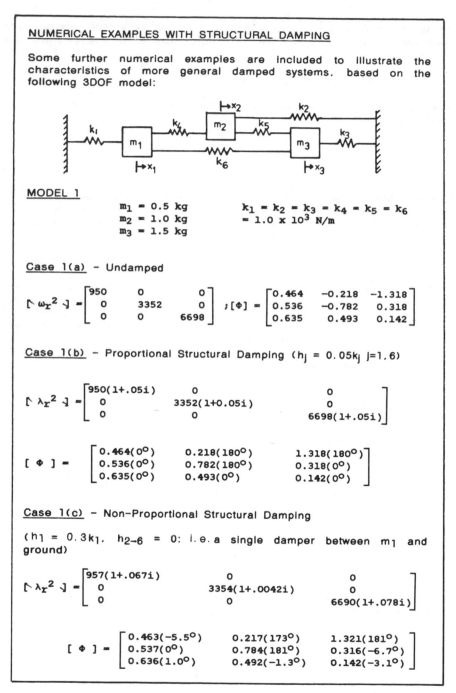

MODEL 1

$m_1 = 0.5$ kg $k_1 = k_2 = k_3 = k_4 = k_5 = k_6$
$m_2 = 1.0$ kg $= 1.0 \times 10^3$ N/m
$m_3 = 1.5$ kg

Case 1(a) – Undamped

$$\lceil \omega_r^2 \rfloor = \begin{bmatrix} 950 & 0 & 0 \\ 0 & 3352 & 0 \\ 0 & 0 & 6698 \end{bmatrix} ; [\Phi] = \begin{bmatrix} 0.464 & -0.218 & -1.318 \\ 0.536 & -0.782 & 0.318 \\ 0.635 & 0.493 & 0.142 \end{bmatrix}$$

Case 1(b) – Proportional Structural Damping ($h_j = 0.05k_j$ j=1,6)

$$\lceil \lambda_r^2 \rfloor = \begin{bmatrix} 950(1+.05i) & 0 & 0 \\ 0 & 3352(1+0.05i) & 0 \\ 0 & 0 & 6698(1+.05i) \end{bmatrix}$$

$$[\Phi] = \begin{bmatrix} 0.464(0^\circ) & 0.218(180^\circ) & 1.318(180^\circ) \\ 0.536(0^\circ) & 0.782(180^\circ) & 0.318(0^\circ) \\ 0.635(0^\circ) & 0.493(0^\circ) & 0.142(0^\circ) \end{bmatrix}$$

Case 1(c) – Non-Proportional Structural Damping

($h_1 = 0.3k_1$, $h_{2-6} = 0$: i.e. a single damper between m_1 and ground)

$$\lceil \lambda_r^2 \rfloor = \begin{bmatrix} 957(1+.067i) & 0 & 0 \\ 0 & 3354(1+.0042i) & 0 \\ 0 & 0 & 6690(1+.078i) \end{bmatrix}$$

$$[\Phi] = \begin{bmatrix} 0.463(-5.5^\circ) & 0.217(173^\circ) & 1.321(181^\circ) \\ 0.537(0^\circ) & 0.784(181^\circ) & 0.316(-6.7^\circ) \\ 0.636(1.0^\circ) & 0.492(-1.3^\circ) & 0.142(-3.1^\circ) \end{bmatrix}$$

NOTES: (i)   Each mode has a different damping factor

(ii)   All eigenvector arguments within 10° of 0° or 180° (ie the modes are almost 'real').

MODEL 2

$m_1 = 1.0$ kg
$m_2 = 0.95$ kg
$m_3 = 1.05$ kg

$k_1 = k_2 = k_3 = k_4 = k_5 = k_6$
$= 1 \times 10^3$ N/m

Case 2(a) – Undamped

$$\lceil \omega_r^2 \rfloor = \begin{bmatrix} 999 & 0 & 0 \\ 0 & 3892 & 0 \\ 0 & 0 & 4124 \end{bmatrix} \; ; \; [\Phi] = \begin{bmatrix} 0.577 & -0.702 & 0.552 \\ 0.567 & -0.215 & -0.826 \\ 0.587 & 0.752 & 0.207 \end{bmatrix}$$

NOTE: This system has two close natural frequencies

Case 2(b) – Proportional Structural Damping ($h_j = 0.05k_j$)

$$\lceil \lambda_r^2 \rfloor = \begin{bmatrix} 999(1+.05i) & 0 & 0 \\ 0 & 3892(1+.05i) & 0 \\ 0 & 0 & 4124(1+.05i) \end{bmatrix}$$

$$[\Phi] = \begin{bmatrix} 0.577(0^o) & 0.702(180^o) & 0.552(0^o) \\ 0.567(0^o) & 0.215(180^o) & 0.827(180^o) \\ 0.587(0^o) & 0.752(0^o) & 0.207(0^o) \end{bmatrix}$$

Case 2(c) – Non-Proportional Structural Damping
($h_1 = 0.3k_1$; $h_{2-6}=0$)

$$\lceil \lambda_r^2 \rfloor = \begin{bmatrix} 1006(1+.10i) & 0 & 0 \\ 0 & 3942(1+.031i) & 0 \\ 0 & 0 & 4067(1+.019i) \end{bmatrix}$$

$$[\Phi] = \begin{bmatrix} 0.578(-4^o) & 0.851(162^o) & 0.685(40^o) \\ 0.569(2^o) & 0.570(101^o) & 1.019(176^o) \\ 0.588(2^o) & 0.848(12^o) & 0.560(-50^o) \end{bmatrix}$$

Forced Response Analysis

We turn next to the analysis of forced vibration for the particular case of harmonic excitation and response, for which the governing equation of motion is:

$$[K + iH - \omega^2 M]\ \{x\}e^{i\omega t} = \{f\}e^{i\omega t} \tag{2.62}$$

As before, a direct solution to this problem may be obtained by using the equations of motion to give:

$$\{x\} = [K + iH - \omega^2 M]^{-1}\ \{f\} = [\alpha(\omega)]\ \{f\} \tag{2.63}$$

but again this is very inefficient for numerical application and we shall make use of the same procedure as before by multiplying both sides of the equation by the eigenvectors. Starting with (2.63), and following the same procedure as between equations (2.37) and (2.39), we can write:

$$[\alpha(\omega)] = [\Phi]\ \lceil (\lambda_r^2 - \omega^2)\ \rfloor^{-1}\ [\Phi]^T \tag{2.64}$$

and from this full matrix equation we can extract any one FRF element, such as $\alpha_{jk}(\omega)$, and express it explicitly in a series form:

$$\alpha_{jk}(\omega) = \sum_{r=1}^{N} \frac{{}_r\phi_j\ {}_r\phi_k}{\omega_r^2 - \omega^2 + i\eta_r\omega_r^2} \tag{2.65}$$

which may also be rewritten in various alternative ways, such as:

$$\alpha_{jk}(\omega) = \sum_{r=1}^{N} \frac{{}_r\psi_j\ {}_r\psi_k}{m_r(\omega_r^2 - \omega^2 + i\eta_r\omega_r^2)}$$

or

$$= \sum_{r=1}^{N} \frac{{}_rA_{jk}}{\omega_r^2 - \omega^2 + i\eta_r\omega_r^2}$$

In these expressions, the numerator (as well as the denominator) is now complex as a result of the complexity of the eigenvectors. It is in this respect that the general damping case differs from that for proportional damping.

Excitation by a General Force Vector

Having derived an expression for the general term in the frequency response function matrix $\alpha_{jk}(\omega)$, it is appropriate to consider next the analysis of a situation where the system is excited simultaneously at several points (rather than at just one, as is the case for the individual FRF expressions).

The general behaviour for this case is governed by equation (2.62) and the solution in (2.63). However, a more explicit (and perhaps useful) form of this solution may be derived from (2.63) – although not very easily! – as:

$$\{x\} = \sum_{r=1}^{N} \frac{\{\phi\}_r^T \{f\} \{\phi\}_r}{\omega_r^2 - \omega^2 + i\eta_r\omega_r^2} \qquad (2.66)$$

This equation permits the calculation of one or more individual responses to an excitation of several simultaneous harmonic forces (all of which must have the same frequency but may vary in magnitude and phase) and it may be seen that the special case of one single response to a single force (a frequency response function) is clearly that quoted in (2.65).

Before leaving this section, it is worth mentioning another special case of some interest, namely that where the excitation is a vector of mono-phased forces. Here, the complete generality admitted in the previous paragraph is restricted somewhat by insisting that all forces have the same frequency _and_ phase, although their magnitudes may vary. What is of interest in this case is to see whether there exist any conditions under which it is possible to obtain a similarly mono-phased response (the whole system responding with a single phase angle). This is not generally the case in the solution to equation (2.66) above.

Thus, let the force and response vectors be represented by

$$\{f\} = \{\hat{F}\}e^{i\omega t} \qquad (2.67)$$

$$\{x\} = \{\hat{x}\}e^{i(\omega t + \theta)}$$

where both $\{\hat{F}\}$ and $\{\hat{x}\}$ are vectors of real quantities, and substitute these into the equation of motion (2.62). This leads to a complex equation which can be split into real and imaginary parts to give:

$$((-\omega^2[M] + [K]) \cos\theta + [H] \sin\theta)\{\hat{x}\} = \{\hat{F}\}$$
$$((-\omega^2[M] + [K]) \sin\theta - [H] \cos\theta)\{\hat{x}\} = \{o\} \qquad (2.68)$$

The second of this pair of equations can be treated as an eigenvalue problem which has 'roots' θ_s and corresponding 'vectors' $\{x\}_s$. These may be inserted back into the first of the pair of equations (2.68) in order to establish the form of the (mono-phased) force vector necessary to bring about the (mono-phased) response vector described by $\{x\}_s$. Thus we find that there exist a set of N mono-phased force vectors each of which, when applied as excitation to the system, results in a mono-phased response characteristic.

It must be noted that this analysis is even more complicated than it appears at first, mainly because the equations used to obtain the above mentioned solution are functions of frequency. Thus, each solution obtained as described above applies only at one specific frequency, ω_s. However, it is particularly interesting to determine what frequencies must be considered in order that the characteristic phase lag (θ) between (all) the forces and (all) the responses is exactly 90 degrees. Inspection of equation (2.68) shows that if θ is to be 90°, then that equation reduces to:

$$(-\omega^2[M] + [K]) \hat{\{x\}} = 0 \qquad (2.69)$$

which is clearly the equation to be solved to find the undamped system natural frequencies and mode shapes. Thus, we have the important result that it is always possible to find a set of mono-phased forces which will cause a mono-phased set of responses and, moreover, if these two sets of mono-phased parameters are separated by exactly 90°, then the frequency at which the system is vibrating is identical to one of its undamped natural frequencies and the displacement 'shape' is the corresponding undamped mode shape.

This most important result is the basis for many of the multi-shaker test procedures used (particularly in the aircraft industry) to isolate the undamped modes of structures for comparison with theoretical predictions. It is also noteworthy that this is one of the few methods for obtaining directly the undamped modes as almost all other methods extract the actual damped modes of the system under test. The physics of the technique are quite simple: the force vector is chosen so that it exactly balances all the damping forces, whatever these may be, and so the principle applies equally to other types of damping.

POSTSCRIPT

It is often observed that the analysis for hysteretic damping is less than rigorous when applied to the free-vibration situation, as we have done above. However, it is an admissible model of damping for describing harmonic forced vibration and this is the objective of most of our studies. Moreover, it is always possible to express each of the receptance (or other FRF) expressions either as a ratio of two polynomials (as explained in Section 2.3) or as a series of simple terms such as those we have used above. Each of the terms in the series may be identified with one of the 'modes' we have defined in the earlier free-vibration analysis for the system. Thus, whether or not the solution is strictly valid for a free vibration analysis, we can usefully and confidently consider each of the uncoupled terms or modes as being a genuine characteristic of the system. As will be seen in the next section, the analysis required for the general case of viscous damping – which is more rigorous – is considerably more complicated than that used here which is, in effect, a very simple extension of the undamped case.

2.6 VISCOUS DAMPING – GENERAL CASE

We turn now to a corresponding treatment for the case of general viscous damping. Exactly the same introductory comments apply in this case as were made at the beginning of Section 2.5 and the only difference is in the specific model chosen to represent the damping behaviour.

The general equation of motion for a MDOF system with viscous damping and harmonic excitation is:

$$[M] \{\ddot{x}\} + [C] \{\dot{x}\} + [K] \{x\} = \{f\} \qquad (2.70)$$

As before, we consider first the case where there is zero excitation in order to determine the natural modes of the system and to this end we assume a solution to the equations of motion which has the form

$$\{x\} = \{x\}e^{st} \qquad (2.71)$$

Substituting this into the appropriate equation of motion gives:

$$(s^2[M] + s[C] + [K]) \{x\} = \{0\} \qquad (2.72)$$

the solution of which constitutes a complex eigenproblem, although one with a somewhat different solution to that of the corresponding stage for the previous case with hysteretic damping. In this case, there are 2N eigenvalues, s_r (as opposed to N values of λ_r^2 before) but these now occur in complex conjugate pairs. (This is an inevitable result of the fact that all the coefficients in the matrices are real and thus any characteristic values, or roots, must either be real or occur in complex conjugate pairs.) As before, there is an eigenvector corresponding to each of these eigenvalues, but these also occur as complex conjugates. Hence, we can describe the eigensolution as:

$$\text{and} \quad \left. \begin{array}{c} s_r, \ s_r^* \\ \{\psi\}_r, \ \{\psi^*\}_r \end{array} \right\} \quad r = 1, N \qquad (2.73)$$

It is customary to express each eigenvalue s_r in the form:

$$s_r = \omega_r(-\zeta_r + i\sqrt{1-\zeta_r^2})$$

where ω_r is the 'natural frequency' and ζ_r is the critical damping ratio for that mode. Sometimes, the quantity ω_r is referred to as the 'undamped natural frequency' but this is not strictly correct except in the case of proportional damping (or, of course, of a single-degree-of-freedom system).

The eigensolution possesses orthogonality properties although these, also, are different to those of the earlier cases. In order to examine these, we first note that any eigenvalue/eigenvector pair satisfies the equation

$$(s_r^2[M] + s_r[C] + [K]) \{\psi\}_r = \{0\} \qquad (2.74)$$

and then we premultiply this equation by $\{\psi\}_q^T$ so that we have:

$$\{\psi\}_q^T (s_r^2[M] + s_r[C] + [K]) \{\psi\}_r = 0 \qquad (2.75)$$

A similar expression to (2.74) can be produced by using λ_q and $\{\psi\}_q$:

$$(s_q{}^2[M] + s_q[C] + [K]) \{\psi\}_q = \{0\} \qquad (2.76)$$

which can be transposed, taking account of the symmetry of the system matrices, to give:

$$\{\psi\}_q{}^T (s_q{}^2[M] + s_q[C] + [K]) = \{0\}^T \qquad (2.77)$$

If we now postmultiply this expression by $\{\psi\}_r$ and subtract the result from that in equation (2.75), we obtain:

$$(s_r{}^2 - s_q{}^2) \{\psi\}_q{}^T[M]\{\psi\}_r + (s_r - s_q) \{\psi\}_q{}^T[C]\{\psi\}_r = 0 \qquad (2.78)$$

and, provided s_r and s_q are different, this leads to the first of a pair of orthogonality equations:

$$(s_r + s_q) \{\psi\}_q{}^T[M]\{\psi\}_r + \{\psi\}_q{}^T[C]\{\psi\}_r = 0 \qquad (2.79a)$$

A second equation can be derived from the above expressions as follows: Multiply (2.75) by s_q and (2.77) by s_r and subtract one from the other to obtain:

$$s_r s_q \{\psi\}_q{}^T[M]\{\psi\}_r - \{\psi\}_q{}^T[K]\{\psi\}_r = 0 \qquad (2.79b)$$

These two equations – (2.79a) and (2.79b) – constitute the orthogonality conditions of the system and it is immediately clear that they are far less simple than those we have encountered previously. However, it is interesting to examine the form they take when the modes r and q are a complex conjugate pair. In this case, we have that

$$s_q = \omega_r(- \zeta_r - i\sqrt{1 - \zeta_r{}^2}) \qquad (2.80)$$

and also that

$$\{\psi\}_q = \{\psi^*\}_r \qquad (2.81)$$

Inserting these into equation (2.79a) gives

$$-2\omega_r \zeta_r \{\psi^*\}_r{}^T[M]\{\psi\}_r + \{\psi^*\}_r{}^T[C]\{\psi\}_r = 0 \qquad (2.82)$$

from which we obtain:

$$2\omega_r \zeta_r = \frac{\{\psi^*\}_r{}^T[C]\{\psi\}_r}{\{\psi^*\}_r{}^T[M]\{\psi\}_r} = \frac{c_r}{m_r} \qquad (2.83)$$

Similarly, inserting (2.80) and (2.81) into (2.79b) gives

$$\omega_r{}^2 \{\psi^*\}_r{}^T[M]\{\psi\}_r - \{\psi^*\}_r{}^T[K]\{\psi\}_r = 0 \qquad (2.84)$$

from which

$$\omega_r{}^2 = \frac{(\psi^*)_r{}^T[K]\{\psi\}_r}{(\psi^*)_r{}^T[M]\{\psi\}_r} = \frac{k_r}{m_r} \qquad (2.85)$$

In these expressions, m_r, k_r, and c_r may be described as modal mass, stiffness and damping parameters respectively although the meaning is slightly different to that used in the other systems.

Forced Response Analysis

In this stage of the analysis, this case of general viscous damping again presents a more complex task. Returning to the basic equation, (2.70), and assuming a harmonic response:

$$\{x(t)\} = \{x\}e^{i\omega t} \qquad (2.86)$$

we can write the forced response solution directly as

$$\{x\} = [[K] - \omega^2[M] + i\omega[C]]^{-1} \{f\} \qquad (2.87)$$

but as in previous cases, this expression is not particularly convenient for numerical application. We shall seek a similar series expansion to that which has been used in the earlier cases of undamped, proportionally-damped and hysteretically-damped systems but now we find that the eigenvalue solution presented in the above equations is not directly amenable to this task. In fact, it is necessary to recast the equations in order to achieve our aim.

Define a new coordinate vector $\{y\}$ which is of order $2N$ and which contains both the displacements $\{x\}$ and the velocities $\{\dot{x}\}$:

$$\{y\} = \begin{Bmatrix} x \\ \dot{x} \end{Bmatrix} \qquad (2.88)$$
$$\quad (2Nx1)$$

Equation (2.70) can then be written as:

$$[C:M] \quad \{\dot{y}\} \quad + \quad [K:0] \quad \{y\} = \{0\} \qquad (2.89)$$
$$Nx2N \quad 2Nx1 \qquad\qquad Nx1$$

However, in this form we have N equations and $2N$ unknowns and so we add an identity equation of the type:

$$[M:0] \{\dot{y}\} + [0:-M] \{y\} = \{0\} \qquad (2.90)$$

which can be combined to form a set of $2N$ equations

$$\begin{bmatrix} C & M \\ M & 0 \end{bmatrix} \{\dot{y}\} + \begin{bmatrix} K & 0 \\ 0 & -M \end{bmatrix} \{y\} = \{0\} \qquad (2.91a)$$

which can be simplified to:
$$[A] \{\dot{y}\} + [B] \{y\} = \{0\} \qquad (2.91b)$$

These equations are now in a standard eigenvalue form and by assuming a trial solution of the form $\{y\} = \{y\}e^{st}$, we can obtain the 2N eigenvalues and eigenvectors of the system, λ_r and $\{\theta\}_r$, which together satisfy the general equation:

$$(\lambda_r [A] + [B]) \ \{\theta\}_r = \{0\}; \qquad r = 1, \ 2N \qquad (2.92)$$

These eigenproperties will, in general, be complex although for the same reasons as previously they will always occur in conjugate pairs. They possess orthogonality properties which are simply stated as

$$[\theta]^T \ [A] \ [\theta] = \lceil a_r \rfloor$$
$$[\theta]^T \ [B] \ [\theta] = \lceil b_r \rfloor \qquad (2.93)$$

and which have the usual characteristic that

$$\lambda_r = - \frac{b_r}{a_r} \qquad r = 1, \ 2N \qquad (2.94)$$

Now we may express the forcing vector in terms of the new coordinate system as:

$$\{P\}_{2N \times 1} = \begin{Bmatrix} f \\ 0 \end{Bmatrix} \qquad (2.95)$$

and, assuming a similarly harmonic response and making use of the previous development of a series form expression of the response (equations 2.34 to 2.40), we may write:

$$\begin{Bmatrix} x \\ \cdots \\ i\omega x \end{Bmatrix}_{2N \times 1} = \sum_{r=1}^{2N} \frac{\{\theta\}_r^T \{P\}\{\theta\}_r}{a_r(i\omega - s_r)} \qquad (2.96)$$

However, because the eigenvalues and vectors occur in complex conjugate pairs, this last equation may be rewritten as:

$$\begin{Bmatrix} x \\ \cdots \\ i\omega x \end{Bmatrix} = \sum_{r=1}^{N} \left(\frac{\{\theta\}_r^T \{P\}\{\theta\}_r}{a_r(i\omega - s_r)} + \frac{\{\theta^*\}_r^T \{P\}\{\theta^*\}_r}{a_r^*(i\omega - s_r^*)} \right) \qquad (2.97)$$

At this stage, it is convenient to extract a single response parameter, say x_j, resulting from a single force such as f_k – the receptance frequency response function α_{jk}, and in this case, equation (2.97) leads to:

$$\alpha_{jk}(\omega) = \sum_{r=1}^{N} \left(\frac{{}_r\theta_j \ {}_r\theta_k}{a_r(\omega_r\zeta_r + i(\omega - \omega_r\sqrt{1-\zeta_r^2}))} + \frac{{}_r\theta_j^* \ {}_r\theta_k^*}{a_r^*(\omega_r\zeta_r + i(\omega + \omega_r\sqrt{1-\zeta_r^2}))} \right)$$

$$(2.98)$$

Using the fact that $s_r = \omega_r(-\zeta_r + i\sqrt{1-\zeta_r^2})$, this expression can be further reduced to the form:

$$\alpha_{jk}(\omega) = \sum_{r=1}^{N} \frac{(_rR_{jk}) + i(\omega/\omega_r)(_rS_{jk})}{\omega_r^2 - \omega^2 + 2i\omega\omega_r\zeta_r} \qquad (2.99)$$

where the coefficients R and S are obtained from:

$$\begin{aligned}
(_rR_k) &= 2(\zeta_r \, \text{Re}(_rG_k) - \text{Im}(_rG_k)\sqrt{1-\zeta_r^2}) \, ; \\
(_rS_k) &= 2 \, \text{Re}(_rG_k); \\
(_rG_k) &= (_r\theta_k/a_r)(\theta)_r \qquad (2.100)
\end{aligned}$$

The similarity between this expression and that derived in Section 2.5 (equation 2.65) is evident, the main difference being in the frequency-dependence of the numerator in the case of viscous damping. If we confine our interest to a small range of frequency in the vicinity of one of the natural frequencies (i.e. $\omega \doteq \omega_r$), then it is clear that (2.99) and (2.65) are very similar indeed.

Excitation by General Force Vector

Although we have only fully developed the analysis for the case of a single force, the ingredients already exist for the more general case of multi-point excitation. The particular case of mono-phased forces has effectively been dealt with in Section 2.5 because it was there shown that the results obtained would apply to any type of damping.

2.7   CHARACTERISTICS AND PRESENTATION OF MDOF FRF DATA

2.7.1.   A Note about Natural Frequencies

Having now presented all the basic theory, it is appropriate to comment on the various definitions which have been introduced for 'natural' frequencies. The basic definition derives from the undamped system's eigenvalues which yield the frequencies at which free vibration of the system can take place. These frequencies are identified by the symbol $\bar{\omega}_r$, and this occurs in expressions for both free vibration response:

$$x(t) = \sum_{r=1}^{N} x_r \, e^{i\bar{\omega}_r t}$$

and for forced vibration, the FRF:

$$\alpha(\omega) = \sum_{r=1}^{N} \frac{A_r}{\bar{\omega}_r^2 - \omega^2}$$

For damped systems, the situation is more complicated and leads to two alternative characteristic frequency parameters being defined – both called 'natural' frequencies – one for free vibration (ω_r') and the other for forced vibration (ω_r). The former constitutes the oscillatory part of the free vibration characteristic which, being complex, contains an exponential decay term as well. Thus we have:

$$x(t) = \sum_{r=1}^{N} x_r \, e^{-a_r t} \, e^{i\omega_r' t}$$

where ω_r' may or may not be identical to $\bar{\omega}_r$, depending on the type and distribution of the damping (see Table 2.3). The second definition comes from the general form of the FRF expression which, combining all the previous cases, may be written in the form:

$$\alpha(\omega) = \sum_{r=1}^{N} \frac{C_r}{\omega_r^2 - \omega^2 + iD_r} \qquad (2.101)$$

Here, C_r may be real or complex and D_r will be real, both may be constant or frequency-dependent and ω_r will, in general, be different to both $\bar{\omega}_r$ and ω_r', except in some special cases. Table 2.3 summarises all the different cases which have been included.

| CASE | EQ. FOR FRF | C | D | NATURAL FREQUENCY | |
				FREE ω'_r	FORCED ω_r
UNDAMPED	2.40	REAL, CONST.	0	$\bar{\omega}_r$	$\bar{\omega}_r$
PROP.HYST.	2.55	REAL, CONST.	REAL, CONST.	$\bar{\omega}_r$	$\bar{\omega}_r$
PROP.VISC.	2.49	REAL, CONST.	REAL(ω)	$\bar{\omega}_r\sqrt{1-\zeta_r^2}$	$\bar{\omega}_r$
GEN.HYST.	2.65	COMPLEX, CONST.	REAL, CONST.	ω_r	ω_r
GEN.VISC.	2.99	COMPLEX(ω)	REAL(ω)	$\omega_r\sqrt{1-\zeta_r^2}$	ω_r

Table 2.3   FRF Formulae and Natural Frequencies

2.7.2 Mobility and Impedance Parameters

In every case, the most important feature of the general expression in (2.101) is its close relationship with the FRF expression for the much simpler SDOF system, studied in detail in Section 2.1. We shall now consider the properties of this type of function and then examine the various means used to display the information it contains. It should be emphasised that a thorough understanding of the form of the different plots of FRF data is invaluable to an understanding of the modal analysis processes which are described in Chapter 4.

First, we consider the various forms of FRF. As before, there are three main alternatives, using displacement, velocity or acceleration response to produce respectively receptance, mobility or inertance (or accelerance). These three forms are interrelated in just the same way as described earlier, so that we may write:

$$[Y(\omega)] = i\omega \, [\alpha(\omega)]$$

$$[A(\omega)] = i\omega \, [Y(\omega)] \qquad\qquad (2.102)$$

$$= -\omega^2 \, [\alpha(\omega)]$$

However, the FRF data of multi-degree-of-freedom systems have a more complex form than their SDOF counterparts and this may be seen from the strict definition of the general receptance α_{jk} which is:

$$\alpha_{jk}(\omega) = (x_j/f_k); \; f_m=0, \; m=1,N; \neq k \qquad\qquad (2.103)$$

and it is the footnote qualification which is particularly important.

We saw in Sections 2.1 and 2.2 that there exist a further three formats for FRF data, these being the inverses of the standard receptance, mobility and inertance and generally known as 'dynamic stiffness', 'mechanical impedance' and 'apparent mass' respectively. Whereas with a SDOF system there is no difficulty in using either one or its inverse, the same cannot be said in the case of MDOF systems. It is true to say that for MDOF systems we can define a complete set of dynamic stiffness or impedance data (and indeed such data are used in some types of analysis), but it is not a simple matter to derive these inverse properties from the standard mobility type as the following explanation demonstrates.

In general, we can determine the response of a structure to an excitation using the equation:

$$\{\dot{x}\} = \{v\} = [Y(\omega)]\{f\} \qquad\qquad (2.104a)$$

Equally, we can write the inverse equation using impedances instead of mobilities, as:

$$\{f\} = [Z(\omega)]\{v\} \qquad\qquad (2.104b)$$

The problem arises because the general element in the mobility matrix $(Y_{jk}(\omega))$ is not simply related to its counterpart in the impedance matrix $(Z_{jk}(\omega))$ as was the case for a SDOF system. Stated simply:

$$Y_{jk}(\omega) \equiv Y_{kj}(\omega) \neq 1/Z_{jk}(\omega) \qquad (2.105)$$

and the reason for this unfortunate fact derives from the respective definitions, which are:

$$Y_{kj}(\omega) = (v_k/f_j) ; \quad f_m=0 \qquad \text{and} \qquad Z_{jk}(\omega) = (f_j/v_k) ; \quad v_m=0 \quad (2.106)$$

It is clear from these expressions that while it is entirely feasible to measure the mobility type of FRF by applying just a single excitation force and ensuring that no others are generated, it is far less straightforward to measure an impedance property which demands that all coordinates except one are grounded. Such a condition is almost impossible to achieve in a practical situation.

Thus, we find that the only types of FRF which we can expect to measure directly are those of the mobility or receptance type. Further, it is necessary to guard against the temptation to derive impedance-type data by measuring mobility functions and then computing their reciprocals: these are not the same as the elements in the matrix inverse. We can also see from this discussion that if one changes the number of coordinates considered in a particular case (in practice we will probably only measure at a small fraction of the total number of degrees of freedom of a practical structure), then the mobility functions involved remain exactly the same but the impedances will vary.

Lastly, we should just note some definitions used to distinguish the various types of FRF.

A *point mobility* (or receptance etc) is one where the response coordinate and the excitation coordinate are identical.

A *transfer mobility* is one where the response and excitation coordinates are different.

Sometimes, these are further subdivided into *direct* and *cross mobilities*, which describe whether the types of the coordinates for response and excitation are identical – for example, whether they are both x-direction translations, or one is x-direction and the other is y-direction, etc.

2.7.3 Display for Undamped System FRF Data

As in the earlier section, it is helpful to examine the form which FRF data take when presented in various graphical formats. This knowledge can be invaluable in assessing the validity of and interpreting measured data.

We shall start with the simplest case of undamped systems, for which the receptance expression is given in equation (2.40). Using the type of log-log plot described in Section 2.2, we can plot the individual terms in the FRF series as separate curves, as shown in Figure 2.14 (which is actually a plot of mobility). In this way, we can envisage the form the total FRF curve will take as it is simply the summation of all the individual terms, or curves. However, the exact shape of the curve is not quite so simple to deduce as appears at first because part of the information (the phase) is not shown. In fact, in some sections of each curve, the receptance is actually positive in sign and in others, it is negative but there is no indication of this on the logarithmic plot which only shows the modulus. However, when the addition of the various components is made to determine the complete receptance expression, the signs of the various terms are obviously of considerable importance. We shall examine some of the important features using a simple example with just two modes – in fact, based on the system used in Section 2.3 – and we shall develop the FRF plots for two parameters, the point receptance (or mobility) α_{11} and the transfer α_{21}. Figure 2.15 is a mobility plot showing both the individual terms in the series and applies to both the above-mentioned mobilities. If we look at the expressions for the receptances we have

$$\alpha_{11}(\omega) = 0.5/(\omega_1{}^2-\omega^2) + 0.5/(\omega_2{}^2-\omega^2)$$

and   (2.107)

$$\alpha_{21}(\omega) = 0.5/(\omega_1{}^2-\omega^2) - 0.5/(\omega_2{}^2-\omega^2)$$

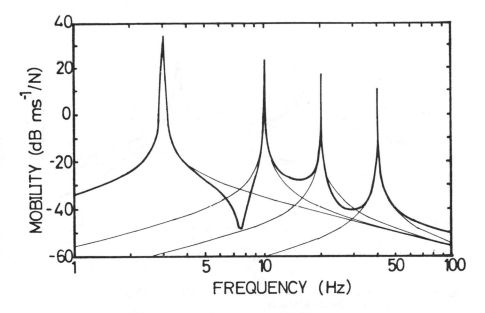

Fig 2.14   *Typical Mobility Plot for Multi-Degree-of-Freedom System (showing individual modal contributions)*

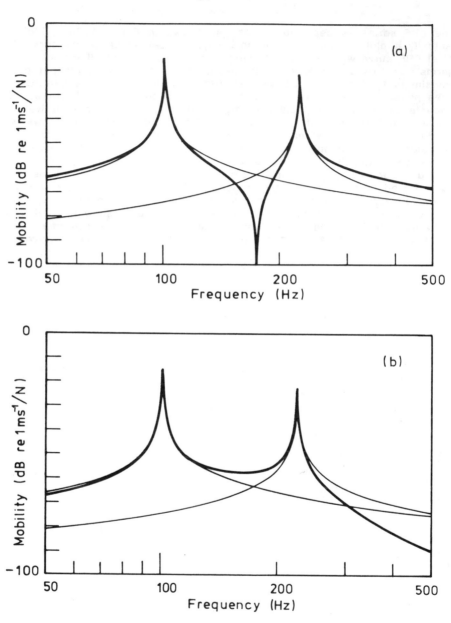

Fig 2.15   Mobility Plot for Undamped 2DOF System
             (a)   Point Mobility
             (b)   Transfer Mobility

from which it can be seen that the only difference between the point and the transfer receptances is in the sign of the modal constant (the numerator) of the second mode and as the plots only show the modulus, they are apparently insensitive to this difference. However, if we consider what happens when the two terms are added to produce the actual FRF for the MDOF system, we find the following characteristics.

Consider first the point mobility, Figure 2.15a. We see from (2.107) that at frequencies below the first natural frequency, both terms have the same sign and are thus additive, making the total FRF curve higher than either component, but we must note that the plot uses a logarithmic scale so that the contribution of the second mode at these low frequencies is relatively insignificant. Hence, the total FRF curve is only slightly above that for the first term. A similar argument and result apply at the high frequency end, above the second natural frequency, where the total plot is just above that for the second term alone. However, in the region between the two resonances, we have a situation where the two components have opposite sign to each other so that they are subtractive, rather than additive, and indeed at the point where they cross, their sum is zero since there they are of equal magnitude but opposite sign. On a logarithmic plot of this type, this produces the antiresonance characteristic which is so similar to the resonance. In the immediate vicinity of either resonance, the contribution of that term whose natural frequency is nearby is so much greater than the other one that the total is, in effect, the same as that one term. Physically, the response of the MDOF system just at one of its natural frequencies is totally dominated by that mode and the other modes have very little influence. (Remember that at this stage we are still concerned with undamped, or effectively undamped, systems.)

Now consider the transfer mobility plot, Figure 2.15b. We can apply similar reasoning as we progress along the frequency range with the sole difference that the signs of the two terms in this case are opposite. Thus, at very low frequencies and at very high frequencies, the total FRF curve lies just below that of the nearest individual component while in the region between the resonances, the two components now have the same sign and so we do not encounter the cancelling-out feature which gave rise to the antiresonance in the point mobility. In fact, at the frequency where the two terms intersect, the total curve has a magnitude of exactly twice that at the crossover.

The principles illustrated here may be extended to any number of degrees of freedom and there is a fundamental rule which has great value and that is that if two consecutive modes have the same sign for the modal constants, then there will be an antiresonance at some frequency between the natural frequencies of those two modes. If they have opposite signs, there will not be an antiresonance, but just a minimum. (The most important feature of the antiresonance is perhaps the fact that there is a phase change associated with it, as well as a very low magnitude.)

It is also very interesting to determine what controls whether a particular FRF will have positive or negative constants, and thus whether it will exhibit antiresonances or not. Considerable insight may be gained by considering the origin of the modal constant: it is the product of two eigenvector elements, one at the response point and the other at the excitation point. Clearly, if we are considering a point mobility, then the modal constant for every mode must be positive, it being the square of a number. This means that for a point FRF, there MUST be an antiresonance following every resonance, without exception.

The situation for transfer mobilities is less categoric because clearly the modal constant will sometimes be positive and sometimes negative. Thus, we expect transfer measurements to show a mixture of antiresonances and minima. However, this mixture can be anticipated to some extent because it can be shown that, in general, the further apart are the two points in question, the more likely are the two eigenvector elements to alternate in sign as one progresses through the modes. Thus, we might expect a transfer mobility between two positions widely separate on the structure to exhibit less antiresonances than one for two points relatively close together. A clear example of this is given in Figure 2.16 for a 6 degrees-of-freedom system, showing a complete set of mobilities for excitation at one extremity.

Finally, it should be noted that if either the excitation or the response coordinates happen to coincide with a node for one of the modes (ie $_r\phi_j{_r}\phi_k = 0$), then that mode will not appear as a resonance on the FRF plot. This arises since, for such a case, we shall have $_rA_{jk} = 0$ and so the only response which will be encountered at or near $\omega = \overline{\omega}_r$ will be due to the off-resonant contribution of all the other modes.

2.7.4 Display of FRF Data for Damped Systems

If we turn our attention now to damped systems, we find that the form of the FRF plot of the type just discussed is rather similar to that for the undamped case. The resonances and antiresonances are blunted by the inclusion of damping, and the phase angles (not shown) are no longer exactly 0° or 180°, but the general appearance of the plot is a natural extension of that for the system without damping. Figure 2.17 shows a plot for the same mobility parameter as appears in Figure 2.15 but here for a system with damping added. Most mobility plots have this general form as long as the modes are relatively well-separated. This condition is satisfied unless the separation between adjacent natural frequencies (expressed as a percentage of their mean) is of the same order as, or less than, the modal damping factors, in which case it becomes difficult to distinguish the individual modes.

However, as for the SDOF case, it is interesting to examine the nature of the other types of plot for FRF data, and the most profitable alternative version is again the Nyquist or Argand diagram plot. We saw earlier how one of the standard FRF parameters of a SDOF system produced a circle when plotted in the Nyquist format (and that by choosing the appropriate FRF parameter, an exact circle can be formed for either type of damping). This also applies to the MDOF system in that each of its frequency responses is composed of a number of SDOF components.

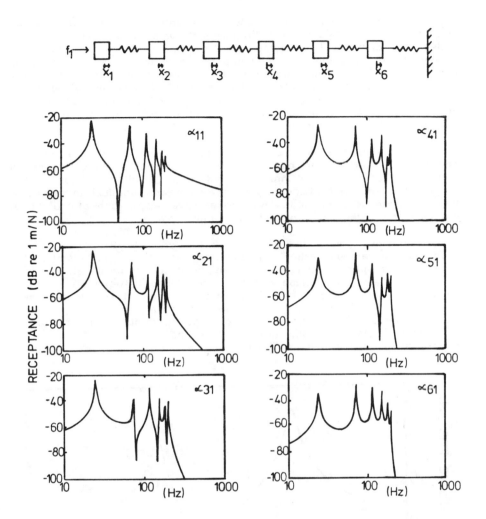

Fig 2.16   Point and Transfer FRF Plots for a 6DOF System

Figure 2.18 shows the result of plotting the point receptance α_{11} for the 2DOF system described above. Proportional hysteretic damping has been added with damping loss factors of 0.02 and 0.04 for the first and second modes respectively. It should be noted that it is not always as easy to visualise the total curve from the individual components as is the case here (with well-separated modes) although it is generally found that the basic characteristics of each (mainly the diameter and the frequency at which the local maximum amplitude is reached) are carried through into the complete expression.

A corresponding plot for the transfer receptance α_{21} is presented in Figure 2.19 where it may be seen that the opposing signs of the modal constants (remember that these are still real quantities because for a proportionally-damped system the eigenvectors are identical to those for the undamped version) of the two modes have caused one of the modal circles to be in the upper half of the complex plane.

The examples given in Figures 2.18 and 2.19 were for a proportionally-damped system. In the next two figures, 2.20 and 2.21, we show corresponding data for an example of non-proportional damping. In this case a relative phase has been introduced between the first and second elements of the eigenvectors: of 30° in mode 1 (previously it was 0°) and of 150° in mode 2 (where previously it was 180°). Now we find that the individual modal circles are no longer 'upright' but are rotated by an amount dictated by the complexity of the modal constants. The general shape of the resulting Nyquist plot is similar to that for the

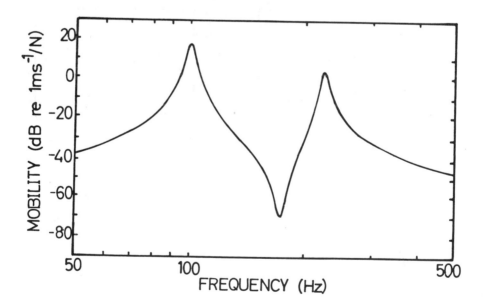

Fig 2.17   *Mobility Plot for Damped 2DOF System*

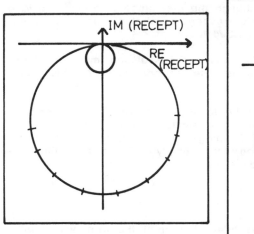

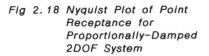

Fig 2.18 Nyquist Plot of Point
Receptance for
Proportionally-Damped
2DOF System

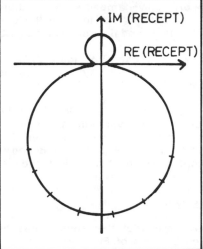

Fig 2.19 Nyquist Plot of Transfer
Receptance for
Proportionally-Damped
2DOF System

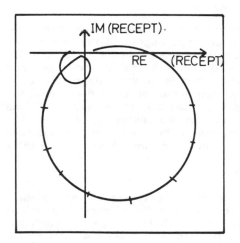

Fig 2.20 Nyquist Plot of Point
Receptance for
Nonproportionally-Damped
2DOF System

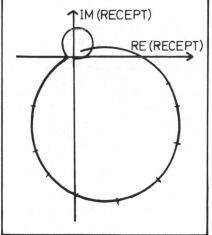

Fig 2.21 Nyquist Plot of Transfer
Receptance for
Nonproportionally-Damped
2DOF System

proportionally–damped system although the resonance points are no longer at the 'bottom' (or 'top') of the corresponding circles. The properties of an isolated modal circle are described in Chapter 4.

Lastly, we present in Figure 2.22 plots of the Real and Imaginary Parts of the FRF vs Frequency to illustrate the general form of this type of display.

The plots shown in Figures 2.17 to 2.22 all refer to systems with structural or hysteretic damping. A similar set of results would be obtained for the case of viscous damping with the difference that the exact modal circles will be produced for mobility FRF data, rather than receptances, as has been the case here.

SUMMARY

The purpose of this section has been to predict the form which will be taken by plots of FRF data using the different display formats which are in current use. Although we may have a working familiarity with measured FRF plots, the results shown above have been derived entirely from consideration of the theoretical basis of structural vibration theory and the exercise in so doing proves to be invaluable when trying to understand and interpret actual measured data.

2.8   COMPLETE AND INCOMPLETE MODELS

All the preceding theory has been concerned with complete models; that is, the analysis has been presented for an N-degree-of-freedom system with the implicit assumption that all the mass, stiffness and damping properties are known and that all the elements in the eigenmatrices and the FRF matrix are available. While this is a valid approach for a theoretical study, it is less generally applicable for experimentally–based investigations where it is not usually possible to measure all the coordinates, or to examine all the modes possessed by a structure. Because of this limitation, it is necessary to extend our analysis to examine the implications of having access to something less than a complete set of data, or model, and this leads us to the concept of a 'reduced' or incomplete type of model.

As intimated, there are two ways in which a model can be incomplete – by the omission of some modes, or by the omission of some coordinates (or both) – and we shall examine these individually, paying particular attention to the implications for the response model (in the form of the FRF matrix). Consider first the complete FRF matrix, which is NxN:

$$[Y(\omega)]_{NxN}$$

and then suppose that we decide to limit our description of the system to include certain coordinates only (and thus to ignore what happens at the others, which is not the same as supposing they do not exist). Our

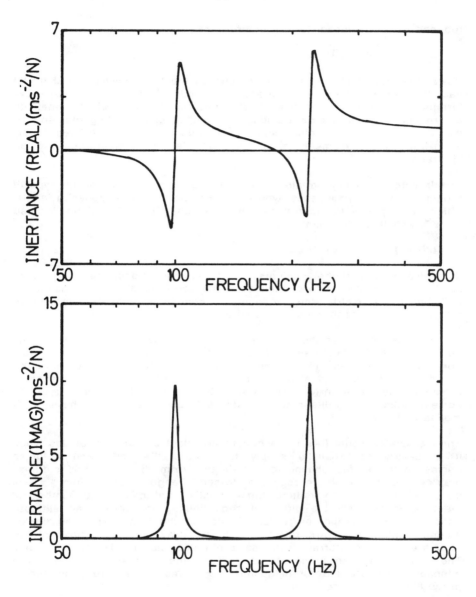

Fig 2. 22   Real and Imaginary Receptance for Damped 2DOF System

reduced response model is now of order nxn, and is written as:

$$[Y^R(\omega)]_{nxn}$$

Now, it is clear that as we have not altered the basic system, and it still has the same number of degrees of freedom even though we have foregone our ability to describe all of them, the elements which remain in the reduced mobility matrix are identical to the corresponding elements in the full NxN matrix. In other words, the reduced matrix is formed simply by extracting the elements of interest and leaving behind those to be ignored.

At this point, it is appropriate to mention the consequences of this type of reduction on the impedance type of FRF data. The impedance matrix which corresponds to the reduced model defined by $[Y^R]$ will be denoted as $[Z^R]$ and it is clear that

$$[Z^R(\omega)] = [Y^R(\omega)]^{-1} \qquad (2.108)$$

It is also clear that the elements in the reduced impedance matrix such as Z^R_{jk} are not the same quantities as the corresponding elements in the full impedance matrix and, indeed, a completely different impedance matrix applies to each specific reduction.

We can also consider the implications of this form of reduction on the other types of model, namely the modal model and the spatial model. For the modal model, elimination of the data pertaining to some of the coordinates results in a smaller eigenvector matrix, which then becomes rectangular of order nxN. This matrix still retains N columns, and the corresponding eigenvalue matrix is still NxN because we still have all N modes included.

For the spatial model it is more difficult to effect a reduction of this type. It is clearly not realistic simply to remove the rows and columns corresponding to the eliminated coordinates from the mass and stiffness matrices as this would represent a drastic change to the system. It is possible, however, to reduce these spatial matrices by a number of methods which have the effect of redistributing the mass and stiffness (and damping) properties which relate to the redundant coordinates amongst those which are retained. In this way, the total mass of the structure and its correct stiffness properties can be largely retained. The Guyan reduction procedure is perhaps the best known of this type although there are several modelling techniques. Such reduced spatial properties will be denoted as:

$$[M^R], \quad [K^R]$$

Next, we shall consider the other form of reduction in which not all the N modes of the system are included. Frequently, this is a necessary approach in that many of the high-frequency modes will be of little interest and almost certainly very difficult to measure. Consider first the FRF matrix and include initially all the coordinates but suppose that each element in the matrix is computed using not all the N terms in the summation, i.e.:

$$Y_{jk}(\omega) = i\omega \sum_{r=1}^{m \leqslant N} \frac{rA_{jk}}{\omega_r^2 - \omega^2 + i\eta_r\omega_r^2} \qquad (2.109)$$

In full, we can thus write the FRF matrix as:

$$[Y(\omega)] = i\omega [\Phi] \lceil (\lambda_r^2 - \omega^2) \rfloor^{-1} [\Phi]^T \qquad (2.110)$$
$$ \; NxN \quad\quad Nxm \quad\quad mxm \quad\quad mxN$$

Of course, both types of reduction can be combined when the resulting matrix would be denoted:

$$[Y^R(\omega)]_{nxn}$$

Sometimes, it is convenient to attempt to provide an approximate correction to the FRF data to compensate for the errors introduced by leaving out some of the terms. This is usually effected by adding a constant or 'residual' term to each FRF, as shown in the following equation:

$$[Y(\omega)] = [Y^R(\omega)] + [R] \qquad (2.111)$$

The consequence of neglecting some of the modes on the modal model is evident in that the eigenvalue matrix becomes of order mxm and the eigenvector matrix is again rectangular, although in the other sense, and we have:

$$\lceil \lambda_r^2 \rfloor_{mxm}; \quad [\Phi]_{Nxm}$$

There is no immediate implication for the spatial type of model of omitting some of the modes.

Figure 2.23 shows the relationship between different forms of complete and incomplete models.

2.9 NON-SINUSOIDAL VIBRATION AND FRF PROPERTIES

With receptance and other FRF data we have a means of computing the response of a MDOF system to an excitation which consists of a set of harmonic forces of different amplitudes and phases but all of the same frequency. In the general case, we can simply write

$$\{x\}e^{i\omega t} = [\alpha(\omega)] \{f\}e^{i\omega t} \qquad (2.112)$$

We shall now turn our attention to a range of other excitation/response situations which exist in practice and which can be analysed using the same frequency response functions. Also, we shall indicate how the FRF properties can be obtained from measurements made during non-sinusoidal vibration tests.

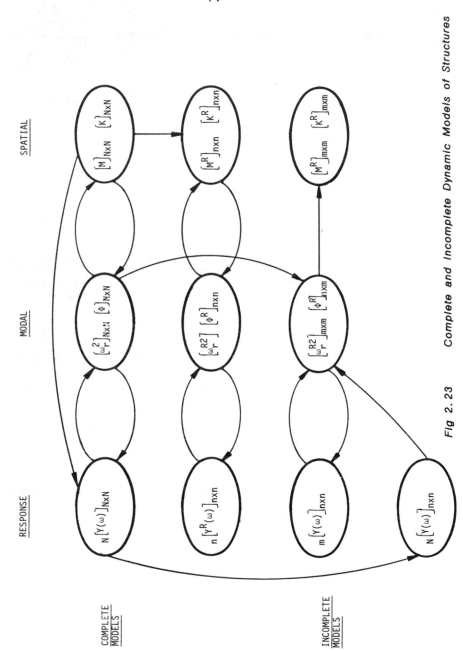

Fig 2. 23   Complete and Incomplete Dynamic Models of Structures

2.9.1 Periodic Vibration

The first of these cases is that of periodic vibration, in which the excitation (and thus the response) is not simply sinusoidal although it does retain the property of periodicity. Such a case is illustrated in the sketch of Figure 2.24a which shows a sawtooth type of excitation and two of the responses it produces from a system. Clearly, in this case there is no longer a simple relationship between the input and the outputs, such as exists for harmonic vibration where we simply need to define the amplitude and phase of each parameter. As a result, any function relating input and output in this case will necessarily be quite complex.

It transpires that the easiest way of computing the responses in such a case as this is by means of Fourier Series. The basic principle of the Fourier Analysis is that any periodic function (such as $f_0(t)$, $x_1(t)$ or $x_2(t)$ in Fig 2.24a) can be represented by a series of sinusoids of suitable frequencies, amplitudes and phases, as illustrated in Fig 2.24b. (A more detailed discussion of Fourier Series is given in Appendix 3). So

$$f_0(t) = \sum_{n=1}^{\infty} {}_0F_n \, e^{i\omega_n t} \; ; \; \omega_n = 2\pi n/T \qquad (2.113)$$

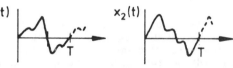

(a)

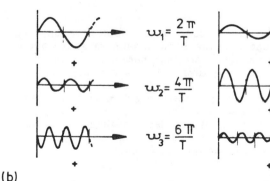

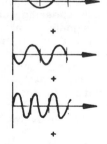

(b)

Fig 2.24   Periodic Signals and their Sinusoidal Components

Once a frequency decomposition of the forcing function has been obtained, we may use the corresponding FRF data, computed at the specific frequencies present in the forcing spectrum, in order to compute the corresponding frequency components of the responses of interest:

$$x_j(t) = \sum_{n=1}^{\infty} \alpha_{jo}(\omega_n) \, _oF_n \, e^{i\omega_n t} \; ; \; \omega_n = 2\pi n/T \qquad (2.114)$$

What must be noted here is that although the response contains exactly the same frequencies in its spectrum as does the forcing, the relative magnitudes of the various components are different in the two cases because the FRF data vary considerably with frequency. Thus, we obtain response time histories which are periodic with the same period as the excitation but which have a quite different shape to it and, incidentally, to each other (see Figure 2.24).

TO DERIVE FRF FROM PERIODIC VIBRATION

It is possible to determine a system's FRF properties from excitation and response measurements when the vibration is periodic. To do this, it is necessary to determine the Fourier Series components of both the input force signal and of the relevant output response signal(s). Both of these series will contain components at the same set of discrete frequencies; these being integer multiples of $2\pi/T$, where T is the fundamental period.

Once these two series are available, the frequency response function can be defined at the same set of frequency points by computing the ratio of the response component to the input component. For both data sets, there will be two parts to each component – magnitude and phase (or sine and cosine).

2.9.2 Transient Vibration

We shall next turn our attention to the case of transient vibration which, strictly speaking, cannot be treated by the same means as above because the signals of excitation and response are not periodic. However, as discussed in the Appendix on Fourier Analysis, it is sometimes possible to extend the Fourier Series approach to a Fourier Transform for the case of an infinitely long period. Here, it is generally possible to treat both the transient input and response in this way and to obtain an input/output equation in the frequency domain. It is also possible to derive an alternative relationship working in the time domain directly and we shall see that these two approaches arrive at the same solution.

Analysis via Fourier Transform

For most transient cases, the input function f(t) will satisfy the Dirichlet condition and so its Fourier Transform $F(\omega)$ can be computed from:

$$F(\omega) = (1/2\pi) \int_{-\infty}^{\infty} f(t) e^{-i\omega t} \, dt \qquad (2.115)$$

Now, at any frequency ω, the corresponding Fourier Transform of the response, X(ω), can be determined from:

$$X(\omega) = H(\omega)\ F(\omega) \tag{2.116}$$

where H(ω) represents the appropriate version of the FRF for the particular input and output parameters considered. We may then derive an expression for the response itself, x(t), from the Inverse Fourier Transform of X(ω):

$$x(t) = \int_{-\infty}^{\infty} (H(\omega)\ F(\omega))\,e^{j\omega t}d\omega \tag{2.117}$$

Response Via Time Domain (Superposition)

This alternative analysis is sometimes referred to as 'Duhamel's Method' and is based on the ability to compute the response of a system to a simple (unit) impulse. Fig 2.25(a) shows a typical unit impulse excitation applied at time t=t' which has the property that although the function has infinite magnitude and lasts for an infinitesimal time, the area underneath it (or the integral f(t)dt) is equal to unity. The response of a system at time t (after t') is defined as the system's unit Impulse Response Function (IRF) and has a direct relationship to the Frequency Response Function (FRF) – one being in the time domain and the other in the frequency domain. The IRF is written as:

$$h(t-t')$$

If we now consider a more general transient excitation or input function, as shown in Fig 2.25b, we see that it is possible to represent this as the superposition of several impulses, each of magnitude (f(t')dt') and occurring at different instants in time. The response of a system to just one of these incremental impulses can be written as:

$$\delta x(t) = h(t-t')\ f(t')dt' \tag{2.118}$$

and the total response of the system will be given by adding or superimposing all the incremental responses as follows:

$$x(t) = \int_{-\infty}^{\infty} h(t-t')\ f(t')dt'\ ;\ h(t-t') = 0;\,t\le t' \tag{2.119}$$

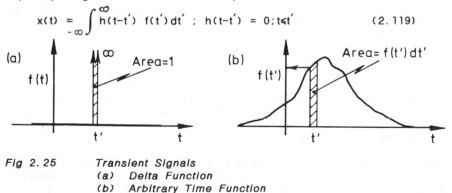

Fig 2.25   Transient Signals
             (a)   Delta Function
             (b)   Arbitrary Time Function

This input/output relationship appears somewhat different to that obtained via the Fourier Transform method, eq. (2.117), but we shall find that there is in fact a very close relationship between them. This we can do by using the Fourier Transform approach to compute the response of a system to a unit impulse. Thus, let $f(t) = \delta(0)$ and determine its Fourier Transform $F(\omega)$. In this case, application of equation (2.115) is relatively easy and yields:

$$F(\omega) = 1/2\pi$$

If we now insert this expression into the general response equation, (2.117), and note that, by definition, this must be identical to the impulse response function, we obtain:

$$x(t) = h(t) = (1/2\pi) \int_{-\infty}^{\infty} H(\omega) e^{i\omega t} d\omega \qquad (2.120)$$

Thus we arrive at a most important result in finding the Impulse and Frequency Response Functions to constitute a Fourier Transform pair.

Following from this derivation, we can also see that the IRF can also be expressed as a modal series, just as is possible for the FRF. Thus, if we write;

$$H(\omega) = \Sigma\ H_r(\omega)$$

where $H_r(\omega)$ is the contribution for a single mode, we can likewise write:

$$h(t) = \Sigma\ h_r(t)$$

where, for a viscously-damped system, $h_r(t) = A_r e^{s_r t}$.

TO DERIVE FRF FROM TRANSIENT VIBRATION

As before, we are able to prescribe a formula for obtaining a structure's FRF properties from measurements made during a transient vibration test. What is required is the calculation of the Fourier Transforms of both the excitation and the response signals. The ratio of these two functions (both of frequency) can be computed in order to obtain an expression for the corresponding frequency response function:

$$H(\omega) = X(\omega)/F(\omega) \qquad (2.121)$$

In practice, it is much more common to compute a Discrete Fourier Transform (DFT) or Series and thus to perform the same set of calculations as described in the previous section for periodic vibration. Indeed, such an approach using a DFT assumes that the complete transient event is periodic.

Alternatively, the spectrum analyser may be used to compute the FRF in the same way as it would for random vibration (see below), namely by taking the ratio of the spectra. This is only useful if a succession of repeated transients are applied − nominally, the same as each other − in which case any noise on individual measurements will be averaged out.

2.9.3 Random Vibration

We come now to the most complex type of vibration − where both excitation and response are described by random processes.   Although it might be thought that this case could be treated in much the same way as the previous one − by considering the random signals to be periodic with infinite period − this is not possible because the inherent properties of random signals cause them to violate the Dirichlet condition.   As a result, neither excitation nor response signals can be subjected to a valid Fourier Transform calculation and another approach must be found.

It will be necessary to introduce and define two sets of parameters which are used to describe random signals: one based in the time domain − the Correlation Functions − and the other in the frequency domain − the Spectral Densities.   We shall attempt here to provide some insight into these quantities without necessarily detailing all the background theory.

Consider a typical random vibration parameter, $f(t)$, illustrated in Fig 2.26a, which will be assumed to be ergodic.   We introduce and

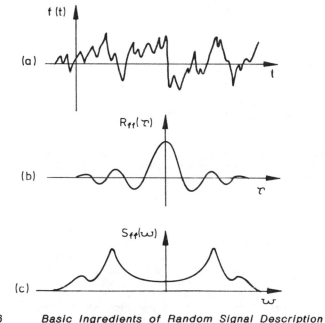

Fig 2.26   Basic Ingredients of Random Signal Description
(a)   Time History
(b)   Autocorrelation Function
(c)   Power Spectral Density

define the Autocorrelation Function $R_{ff}(\tau)$ as the 'expected' (or average) value of the product $(f(t).f(t+\tau))$, computed along the time axis. This will always be a real and even function of time, and is written:

$$R_{ff}(\tau) = E[f(t).f(t+\tau)] \qquad (2.122)$$

and will generally take the form illustrated in the sketch of Fig 2.26b. This correlation function, unlike the original quantity $f(t)$, does satisfy the requirements for Fourier transformation and thus we can obtain its Fourier Transform by the usual equation. The resulting parameter we shall call a Spectral Density, in this case the Auto- or Power Spectral Density (PSD), which is defined as:

$$S_{ff}(\omega) = (1/2\pi) \int_{-\infty}^{\infty} R_{ff}(\tau) e^{-i\omega\tau} d\tau \qquad (2.123)$$

The Auto-Spectral Density is a real and even function of frequency, and does in fact provide a frequency description of the original function $f(t)$. It has units of (f^2/ω) and would generally appear as in the plot of Fig 2.26c.

A similar concept can be applied to a pair of functions such as $f(t)$ and $x(t)$ to produce cross correlation and cross spectral density functions. The cross correlation function $R_{xf}(\tau)$ is defined as:

$$R_{xf}(\tau) = E[x(t).f(t+\tau)] \qquad (2.124)$$

and the cross spectral density (CSD) is defined as its Fourier Transform:

$$S_{xf}(\omega) = (1/2\pi) \int_{-\infty}^{\infty} R_{xf}(\tau) e^{-i\omega\tau} d\tau \qquad (2.125)$$

Cross correlation functions are real, but not always even, functions of time and cross spectral densities, unlike auto spectral densities, are generally complex functions of frequency with the particular conjugate property that:

$$S_{xf}(\omega) = S_{fx}^*(\omega) \qquad (2.126)$$

Now that we have established the necessary parameters to describe random processes in general, we are in a position to define the input/output relationships for systems undergoing random vibration. In deriving the final equations which permit the calculation of response from known excitations, we shall not present a full analysis; rather, we shall indicate the main path followed without detailing all the algebra. In this way, we hope to demonstrate the basis of the analysis and the origins of the final expressions, which are the only ones required in normal modal testing practice.

The analysis is based on the general excitation/response relationship in the time domain, quoted above in equation (2.119) and repeated here:

$$x(t) = \int_{-\infty}^{\infty} h(t-t')f(t')dt' \qquad (2.127)$$

Using this property, it is possible to derive an expression for $x(t)$ and another for $x(t+\tau)$ and thus to calculate the response autocorrelation, $R_{xx}(\tau)$:

$$R_{xx}(\tau) = E[x(t).x(t+\tau)] \qquad (2.128)$$

This equation can be manipulated to describe the response autocorrelation in terms of the corresponding property of the excitation, $R_{ff}(\tau)$, but the result is a complicated and unusable triple integral. However, this same equation can be transformed to the frequency domain to emerge with the very simple form:

$$S_{xx}(\omega) = |H(\omega)|^2 S_{ff}(\omega) \qquad (2.129)$$

Although apparently very convenient, equation (2.129) does not provide a complete description of the random vibration conditions. Further, it is clear that it could not be used to determine the FRF from measurements of excitation and response because it contains only the modulus of $H(\omega)$, the phase information being omitted from this formula. A second equation is required and this may be obtained by a similar analysis based on the cross correlation between the excitation and the response, the frequency domain form of which is:

$$S_{fx}(\omega) = H(\omega) \; S_{ff}(\omega)$$
or, alternatively: $\qquad\qquad\qquad\qquad\qquad\qquad\qquad\qquad (2.130)$
$$S_{xx}(\omega) = H(\omega) \; S_{xf}(\omega)$$

So far, all the analysis in this section has been confined to the case of a single excitation parameter, although it is clear that several responses can be considered by repeated application of the equations (2.129) and (2.130). In fact, the analysis can be extended to situations where several excitations are applied simultaneously, whether or not these are correlated with each other. This analysis involves not only the auto spectra of all the individual excitations, but also the cross spectra which link one with the others. The general input/output equation for this case is:

$$[S_{fx}(\omega)] = [S_{ff}(\omega)][H(\omega)] \qquad (2.131)$$

TO DERIVE FRF FROM RANDOM VIBRATION

The pair of equations (2.130) provides us with the basis for a method of determining a system's FRF properties from the measurement and analysis of a random vibration test. Using either of them, we have a simple formula for determing the FRF from estimates of the relevant spectral densities:

$$H(\omega) = S_{fx}(\omega)/S_{ff}(\omega)$$

or   (2.132)

$$H(\omega) = S_{xx}(\omega)/S_{xf}(\omega)$$

In fact, the existence of two equations (and a third, if we include (2.129)) presents an opportunity to check the quality of calculations made using measured (and therefore imperfect) data, as will be discussed in more detail in Chapter 3.

2.10   ANALYSIS OF WEAKLY NON-LINEAR STRUCTURES

2.10.1   General

Before concluding our review of the theoretical basis of the subject, it is appropriate to include a consideration of the possibility that not all the systems or structures encountered in practice will be linear.   All the preceding analysis and, indeed, the whole basis of the subject, assumes linearity, an assumption which has two main implications in the present context:

(i)   that doubling the magnitude of the excitation force would simply result in a doubling of the response, and so on (response linearity related to excitation), and

(ii)   that if two or more excitation patterns are applied simultaneously then the response thus produced will be equal to the sum of the responses caused by each excitation individually (i.e. the principle of linear superposition applies).

We shall now introduce some of the characteristics exhibited by weakly (i.e. slightly) non-linear systems, not in order to provide detailed analysis but so that such structural behaviour can be recognised and identified if encountered during a modal test.   Thus we shall seek to derive and illustrate the frequency response characteristics of such a system.

The equation of motion for a single-degree-of-freedom system with non-linear displacement and/or velocity dependent non-linearity is:

$$m(\ddot{x} + 2\zeta\omega_0\dot{x} + \omega_0^2 x + \mu(x,x)) = f(t)$$ (2.133)

This equation can be expressed as

$$m(\ddot{x} + \tilde{\lambda}\dot{x} + \tilde{\omega}_0^2 x) = f(t)$$ (2.134)

where $\tilde{\lambda}$ and $\tilde{\omega}_0^2$ depend on the amplitude (a) and frequency (ω) of vibration, according to:

$$\tilde{\lambda} = - \frac{1}{\pi a \omega_0} \quad \mu(a \cos \phi, - a\omega_0 \sin \phi) \sin \phi \ d\phi$$

$$\tilde{\omega}_0{}^2 = \omega_0{}^2 + \frac{1}{\pi a} \quad \mu \ (a \cos \phi, - a\omega_0 \sin \phi) \cos \phi \ d\phi \qquad (2.135)$$

We shall confine our attention here to two specific cases of practical interest, namely

(a)   cubic stiffness, where the spring force is given by $k(x + \beta x^3)$, and

(b)   coulomb friction, where the (or some of the) damping is provided by dry friction.

2.10.2   Cubic Stiffness

In this case, we have a basic equation of motion of the form

$$m(\ddot{x} + 2\zeta\omega_0\dot{x} + \omega_0{}^2(x + \beta x^3)) = f(t) \qquad (2.136)$$

or

$$m(\ddot{x} + \tilde{\lambda}\dot{x} + \tilde{\omega}_0{}^2 x) = f(t)$$

where

$$\tilde{\lambda} = 2\zeta\omega_0 \quad \text{and}$$

$$\tilde{\omega}_0{}^2 = \omega_0{}^2 \ (1 + 3\beta a^2/4) \qquad (2.137)$$

In the case of harmonic excitation, $f(t) = f \ e^{i\omega t}$, we find that in fact the response $x(t)$ is not simply harmonic – the non-linearity causes the generation of some response (generally small) at multiples of the excitation frequency – but it is convenient to examine the component of the response at the excitation frequency. (Note that this is just what would be measured in a sinusoidal test, though not with a random, periodic or transient test). Then we shall find:

$$x(t) \simeq ae^{i\omega t} \ ; \ a = \frac{f/m}{\tilde{\omega}_0{}^2 - \omega^2 + i\tilde{\lambda}} \qquad (2.138)$$

where $\tilde{\omega}_0{}^2$ and $\tilde{\lambda}$ are themselves functions of a.   Equation (2.138) needs further processing to find an explicit expression for a.   This is obtained from:

$$(3\beta\omega_0{}^2/4)^2 a^6 - (3(\omega_0{}^2 - \omega^2)\beta\omega_0{}^2/2) a^4$$

$$+ ((\omega_0{}^2 - \omega^2) + (2\zeta\omega_0\omega)^2) a^2 - (f/m)^2 = 0 \qquad (2.139)$$

which shows that there can either be one or three real roots.   All cubic stiffness systems exhibit this characteristic although the existence of the two types of solution (one possible value for a, or three) depends upon the frequency and the magnitude of the excitation and/or the nonlinearity. Some typical plots are shown in Figure 2.27, computed using the above expressions.

2.10.3 Coulomb Friction

In this case, we have a basic equation of motion of the type:

$$m(\ddot{x} + 2\zeta\omega_0\dot{x} + \omega_0^2 x) + \frac{R\dot{x}}{|\dot{x}|} = f(t) \qquad (2.140)$$

or

$$m(\ddot{x} + \tilde{\lambda}\dot{x} + \tilde{\omega}_0^2 x) = f(t) \quad = mF(t)$$

where

$$\tilde{\lambda} = 2\zeta\omega_0 + 4R/(\pi a\omega_0)$$

$$\tilde{\omega}_0^2 = \omega_0^2 \qquad (2.141)$$

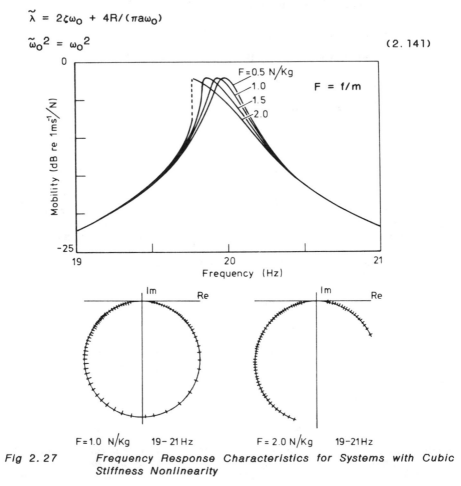

Fig 2.27   *Frequency Response Characteristics for Systems with Cubic Stiffness Nonlinearity*

Once again, a harmonic excitation will produce a more complex, though periodic, response whose fundamental component is given by

$$x(t) \simeq ae^{i\omega t}$$

where a is obtained from

$$((\omega_0^2 - \omega^2)^2 + (2\zeta\omega_0\omega)^2) \, a^2 + (8\zeta\omega^2 R/\pi) a$$

$$+ ((4R\omega/\pi\omega_0)^2 - (f/m)^2) = 0 \qquad (2.142)$$

Further analysis of this expression shows that only a single value of a applies. Plots of $\frac{\dot{a}}{f}$ for various values of f and/or R are illustrated in Figure 2.28.

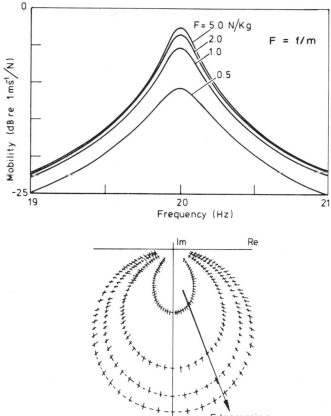

Fig 2.28   *Frequency Response Characteristics of System with Coulomb Friction*

CHAPTER 3
Mobility Measurement
Techniques

3.0 INTRODUCTION

In this chapter we shall be concerned with the measurement techniques which are used for modal testing. First, it is appropriate to consider vibration measurement methods in general in order to view the context of those used for our particular interest here. Basically, there are two types of vibration measurement:

(i)   those in which just one parameter is measured (usually a response level), and
(ii)   those in which both input and response output are measured.

Recalling the basic relationship:

$$\boxed{\text{RESPONSE}} \quad = \quad \boxed{\text{PROPERTIES}} \quad \text{x} \quad \boxed{\text{INPUT}}$$

we can see that only when two of the three terms in this equation have been measured can we define completely what is going on in the vibration of the test object. If we measure only the response, then we are unable to say whether a particularly large response level is due to a strong excitation or to a resonance of the structure. Nevertheless, both types of measurement have their applications and much of the equipment and instrumentation used is the same in both cases.

We shall be concerned here with the second type of measurement, where both excitation and response are measured simultaneously so that the basic equation can be used to deduce the system properties directly from the measured data. Within this category there are a number of different approaches which can be adopted but we shall concentrate heavily on one which we refer to as the 'single-point excitation' method. All the others involve simultaneous excitation at several points on the structure and although we shall discuss these briefly at the end of this chapter, our interest will be focused on the more straightforward approach (at least from the viewpoint of the experimenter) where the excitation is applied at a single point (although in the course of a test, this point may be varied around the structure). This type of measurement is often referred to as 'mobility measurement', and that is the name we shall use throughout this work.

3.1 BASIC MEASUREMENT SYSTEM

The experimental setup used for mobility measurement is basically quite simple although there exist a great many different variants on it, in terms of the specific items used. There are three major items:

(i)   an excitation mechanism
(ii)   a transduction system (to measure the various parameters of interest), and
(iii)   an analyser, to extract the desired information (in the presence of the inevitable imperfections which will accumulate on the measured signals).

Figure 3.1 shows a typical layout for the measurement system, detailing some of the 'standard' items which are usually found. An additional component has been included in this illustration in the form of a Controller. This is now a common feature in many if not most modern measurement 'chains' and can be provided by a desktop, mini- or micro-computer. As many of the detailed procedures in mobility measurements are repetitive and tedious, some form of automation is highly desirable and, if provided by a computer, this can also serve to process the measured data as required for the modal analysis stage, later in the overall process.

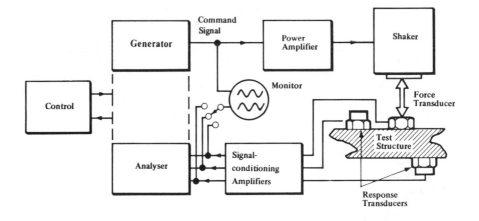

Fig 3.1   General Layout of Mobility Measurement System

The main items in the measurement chain are then:

(a) a source for the excitation signal. This will depend on the type of test being undertaken and can be any of the following:
- sinusoidal (from an oscillator)
- random (from a noise generator)
- transient (from a special pulse generating device, or by applying an impact with a hammer)
- periodic (from a special signal generator capable of producing a specific frequency content).

(b) Power Amplifier. This component will be necessary in order to drive the actual device used to vibrate the structure which, in turn, will take one of a number of different forms, as discussed below. The power amplifier will necessarily be selected to match the excitation device.

(c) Exciter. The structure can be excited into vibration in several ways, although the two most commonly (and successfully) used are by an attached shaker or by a hammer blow. Other possibilities exist by step relaxation (releasing from a deflected position) and by ambient excitation (such as wave, wind or roadway excitations), but these are relatively special cases which are only used when the more conventional methods are not possible.

(d) Transducers. Here again, there are a great many different possibilities for the devices available to measure the excitation forces and the various responses of interest. For the most part, piezoelectric transducers are widely used for both types of parameter although strain gauges are often found to be convenient because of their minimal interference with the test object.

(e) Conditioning Amplifiers. The choice of amplifier depends heavily on the type of transducer used and should, in effect, be regarded as part of it. In all cases, its role is to strengthen the (usually) small signals generated by the transducers so that they can be fed to the analyser for measurement.

(f) Analyser. The function of this item is simply to measure the various signals developed by the transducers in order to ascertain the magnitudes of the excitation force(s) and responses. In essence, it is a voltmeter but in practice it is a very sophisticated one. There are different types of analyser available and the choice will depend on the type of excitation which has been used: sinusoidal, random, transient, periodic. The two most common devices are Spectrum (Fourier) Analysers and Frequency Response Analysers although the same functions as provided by these can be performed by a tunable narrow-band filter, a voltmeter and a phase meter plus a great deal of time and patience!

3.2   STRUCTURE PREPARATION

3.2.1   Free and Grounded Supports

One important preliminary to the whole process of mobility measurement is the preparation of the test structure itself.   This is often not given the attention it deserves and the consequences which accrue can cause an unnecessary degradation of the whole test.

The first decision which has to be taken is whether the structure is to be tested in a 'free' condition or 'grounded'.   By 'free' is meant that the test object is not attached to ground at any of its coordinates and is, in effect, freely suspended in space.   In this condition, the structure will exhibit rigid body modes which are determined solely by its mass and inertia properties and in which there is no bending or flexing at all. Theoretically, any structure will possess 6 rigid-body modes and each of these has a natural frequency of 0 Hz.   By testing a structure in this free condition, we are able to determine the rigid-body modes and thus the mass and inertia properties which can themselves be very useful data.

In practice, of course, it is not feasible to provide a truly free support – the structure must be held in some way – but it is generally feasible to provide a suspension system which closely approximates to this condition. This can be achieved by supporting the testpiece on very soft 'springs', such as might be provided by light elastic bands, so that the rigid body modes, while no longer having zero natural frequencies, have values which are very low in relation to those of the bending modes.   ('Very low' in this context means that the highest rigid-body mode frequency is less than 10-20% of that for the lowest bending mode.)   If we achieve a suspension system of this type, then we can still derive the rigid body (inertia) properties from the very low frequency behaviour of the structure without having any significant influence on the flexural modes that are the object of the test.   (In fact, there are several instances where a test of this type may be carried out only to examine the rigid body modes as this is an effective way of determining the full inertia properties of a complex structure.)   One added precaution which can be taken to ensure minimum interference by the suspension on the lowest bending mode of the structure – the one most vulnerable – is to attach the suspension as close as possible to nodal points of the mode in question.   Lastly, particular attention should be paid to the possibility of the suspension adding significant damping to otherwise lightly-damped testpieces.

As a parting comment on this type of suspension, it is necessary to note that any rigid body will possess no less than 6 modes and it is necessary to check that the natural frequencies of all of these are sufficiently low before being satisfied that the suspension system used is sufficiently soft. To this end, suspension wires etc. should generally be normal to the primary direction of vibration, as in Figure 3.6b rather than the case shown in Figure 3.6a.

The other type of support is referred to as 'grounded' because it attempts to fix selected points on the structure to ground.   While this condition is extremely easy to apply in a theoretical analysis, simply by deleting the appropriate coordinates, it is much more difficult to implement in the practical case. The reason for this is that it is very difficult to provide a base or foundation on which to attach the test structure which is sufficiently rigid to provide the necessary grounding. All structures have a finite impedance (or a non-zero mobility) and thus cannot be regarded as truly rigid but whereas we are able to approximate the free condition by a soft suspension, it is less easy to approximate the grounded condition without taking extraordinary precautions when designing the support structure. Perhaps the safest procedure to follow is to measure the mobility of the base structure itself over the frequency range for the test and to establish that this is a much lower mobility than the corresponding levels for the test structure at the point of attachment. If this condition can be satisfied for all the coordinates to be grounded then the base structure can reasonably be assumed to be grounded. However, as a word of caution, it should be noted that the coordinates involved will often include rotations and these are notoriously difficult to measure.

From the above comments, it might be concluded that we should always test structures in a freely-supported condition. Ideally, this is so but there are numerous practical situations where this approach is simply not feasible and again others where it is not the most appropriate. For example, very large testpieces, such as parts of power generating stations or civil engineering structures, could not be tested in a freely-supported state. Further, in just the same way that low frequency properties of a freely supported structure can provide information on its mass and inertia characteristics, so also can the corresponding parts of the mobility curves for a grounded structure yield information on its static stiffness. Another consideration to be made when deciding on the format of the test is the environment in which the structure is to operate. For example, if we consider a turbine blade it is clear that in its operating condition the vibration modes of interest will be much closer to those of a cantilevered root fixing than to those of a completely free blade. Whereas it is possible to test and to analyse a single blade as a free structure, the modes and frequencies which will then form the basis of the test/analysis comparison will be quite different from those which obtain under running conditions. Of course, theoretically, we can validate or obtain a model of the blade using its free properties and expect this to be equally applicable when the root is grounded, but in the real world, where we are dealing with approximations and less-than-perfect data, there is additional comfort to be gained from a comparison made using modes which are close to those of the functioning structure, i.e. with a grounded root. A compromise procedure can be applied in some cases in which the test object (such as the blade) is connected at certain coordinates to another simple component of known mobility, such as a known mass. This modified testpiece is then studied experimentally and the effects of the added component 'removed' analytically.

In the above paragraphs, we have presented a number of considerations which must be made in deciding what is the best way to support the test structure for mobility measurements. There is no universal method: each test must be considered individually and the above points taken into account. Perhaps as a final comment for those cases in which a decision is difficult we should observe that, at least from a theoretical standpoint, it is always possible to determine the grounded structure's properties from those in a free condition while it is not possible to go in the opposite direction. (This characteristic comes from the fact that the free support involves more degrees of freedom, some of which can later be deleted, while it is not possible – without the addition of new data – to convert the more limited model of a grounded structure to one with greater freedom as would be necessary to describe a freely-supported structure.)

Examples of both types of test configuration are shown in Figure 3.2.

3.2.2   Local stiffening

If it is decided to ground the structure, care must be taken to ensure that no local stiffening or other distortion is introduced by the attachment, other than that which is an integral part of the structure itself. In fact, great care must be paid to the area of the attachment if a realistic and reliable test configuration is to be obtained and it is advisable to perform some simple checks to ensure that the whole assembly gives repeatable results when dismantled and reassembled again. Such attention to detail will be repaid by confidence in the eventual results.

Fig 3.2a   *Example of Grounded Structure*

Fig 3. 2 b   *Examples of Freely-Supported Structures*

3.3 EXCITATION OF THE STRUCTURE

3.3.1 General

Various devices are available for exciting the structure and several of these are in widespread use. Basically, they can be divided into two types: contacting and non-contacting. The first of these involves the connection of an exciter of some form which remains attached to the structure throughout the test, whether the excitation type is continuous (sinusoidal, random etc.) or transient (pulse, chirp). The second type includes devices which are either out of contact throughout the vibration (such as provided by a non-contacting electromagnet) or which are only in contact for a short period, while the excitation is being applied (such as a hammer blow).

We shall discuss first the various types of vibrator, or shaker, of which there are three in use:

mechanical (out-of-balance rotating masses),
electromagnetic (moving coil in magnetic field),
electrohydraulic.

Each has its advantages and disadvantages – which we shall attempt to summarise below – and each is most effective within a particular operating range, as illustrated by some typical data shown in Figure 3.3. It should be noted that exciters are often limited at very low frequencies by the stroke (displacement) rather than by the force generated.

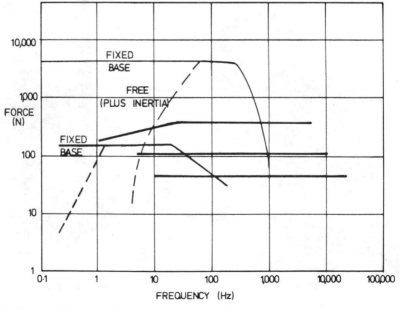

Fig 3.3   *Typical Exciter Characteristics*

3.3.2 Mechanical Exciters

The mechanical exciter is capable of generating a prescribed force at a variable frequency although there is relatively little flexibility or control in its use. The magnitude of the force is restricted by the out-of-balance and is only variable by making adjustments to this quantity – not something which can be done while the vibration is continuing. Also, this type of excitation mechanism is relatively ineffective at low frequencies because of the speed-squared dependence. However, unless the amplitude of vibration caused by the exciter becomes large relative to the orbit of the out-of-balance masses, the magnitude and phase of the excitation force is known quite accurately and does not need further measurement, as is the case for the other types of exciter.

3.3.3 Electromagnetic Exciters

Perhaps the most common type of exciter is the electromagnetic (or 'electrodynamic') shaker in which the supplied input signal is converted to an alternating magnetic field in which is placed a coil which is attached to the drive part of the device, and to the structure. In this case, the frequency and amplitude of excitation are controlled independently of each other, giving more operational flexibility – especially useful as it is generally found that it is better to vary the level of the excitation as resonances are passed through. However, it must be noted that the electrical impedance of these devices varies with the amplitude of motion of the moving coil and so it is not possible to deduce the excitation force from a measurement of the voltage applied to the shaker. Nor, in fact, is it usually appropriate to deduce the excitation force by measuring the current passing through the shaker because this measures the force applied not to the structure itself, but to the assembly of structure and shaker drive. Although it may appear that the difference between this force (generated within the shaker) and that applied to the structure is likely to be small, it must be noted that just near resonance very little force is required to produce a large response and what usually happens is that without altering the settings on the power amplifier or signal generator, there is a marked reduction in the force level at frequencies adjacent to the structure's natural frequencies. As a result, the true force applied to the structure becomes the (small) difference between the force generated in the exciter and the inertia force required to move the drive rod and shaker table and is, in fact, much smaller than either. See Figure 3.4a.

As this is an important feature of most attached-shaker tests using continuous sinusoidal, random or periodic excitation, it is worth illustrating the point by the following example.

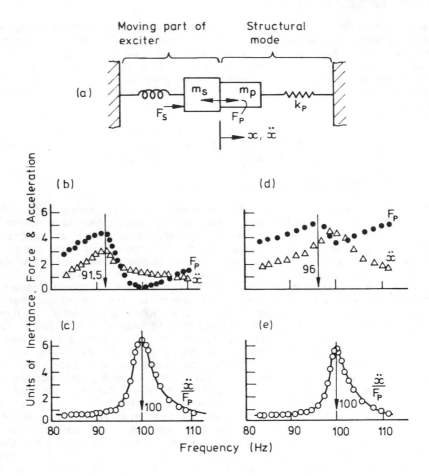

Fig 3. 4   Parameter Variations Around Resonance
                  (a)   Shaker/Structure Model
                  (b)   Measured Data at Point 1
                  (c)   Inertance Measured at Point 1
                  (d)   Measured Data at Point 2
                  (e)   Inertance Measured at Point 2

Suppose we are testing a plate and are trying to determine the properties of one of its modes. In one measurement, where the excitation and response are measured at the same point (a point mobility) and in the immediate vicinity of a natural frequency, the plate behaves very similarly to a single-degree-of-freedom oscillator with an apparent mass of m_{p1} and an apparent stiffness of k_{p1}. (Note that the natural frequency of this mode is given by $(k_{p1}/m_{p1})^{1/2}$.) Suppose also that the mass of the moving part of the shaker and its connection to the structure (which is not part of the structure proper) is m_s. Now, let the force generated in the shaker be F_s and the force actually applied to the structure (the one we want to measure) be F_p. If the acceleration of the structure is denoted by $\ddot{x}$, and we consider the vibration test to be conducted at various sinusoidal frequencies ω, then we may write the simple relationship:

$$F_p = F_s - m_s \, \ddot{x}$$

Taking some typical data, we show in Figure 3.4b the magnitudes of the various quantities which are, or which could be, measured. Also shown in Figure 3.4c is the curve for the mobility quantity of interest, in this case the inertance $\ddot{x}/F_p$, and it is particularly interesting to see how the true natural frequency (indicated when the inertance reaches a maximum) is considerably displaced from that suggested by the apparent resonance when the response alone reaches a maximum.

We now move to a different point on the structure which, for the same mode, will have different values for the apparent mass and stiffness, m_{p2} and k_{p2}, although these two quantities will necessarily stay in the same ratio (i.e. $k_{p1}/m_{p1} = k_{p2}/m_{p2} = \omega_o{}^2$). Another plot of the various quantities in this case is shown in Figure 3.4d and 3.4e from which it is clear that although the mobility parameter shows the natural frequency to be at the same value as before, the system resonance is now at a different frequency to that encountered in the first measurement simply because of the different balance between the structure's apparent properties (which vary from point to point) and those of the shaker (which remain the same throughout).

This example serves to illustrate the need for a direct measurement of the force applied to the structure as close to the surface as possible in order to obtain a reliable and accurate indication of the excitation level, and hence the mobility properties. It also illustrates a characteristic which gives rise to some difficulties in making such measurements: namely, that the (true) applied excitation force becomes very small in the vicinity of the resonant frequency with the consequence that it is particularly vulnerable to noise or distortion, see Figure 3.4b.

Generally, the larger the shaker, the greater the force which may be generated for exciting the structure. However, besides the obvious penalty of expense incurred by using too large an exciter, there is a limitation imposed on the working frequency range. The above discussion, which shows how the force generated in the exciter itself finds its way out to the structure, applies only as long as the moving parts of the shaker remain a rigid mass. Once the frequency of vibration approaches and passes the first natural frequency of the shaker coil and drive platform then there is a severe attenuation of the force which is available for driving the test object and although some excitation is possible above this critical frequency, it does impose a natural limit on the useful working range of the device. Not surprisingly, this frequency is lower for the larger shakers. Figure 3.3 shows, approximately, the relationship between maximum force level and upper frequency limit for a typical range of shakers of this type.

3.3.4 Electrohydraulic Exciters

The next type of exciter to be considered is the hydraulic (or electrohydraulic, to be precise). In this device, the power amplification to generate substantial forces is achieved through the use of hydraulics and although more costly and complex than their electromagnetic counterparts, these exciters do have one potentially significant advantage. That is their ability to apply simultaneously a static load as well as the dynamic vibratory load and this can be extremely useful when testing structures or materials whose normal vibration environment is combined with a major static load which may well change its dynamic properties or even its geometry. Without the facility of applying both static and dynamic loads simultaneously, it is necessary to make elaborate arrangements to provide the necessary static forces and so in these cases hydraulic shakers have a distinct advantage.

Another advantage which they may afford is the possibility of providing a relatively long stroke, thereby permitting the excitation of structures at large amplitudes – a facility not available on the comparably-sized electromagnetic shakers. On the other hand, hydraulic exciters tend to be limited in operational frequency range and only very specialised ones permit measurements in the range above 1 kHz, whereas electromagnetic exciters can operate well into the 30-50 kHz region, depending on their size. Also, as mentioned earlier, hydraulic shakers are more complex and expensive, although they are generally compact and lightweight compared with electromagnetic devices.

The comments made above concerning the need to measure force at the point of application to the structure also apply to this type of exciter, although the relative magnitudes of the various parameters involved will probably be quite different.

3.3.5 Attachment to the structure

For the above excitation devices, it is necessary to connect the driving platform of the shaker to the structure, usually incorporating a force transducer. There are one or two precautions which must be taken at this stage in order to avoid the introduction of unwanted excitations or the inadvertent modification of the structure. The first of these is perhaps the most important because it is the least visible. If we return to our definition of a single mobility or frequency response parameter, Y_{jk}, we note that this is the ratio between the harmonic response at point or coordinate j caused by a single harmonic force applied in coordinate k. There is also a stipulation in the definition that this single force must be the <u>only</u> excitation of the structure and it is this condition that we must be at pains to satisfy in our test. Although it may seem that the exciter is capable of applying a force in one direction only — it is essentially a uni-directional device — there exists a problem on most practical structures whose motion is generally complex and multidirectional. The problem is that when pushed in one direction — say, along the x axis — the structure responds not only in that same direction but also in others, such as along the y and z axes and also in the three rotation directions. Such motion is perfectly in order and expected but it is possible that it can give rise to a secondary form of excitation if the shaker is incorrectly attached to the structure. It is usual for the moving part of the shaker to be very mobile along the axis of its drive but for it to be quite the reverse (i.e. very stiff) in the other directions. Thus, if the structure wishes to respond in, say, a lateral direction as well as in the line of action of the exciter, then the stiffness of the exciter will cause resisting forces or moments to be generated which are, in effect, exerted on the structure in the form of a secondary excitation. The response transducers know nothing of this and they pick up the total response which is that caused not only by the driving force (which is known) but also by the secondary and unknown forces.

The solution is to attach the shaker to the structure through a drive rod or similar connector which has the characteristic of being stiff in one direction (that of the intended excitation) while at the same time being relatively flexible in the other five directions. One such device is illustrated in Figure 3.5a. Care must be taken not to over-compensate:

Fig 3.5(a)   Exciter Attachment and Drive Rod Assemblies — Practical Assembly

If the drive rod or 'stinger' is made too long, or too flexible, then it begins to introduce the effects of its own resonances into the measurements and these can be very difficult to extricate from the genuine data. For most general structures, an exposed length of some 5-10 mm of 1 mm dia. wire is found to be satisfactory, although by experience rather than by detailed analysis. Various alternative arrangements are sometimes found, as illustrated in Figure 3.5b,c,d and e. Of these, b is unsatisfactory while c and d are acceptable, if not ideal, configurations. It is always necessary to check for the existence of an internal resonance of the drive rod - either axially or in flexure - as this can introduce spurious effects on the measured mobility properties. Futhermore, in the case of an axial resonance, it will be found that very little excitation force will be delivered to the test structure at frequencies above the first axial mode. (This should also be noted as it applies to cases where a non-flexible extension rod is used to overcome problems of access, Figure 3.5e).

Another consideration which concerns the shaker is the question of how it should be supported, or mounted, in relation to the test structure. Of the many possibilities, some of which are illustrated in Figure 3.6, two are generally acceptable while others range from 'possible-with-care' to unsatisfactory. The setup shown in Figure 3.6a presents the most satisfactory arrangement in which the shaker is fixed to ground while the test structure is supported by a soft suspension. Figure 3.6b shows an alternative configuration in which the shaker itself is resiliently supported.

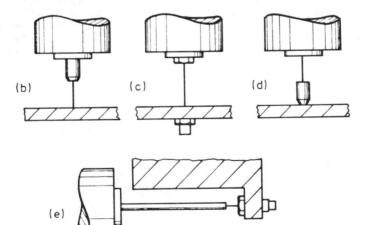

Fig 3.5   *Exciter Attachment and Drive Rod Assembly*
      (b)   Unsatisfactory Assembly with Impedance Head
      (c)   Acceptable Assembly
      (d)   Acceptable Assembly
      (e)   Use of Extension Rod

In this arrangement, the structure can be grounded or ungrounded, but it may be necessary to add an additional inertia mass to the shaker in order to generate sufficient excitation forces at low frequencies. The particular problem which arises here is that the reaction force causes a movement of the shaker body which, at low frequencies, can be of large displacement. This, in turn, causes a reduction in the force generation by the shaker so that its effectiveness at driving the test structure is diminished.

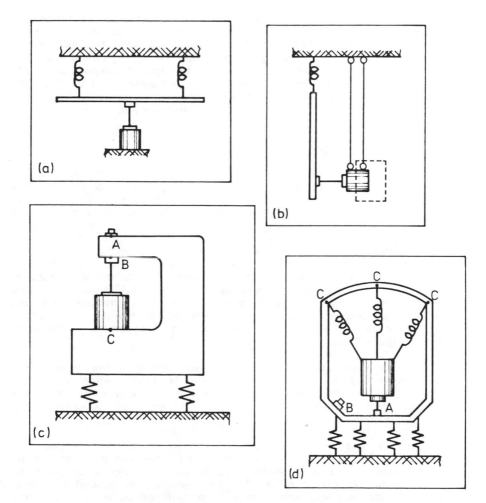

Fig 3.6   *Various Mounting Arrangments for Exciter*
   (a)   Ideal Configuration
   (b)   Suspended Exciter Plus Inertia Mass
   (c)   Unsatisfactory Configuration
   (d)   Compromise Configuration

In both cases 3.6a and 3.6b above, we have sought to ensure that the reaction force imposed on the shaker (equal and opposite to that applied to the drive rod) is not transmitted to the test structure. Figure 3.6c shows a set-up which does not meet that requirement with the result that an invalid mobility measurement would be obtained because the response measured at A would not be due solely to the force applied at B (which has been measured), but would, in part, be caused by the (unmeasured) force applied at C.

The final example, Figure 3.6d, shows a compromise which is sometimes necessary for practical reasons. In this case, it is essential to check that the measured response at A is caused primarily by the directly applied force at B and that it is not significantly influenced by the transmission of the reaction on the shaker through its suspension at C. This is achieved by ensuring that the frequency range for the measurements is well above the suspension resonance of the shaker: then, the reaction forces will be effectively attenuated by normal vibration isolation principles.

3.3.6 Hammer or Impactor Excitation

Another popular method of excitation is through use of an impactor or hammer. Although this type of test places greater demands on the analysis phase of the measurement process, it is a relatively simple means of exciting the structure into vibration. The equipment consists of no more than an impactor, usually with a set of different tips and heads which serve to extend the frequency and force level ranges for testing a variety of different structures. The useful range may also be extended by using different sizes of impactor. Integral with the impactor there is usually a load cell, or force transducer, which detects the magnitude of the force felt by the impactor, and which is assumed to be equal and opposite to that experienced by the structure. When applied by hand, the impactor incorporates a handle – to form a hammer (Figure 3.7a). Otherwise, it can be applied with a suspension arrangement, such as is shown in Figure 3.7b.

Basically, the magnitude of the impact is determined by the mass of the hammer head and the velocity with which it is moving when it hits the structure. Often, the operator will control the velocity rather than the force level itself, and so an appropriate way of adjusting the order of the force level is by varying the mass of the hammer head.

The frequency range which is effectively excited by this type of device is controlled by the stiffness of the contacting surfaces and the mass of the impactor head: there is a system resonance at a frequency given by (contact stiffness/impactor mass)$^{1/2}$ above which it is difficult to deliver energy into the test structure. When the hammer tip impacts the test structure, this will experience a force pulse which is substantially that of a half-sine shape, as shown in Figure 3.8a. A pulse of this type can be shown to have a frequency content of the form illustrated in Figure 3.8b which is essentially flat up to a certain frequency (f_c) and then of diminished and uncertain strength thereafter. Clearly, a pulse of this

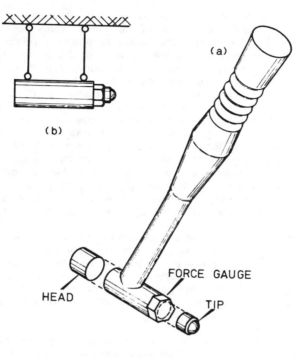

Fig 3. 7   Impactor and Hammer Details

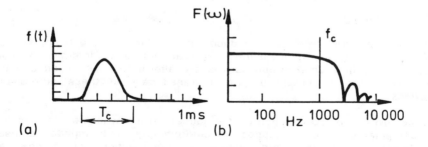

(a)

(b)

Fig 3. 8   Typical Impact Force Pulse and Spectrum
(a)   Time History
(b)   Frequency Spectrum

type would be relatively ineffective at exciting vibrations in the frequency range above f_C and so we need to have some control over this parameter. It can be shown that there is a direct relationship between the first cut-off frequency f_C and the duration of the pulse, T_C, and that in order to raise the frequency range it is necessary to induce a shorter pulse length. This in turn, can be seen to be related to the stiffness (not the hardness) of the contacting surfaces and the mass of the impactor head. The stiffer the materials, the shorter will be the duration of the pulse and the higher will be the frequency range covered by the impact. Similarly, the lighter the impactor mass the higher the effective frequency range. It is for this purpose that a set of different hammer tips and heads are used to permit the regulation of the frequency range to be encompassed. Generally, as soft a tip as possible will be used in order to inject all the input energy into the frequency range of interest: using a stiffer tip than necessary will result in energy being input to vibrations outside the range of interest at the expense of those inside that range.

On a different aspect, one of the difficulties of applying excitation using a hammer is ensuring that each impact is essentially the same as the previous ones, not so much in magnitude (as that is accommodated in the force and response measurement process) as in position and orientation relative to the normal to the surface. At the same time, multiple impacts or 'hammer bounce' must be avoided as these create difficulties in the signal processing stage.

Yet another problem to be considered when using the hammer type of excitation derives from the essentially transient nature of the vibrations under which the measurements are being made. We shall return to this characteristic later but here it is appropriate to mention the possibility of inflicting an overload during the excitation pulse, forcing the structure outside its elastic or linear range.

3.4 TRANSDUCERS AND AMPLIFIERS

3.4.1 General

The piezoelectric type of transducer is by far the most popular and widely-used means of measuring the parameters of interest in modal tests. Only in special circumstances are alternative types used and thus we shall confine our discussion of transducers to these piezoelectric devices.

Three types of piezoelectric transducer are available for mobility measurements – force gauges, accelerometers and impedance heads (although these last are simply a combination of force- and acceleration-sensitive elements in a single unit). The basic principle of operation makes use of the fact that an element of piezoelectric material (either a natural or synthetic crystal) generates an electrical charge across its end faces when subjected to a mechanical stress. By suitable design, such a crystal may be incorporated into a device which induces in it a stress proportional to the physical quantity to be measured (i.e. force or acceleration).

3.4.2 Force Transducers

The force transducer is the simplest type of piezoelectric transducer. The transmitted force F (see Figure 3.9), or a known fraction of it, is applied directly across the crystal which thus generates a corresponding charge, q, proportional to F. It is usual for the sensitive crystals to be used in pairs, arranged so that the negative sides of both are attached to the case, and the positive sides are in mutual contact at their interface. This arrangement obviates the need to insulate one end of the case from the other electrically. One important feature in the design of force gauges is the relative stiffness (in the axial direction) of the crystals and of the case. The fraction of F which is transmitted through the crystals depends directly upon this ratio. In addition, there exists the undesirable possibility of a cross sensitivity – i.e. an electrical output when there is zero force F but, say, a transverse or shear loading – and this is also influenced by the casing.

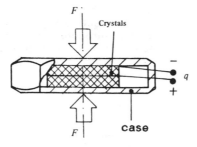

Fig 3.9   Force Transducer

The force indicated by the charge output of the crystals will always be slightly different from the force applied by the shaker, and also from that transmitted to the structure. This is because a fraction of the force detected by the crystals will be used to move the small amount of material between the crystals and the structure. The implications of this effect are discussed later in a section on mass cancellation (Section 3.9), but suffice it to say here that for each force gauge, one end will have a smaller mass than the other, and it is this (lighter) end which should be connected to the structure under test.

3.4.3 Accelerometers

In an accelerometer, transduction is indirect and is achieved using an auxiliary, or seismic, mass (see Figure 3.10a). In this configuration, the force exerted on the crystals is the inertia force of the seismic mass (i.e. $m\ddot{z}$). Thus, so long as the body and the seismic mass move together (i.e. $\ddot{z}$ and $\ddot{x}$ are identical), the output of the transducer will be proportional to the acceleration of its body ($\ddot{x}$), and thus of the structure to which it is attached. Analysis of a simple dynamic model for this device (see Fig 3.10b) shows that the ratio $\ddot{x}/\ddot{z}$ is effectively unity over a wide range of frequency from zero upwards until the first resonant frequency of the transducer is approached. At 20 per cent. of this resonant frequency, the difference (or error in the ratio $\ddot{x}/\ddot{z}$) is 0.04, and at 33 per cent. it has grown to 0.12. Thus, in order to define the working range of an accelerometer, it is necessary to know its lowest resonant frequency. However, this property will depend to some extent upon the characteristics of the structure to which it is fixed, and indeed, upon the fixture itself. Manufacturers' data usually include a value for the 'mounted resonant frequency' and this is the lowest natural frequency of the seismic mass on the stiffness of the crystal when the body is fixed to a rigid base. In the simple model above, this frequency is given by $\sqrt{k/m}$. This value must be regarded as an upper limit (and thus not a conservative one) since in most applications the accelerometer body is attached to something which is less than rigid and so the transducer may possess a lower resonant frequency than that quoted. In any event, the actual attachment to the test structure must always be as rigid as possible and the manufacturer's advice to this end should be followed.

As with force transducers, there is a problem of cross- or transverse sensitivity of accelerometers which can result from imperfections in the crystal geometry and from interaction through the casing. Modern designs aim to minimise these effects and one configuration which tends to be better in this respect is the shear type, a very simple arrangement of which is illustrated in the sketch in Figure 3.10c.

(a)   (b)

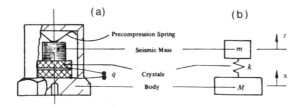

(c)

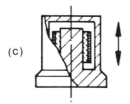

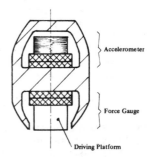

Fig 3.10 Typical Accelerometer Assembly
    (a)   Construction of Compression Type
    (b)   Simple Dynamic Model
    (c)   Construction of Shear Type

Fig 3.11 Impedance Head

3.4.4 Selection of Accelerometers

Accelerometer sensitivities vary between 1 and 10,000 pC/g. How is one to choose the most suitable for any given application? In general, we require as high a sensitivity as possible, but it must be noted that the higher the sensitivity, the heavier and larger the transducer (thus interfering more with the structure) and further, the lower is the transducer's resonant frequency (and thus the maximum working frequency). These considerations, together with any particular environmental requirements, will usually narrow the choice to one of a small range. For accurate measurements, especially on complex structures (which are liable to vibrate simultaneously in several directions), transducers with low transverse sensitivity (less than 1-2 per cent) should be selected.

It must be realised that the addition of even a small transducer to the structure imposes additional and unwanted forces on that structure. The loads are basically the inertia forces and moments associated with the transducer's motion along with the structure and although it may be possible to compensate for some of these (see Section 3.9 on Mass Cancellation, below), it is not possible to account for them all and so, especially at high frequencies and/or for small structures, care should be taken to use the smallest transducer which will provide the necessary signals. To this end, some of the newer transducers with built-in amplifiers offer a considerable improvement.

3.4.5 Impedance Heads

It has been found convenient for some applications to combine both force- and acceleration-measuring elements in a single housing, thereby forming an impedance head. The main reason for using such a device is to facilitate the measurement of both parameters at a single point. We shall discuss the implications of this particular detail of experimental technique later, and confine our attention here to the performance characteristics of impedance heads. A typical, although not unique, construction for an impedance head is shown in Figure 3.11. It is desirable to have both elements as close as possible to the structure – the force gauge in order to minimise the mass 'below the crystal', and the accelerometer to ensure as high a base stiffness as possible. Clearly, a design of the form shown must be a compromise and accordingly, the specifications of these heads should be carefully scrutinised. In particular, the extent of any cross-coupling between the force and acceleration elements should be established, since this can introduce errors in certain frequency and/or mobility ranges.

3.4.6 Conditioning Amplifiers

One of the advantages of the piezoelectric transducer is that it is an active device, and does not require a power supply in order to function. However, this means that it cannot measure truly static quantities and so there is a low frequency limit below which measurements are not practical. This limit is usually determined not simply by the properties of the transducer itself, but also by those of the amplifiers which are necessary to boost the very small electrical charge that is generated by the crystals into a signal strong enough to be measured by the analyser.

Two types of amplifier are available for this role – voltage amplifiers and charge amplifiers – and the essential characteristic for either type is that it must have a very high input impedance. Detailed comparisons of voltage and charge amplifiers are provided by manufacturers' literature. To summarise the main points: voltage amplifiers tend to be simpler (electronically) and to have a better signal/noise characteristic than do charge amplifiers, but they cannot be used at such low frequencies as the latter and the overall gain, or sensitivity, is affected by the length and properties of the transducer cable whereas that for a charge amplifier is effectively independent of the cable.

Increasingly, however, transducers are being constructed with integral amplifiers which make use of microelectronics. These devices require a low voltage power supply to be fed to the transducer but, in return, offer marked advantages in terms of a lower sensitivity to cable noise and fragility.

3.4.7 Attachment and Location of Transducers

Attachment

The correct location and installation of transducers, especially accelerometers, is most important. There are various means of fixing the transducers to the surface of the test structure, some more convenient than others. Some of these methods are illustrated in Figure 3.12 and range from a threaded stud, which requires the appropriate modification of the test structure (not always possible), through various adhesives in conjunction with a stud, to the use of a wax, which is the simplest and easiest to use. These forms of attachment become less reliable as the convenience improves although it is generally possible to define the limits of the usefulness of each and thus to select the correct one in any particular applicaton. Also shown on Figure 3.12 are typical frequency limits for each type of attachment. The particularly high – frequency capability of the screwed stud attachment can only be attained if the transducer is affixed exactly normal to the structure surface so that there is a high stiffness contact between the two components. If, for example, the axis of the tapped hole is not normal to the surface, then the misalignment which results will cause a poor contact region with a corresponding loss of stiffness and of high–frequency range.

Another consideration when attaching the transducer is the extent of local stiffening which is introduced by its addition to the structure. If this is being fixed to a relatively flexible plate–like surface, then there is a distinct possibility that the local stiffness will be increased considerably. The only real solution to this difficulty is to move the transducer to another, more substantial, part of the structure.

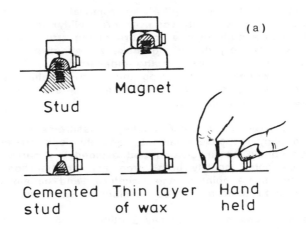

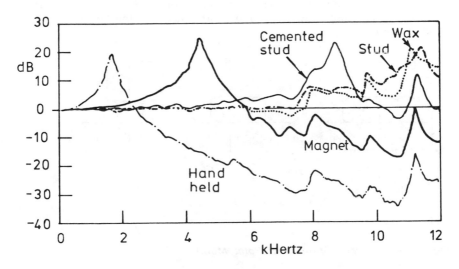

Fig 3.12   Accelerometer Attachment
            (a)   Methods of Attachment
            (b)   Frequency Response of Different Attachments

Location

Another problem which may require the removal of the transducer to another location is the possibility (or even probability) that it is positioned at or very close to a node of one or more of the structure's modes. In this event, it will be very difficult to make an effective measurement of that particular mode. However, if the measurement points are already determined (for example, by matching those on a finite element grid), then it is necessary to make what measurements are possible, even if some of these are less than ideal.

Most modal tests require a point mobility measurement as one of the measured frequency response functions, and this can present a special problem which should be anticipated and avoided. Clearly, in order to measure a true point mobility both force and acceleration transducers should be at the same point on the structure, and equally clearly, this may well be hard to achieve. Three possibilities exist, viz:

(i)   use an impedance head (see Section 3.4.5);
(ii)   place the force and acceleration transducers in line but on opposite sides of the structure as shown in Figure 3.13a (this is only possible if the structure is locally thin);
(iii)   place the accelerometer alongside, but as close as possible to the force gauge, as shown in Figure 3.13b.

(Note that there will be a phase difference of 180° between acceleration measurements made by (ii) and (iii) due to the inversion of the accelerometer.)

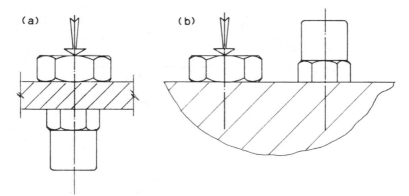

Fig 3.13   *Measurement of Point Mobility*

It is the third alternative which presents the problem, since particular care is required to ensure that the resulting measurements really are representative of a point mobility. A practical example illustrates the problem very clearly. Figure 3.14 shows the result of measuring the 'point' mobility on a model ship's hull structure where the third technique (iii) above was used. Figure 3.14a illustrates a detail of the measurement area, showing four possible sites for the accelerometer. Figure 3.14b presents four curves obtained by placing the accelerometer at each of these four points in turn. It is immediately apparent that two of the positions (B and D) result in very similar curves, and it could be shown later that both gave a good indication of the motion of the point of interest, X. The other two curves, corresponding to the accelerometer being placed at either A or C, show markedly different response characteristics and indeed introduce enormous errors. In this particular case, the trends of these results could be explained by detailed examination of the local stiffness of the structure near the measurement point, but it is possible that similar errors could be incurred in other examples where such an explanation might be less readily available.

One possible approach to reduce errors of this type is to average the outputs of two accelerometers, such as A and C or B and D, but some caution would be advisable when interpreting any results thus obtained.

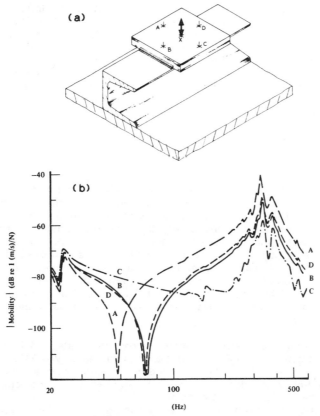

Fig 3.14   Example of Measurements of Point Mobility
(a)   Test Structure
(b)   Measured Curves

3.5   ANALYSERS

3.5.1   Role of the Analyser

Each mobility measurement system incorporates an analyser in order to measure the specific parameters of interest – force, response levels. In principle, each analyser is a form of voltmeter although the signal processing required to extract the necessary information concerning magnitude and phase of each parameter leads to very complex and sophisticated devices. Different measurement systems employ different types of analyser. There are three of these in current use:

–   tracking filters
–   frequency response analysers
–   spectrum analysers.

Of these, the first type is generally an analogue device, the second and third may be either analogue or digital but are most often digital. In all cases, the data are supplied to the analyser in analogue form but with a digital instrument the first stage of the signal processing is analogue-to-digital (A-D) conversion so that the quantities to be processed are then in the form of a string of discrete values, as opposed to a continuous function. The subsequent processing stages are then performed digitally, as in a computer, using a variety of special-purpose routines which are usually hard-wired into the analyser in the form of a microprocessor for maximum speed of execution.

It is appropriate to describe briefly each of these types of device.

3.5.2   Tracking Filter

The tracking filter is the oldest type of analyser used for mobility measurement and is applicable only for the type of excitation where a sinusoidal signal is applied to drive the structure (see Section 3.7). This sinusoid is either swept or stepped slowly through the frequency range of interest. Coupled to the oscillator generating this signal is a set of narrow-band filters through which the transducer signals are passed. The centre frequency of each filter is continuously adjusted so that it is always aligned with the current frequency of the generator output – the command signal. In this way, the analyser is able to indicate the magnitude and phase of the component of each transducer signal which is related to the actual excitation source.

It might seem that such an arrangement is rather elaborate and that these filters are unnecessary: all that should be required is a voltmeter and a phase meter. However, it is quickly found in practice that although the measurement system may start with a pure sine wave as the command signal, this is rapidly polluted by noise and non-linearities so that the transducer signals approaching the analyser contain many spurious components additional to the primary and intended one. Hence it is necessary to provide some means of extracting the desired components from the overall signals. The problem is particularly acute at frequencies near resonance and antiresonance because in these regions, either the force signal or the response signal tends to become very small and is at its most vulnerable to pollution and noise. As our interest is generally drawn most to these regions, the role of the analyser is extremely critical.

3.5.3 Frequency Response Analyser (FRA)

The frequency response analyser (FRA) is a development of the tracking filter concept in that it also is used with sinusoidal excitation. However, in these devices, the heart of the processing is performed digitally, rather than with analogue circuitry as is used in the tracking filter analyser.

The source or 'command' signal – the sinewave at the desired frequency – is first generated digitally within the analyser and then output as an analogue signal via a D-A converter. Within the same device, the two input signals (from the force and response transducers) are digitised and then, one at a time, correlated numerically with the outgoing signal in such a way that all the components of each incoming signal other than that at exactly the frequency of the command signal are eliminated. This is, in effect, a digital filtering process and when completed, permits the accurate measurement of the component of the transducer signals at the current frequency of interest. The advantage which this has over the analogue versions is that both channels are treated in exactly the same way: with the twin analogue tracking filters, it is always necessary to ensure an accurate matching and tuning of the two filters in order to obtain accurate data.

As with all such instruments, the accuracy of the measurements can be controlled to a large extent by the time spent in analysis. In the FRA, it is possible to improve the non-synchronous component rejection simply by performing the correlation (or filtering) over a longer period of time. Sometimes, this is quantified by the number of cycles (of the command signal) during which the computation takes place. Figure 3.15 illustrates the type of dependence of rejection effectiveness versus integration time.

3.5.4 Spectrum Analysers

The spectrum analyser (or frequency analyser, as it is sometimes called) is a quite different type of instrument to the FRA device described above. Whereas that was concerned with extracting just one frequency component at a time, the spectrum analyser seeks to measure simultaneously all the frequency components present in a complex time-varying signal. Its output consists of a spectrum, usually a discrete one containing a finite number of components, describing the relative magnitudes of a whole range of frequencies present in the signal. Perhaps the simplest way to visualise the spectrum analyser is as a set of FRA units, each tuned to a different frequency and working simultaneously.

There are two types of spectrum analyser available, one based on analogue circuitry and the other, more popular, employing digital processing. It is appropriate here to concentrate on this latter type as

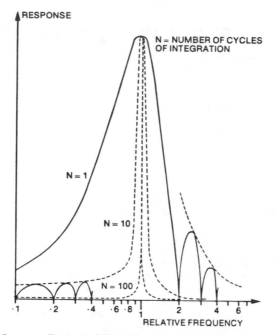

Fig 3.15   *Typical FRA Filtering Capability*

It promises to dominate the scene for some time to come. The digital spectrum analyser (or 'Digital Fourier Analyser' or 'Digital Fourier Transform Analyser') is capable of computing a wide range of properties of incoming signals, including those required for mobility measurements, all of which are based on the Discrete Fourier Transform. In order to appreciate how best to use analysers of this type, it is necessary to understand the basics of their operation and we shall devote the next section to a study of some of the main features. However, it should be remembered that our objective in so doing is specifically to facilitate our use of the analyser to measure the quantities required for mobility measurements. These are listed in Chapter 2: In Section 2.9, equations (2.116), (2.121) and (2.132).

3.6   DIGITAL SIGNAL PROCESSING

3.6.1   Objective

The tasks of the spectrum analyser which concern us here are those of estimating the Fourier Transforms or Spectral Densities of signals which are supplied as inputs.

The basic theory of Fourier analysis is presented in Appendix 3 but it is appropriate here to relate the two versions of the fundamental Fourier equation. In its simplest form, this states that a function $x(t)$, periodic in time T, can be written as an infinite series:

$$x(t) = a_0/2 + \sum_{n=1}^{\infty} (a_n \cos (2\pi nt/T) + b_n \sin (2\pi nt/T)) \quad (3.1a)$$

where a_n and b_n can be computed from knowledge of $x(t)$ via the relationships (3.1b).

$$a_n = (2/T) \int_0^T x(t) \cos (2\pi nt/T) \, dt$$

$$b_n = (2/T) \int_0^T x(t) \sin (2\pi nt/T) \, dt \qquad\qquad (3.1b)$$

In the situation where x(t) is discretised, and is defined only at a set of N particular values of (t_k; k=1,N), then we can write a finite series:

$$x_k (=x(t_k)) = a_0/2 + \sum_{n=1}^{N/2} (a_n \cos (2\pi nt_k/T) + b_n \sin (2\pi nt_k/T)); k=1, N$$

$$(3.1c)$$

The coefficients a_n, b_n are the Fourier or Spectral coefficients for the function $x(t)$ and they are often displayed in modulus (and phase) form, $C_n(=X_n) = (a_n^2+b_n^2)^{1/2}$ (and $\phi_n=tg^{-1}(-b_n/a_n)$).

The signals (accelerometer or force transducer outputs) are in the time domain and the desired spectral properties are in the frequency domain. Figure 3.16 shows the various types of time history encountered, their Fourier Series or Transforms or Spectral Density, and the approximate digitised (or discrete) approximations used and produced by the DFT analyser.

3.6.2 Basics of the DFT

In each case, the input signal is digitised (by an A-D converter) and recorded as a set of N discrete values, evenly spaced in the period T during which the measurement is made.   Then, assuming that the sample in time T is periodic, a Finite Fourier Series (or Transform) is computed as for (3.1c) above as an estimate to the required Fourier Transform. There is a basic relationship between the sample length T, the number of discrete values N, the sampling (or digitising) rate ω_s and the range and resolution of the frequency spectrum (ω_{max}, $\Delta\omega$).   The range of the spectrum is $0-\omega_{max}$ (ω_{max} is the Nyquist frequency) and the resolution of lines in the spectrum is $\Delta\omega$, where

$$\omega_{max} = \omega_s/2 = 1/2 (2\pi N/T) \qquad\qquad (3.2)$$

$$\Delta\omega = \omega_s/N = (2\pi/T) \qquad\qquad (3.3)$$

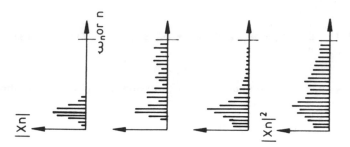

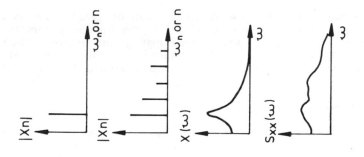

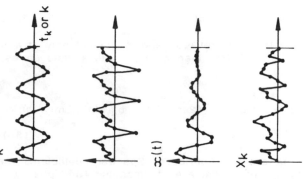

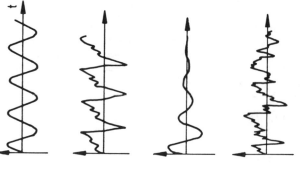

Fig 3.16   Time Histories and Their Spectral Analyses:
Continuous and Discrete Signals

As the size of the transform (N) is generally fixed for a given analyser (and is usually, though not always, a power of 2: 512, 1024 etc), the frequency range covered and the resolution is determined solely by the time length of each sample. This fact introduces constraints on the use of these analysers, as will be seen later.

The basic equation which is solved in order to determine the spectral composition derives from that given in Appendix 3:

$$
\begin{Bmatrix} x_1 \\ x_2 \\ x_3 \\ \cdot \\ \cdot \\ x_N \end{Bmatrix} = \begin{bmatrix} 0.5 & \cos(2\pi/T)\ldots \\ 0.5 & \cos(4\pi/T)\ldots \\ 0.5 & \cos(6\pi/T)\ldots \\ \cdot & \cdot \\ \cdot & \cdot \\ 0.5 & \cos(2N\pi/T) \end{bmatrix} \begin{Bmatrix} a_0 \\ a_1 \\ b_1 \\ \cdot \\ \cdot \\ \cdot \end{Bmatrix} \quad \text{or} \quad \{x_k\} = [C] \, \{a_n\}
$$

(3.4)

Thus, we use $\{a_n\} = [C]^{-1} \{x_k\}$ to determine the unknown spectral or Fourier coefficients contained in $\{a_n\}$. Much of the effort in optimising the calculation of spectral analysis is effectively devoted to equation (3.4) and the most widely used algorithm is the 'Fast Fourier Transform' developed by Cooley and Tukey in the 1960s (Reference [7]). That method requires N to be an integral power of 2 and the value usually taken is between 256 and 4096.

There are a number of features of digital Fourier analysis which, if not properly treated, can give rise to erroneous results. These are generally the result of the discretisation approximation and of the need to limit the length of the time history and in the following sections we shall discuss the specific features of aliassing, leakage, windowing, zooming and averaging.

3.6.3   Aliassing

There is a problem associated with digital spectral analysis known as 'aliassing' and this results from the discretisation of the originally continuous time history (Figure 3.16). With this discretisation process, the existence of very high frequencies in the original signal may well be misinterpreted if the sampling rate is too slow. In fact, such high frequencies will appear as low frequencies or, rather, will be indistinguishable from genuine low frequency components. In Figure 3.17, it can be seen that digitising a 'low' frequency signal (Figure 3.17a) produces exactly the same set of discrete values as result from the same process applied to a higher frequency signal (Figure 3.17b).

Thus, a signal of frequency ω and one of $(\omega_s-\omega)$ are indistiguishable when represented as a discretised time history and this fact causes a distortion of the spectrum measured via the DFT, even when that is computed exactly.

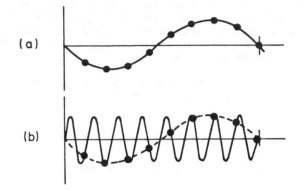

Fig 3.17   The Phenomenon of Aliassing

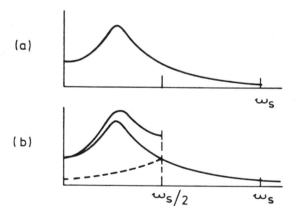

Fig 3.18   Alias Distortion of Spectrum by Finite Fourier Transform
            (a)   Actual Spectrum of Signal
            (b)   Spectrum Indicated by Finite Transform

A signal which has a true frequency content shown in Figure 3.18a will appear in the DFT as the distorted form shown in Figure 3.18b. Note from Section 3.6.2 that the highest frequency which can be included in the spectrum (or transform) is $(\omega_S/2)$ and so the indicated spectrum should stop at that frequency, irrespective of the number of discrete values. The distortion evident in Figure 3.18b can be explained by the fact that the part of the signal which has frequency components above $(\omega_S/2)$ will appear reflected or 'aliassed' in the range $0-(\omega_S/2)$. Thus we see a Fourier Transform composed as illustrated in Figure 3.18b.

The solution to the problem is to use an <u>anti-aliassing</u> filter which subjects the original time signal to a low-pass, sharp cut-off filter with a characteristic of the form shown in Figure 3.19. This has the result of submitting a modified time history to the analyser. Because the filters used are inevitably less than perfect, and have a finite cut-off rate, it remains necessary to reject the spectral measurements in a frequency range approaching the Nyquist frequency, $(\omega_S/2)$. Typical values for that rejected range vary from $0.5-1.0(\omega_S/2)$ for a simple filter to $0.8-1.0(\omega_S/2)$ for a more advanced filter design. It is for this reason that a 1024-point transform does not result in the complete 512-line spectrum being given on the analyser display: only the first 250 to 400 lines will be shown as the higher ones are liable to be contaminated by the imperfect anti-aliassing.

It is essential that the correct anti-aliassing precautions are taken and so they are usually provided as a non-optional feature of the analyser.

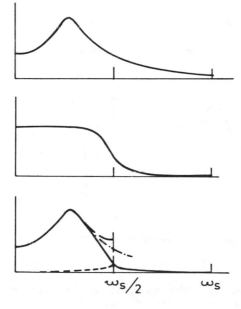

Fig 3.19   Anti-Aliassing Filter Process

3.6.4 <u>Leakage</u>

Leakage is a problem which is a direct consequence of the need to take only a finite length of time history coupled with the assumption of periodicity. The problem is best illustrated by the two examples shown in Figure 3.20 in which two sinusoidal signals of slightly different frequency are subjected to the same analysis process. In the first case, (a), the signal is perfectly periodic in the time window, T, and the resulting spectrum is quite simply a single line – at the frequency of the sine wave. In the second case, (b), the periodicity assumption is not strictly valid and there is a discontinuity implied at each end of the sample. As a result, the spectrum produced for this case does <u>not</u> indicate the single frequency which the original time signal possessed – indeed that frequency is not specifically represented in the specific lines of the spectrum. Energy has 'leaked' into a number of the spectral lines close to the true frequency and the spectrum is spread over several lines or windows. The two examples above represent a best case and a worst case although the problems become most acute when the signal frequencies are lower.

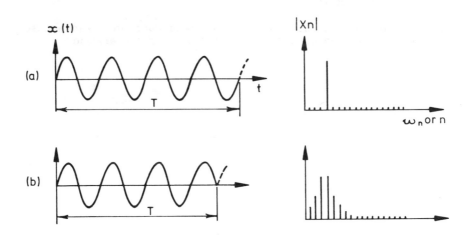

Fig 3.20   Sample Length and Leakage of Spectrum

3.6.5 <u>Windowing</u>

One practical solution to the leakage problem involves the use of windowing and there are a range of different windows for different classes of problem.

Windowing involves the imposition of a prescribed profile on the time signal prior to performing the Fourier Transform and the profiles or 'windows' are generally depicted as a time function, W(t), as shown in Figure 3.21. The analysed signal is $x'(t) = x(t) . W(t)$. The result of using a Hanning or Cosine Taper window is seen in the third column of Figure 3.21 and this in turn produces the improved spectrum shown in Figure 3.22. The Hanning (b) or Cosine Taper (c) windows are typically used for continuous signals, such as produced by steady periodic or random vibration, while the Exponential window (d) is used for transient vibration applications where much of the important information is concentrated in the initial part of the time record and would thus be suppressed by either of the above choices.

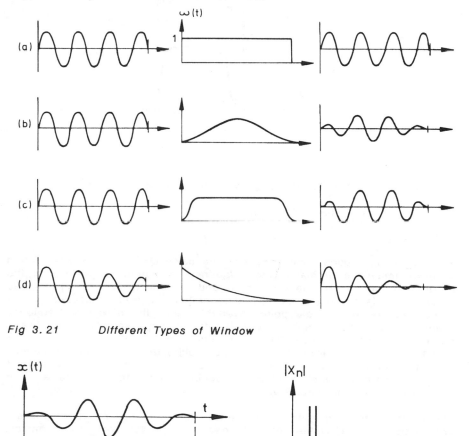

Fig 3.21   Different Types of Window

Fig 3.22   Effect of Hanning Window on Finite Fourier Transform

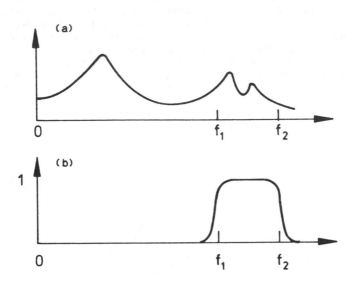

Fig 3.23 *Controlled Aliassing for Frequency Zoom*
     (a) *Signal Spectrum*
     (b) *Band-Pass Filter*

3.6.6 Zoom

So far, we have been concerned with the basic DFT which is often found to have limitations of inadequate frequency resolution, especially at the lower end of the frequency range and especially for lightly-damped systems. This problem arises because of the constraints imposed by the limited number of discrete points available (N), the maximum frequency range to be covered and/or the length of time sample available or necessary to provide good data. An immediate solution to this problem would be to use a larger transform but, although giving finer frequency resolution around the regions of interest, this carries the penalty of providing more information than is required and, anyway, the size of transform is seldom selectable.

The common solution is to 'zoom' in on the frequency range of interest and to concentrate all the spectral lines (256 or 400 etc) into a narrow band between f_{min} and f_{max} (instead of between 0 and f_{max}, as hitherto). There are various ways of achieving this result but perhaps the one which is easiest to understand physically is that which uses a controlled aliassing effect. Suppose a signal $x(t)$ has a spectrum of the type shown in Figure 3.23a and that we are interested in a detailed (zoom) analysis around the second peak – between f_1 and f_2.

In all cases, a rescaling is required to compensate for the attenuation of the signals by the application of the window. However, if both response and excitation signals are subjected to the <u>same</u> window, and the results are used only to compute an FRF ratio, then the rescaling is not necessary. Care should be taken in some cases, especially with transient tests, as the two signals may be treated differently.

If we apply a band-pass filter to the signal, as shown in Figure 3.23b, and perform a DFT between 0 and (f_2-f_1), then because of the aliassing phenomenon described earlier, the frequency components between f_1 and f_2 will appear aliassed in the analysis range $0-(f_2-f_1)$ (see Figure 3.24) with the advantage of a finer resolution – in the example shown here, four times finer resolution than in the original, baseband analysis.

When using zoom to measure FRF in a narrow frequency range, it is important to ensure that there is as little vibration energy as possible <u>outside</u> the frequency range of interest. This means that wherever possible the excitation supplied to drive the structure should be band limited to the analysis range; a feature not provided automatically on some analysers.

As mentioned above, this is not the only way of achieving a zoom measurement, but it serves to illustrate the concept. Other methods are based on effectively shifting the frequency origin of the spectrum by multiplying the original time history by a cos $\omega_1 t$ function and then filtering out the higher of the two components thus produced. For example, suppose the signal to be analysed is:

$x(t) = A \sin \omega t$

Multiplying this by cos $\omega_1 t$ yields

$x'(t) = A \sin \omega t \cos \omega_1 t = (A/2) (\sin(\omega-\omega_1)t + \sin(\omega+\omega_1)t)$ (3.5)

and if we then filter out the second component we are left with the original signal translated down the frequency range by ω_1. The modified signal is then analysed in the range 0 to $(\omega_2-\omega_1)$ yielding a zoom measurement between ω_1 and ω_2 of the original signal.

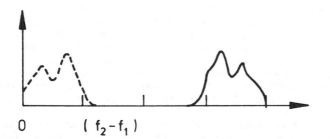

0   (f_2-f_1)

Fig 3.24   Effective Frequency Translation for Zoom

3.6.7 Averaging

We now turn our attention to another feature of digital spectral analysis that concerns the particular requirements for processing random signals. (So far, we have dealt with deterministic data). When analysing random vibration, it is not sufficient to compute Fourier Transforms – strictly, these do not exist for a random process – and we must instead obtain estimates for the spectral densities and correlation functions which are used to characterise this type of signal. Although these properties are computed from the Fourier Transforms, there are additional considerations concerning their accuracy and statistical reliability which must be given due attention. Generally, it is necessary to perform an averaging process, involving several individual time records, or samples, before a result is obtained which can be used with confidence. The two major considerations which determine the number of averages required are the statistical reliability and the removal of spurious random noise from the signals. Detailed guidance on the use of these analysers for valid random signal processing may be obtained from specialist texts, such as Newland (Reference [8]) and Bendat & Piersol (Reference [9]). However, an indication of the requirements from a statistical standpoint may be provided by the 'statistical degrees of freedom' (κ) which is provided by

$$\kappa = 2BT_t$$

where B = frequency bandwidth
T_t = total time encompassing all data
(= mT for m samples each of T duration).

As a guide, this quantity κ should be a minimum of 10 (in which case there is an 80% probability that the estimated spectrum lies between 0.5 and 1.5 times the true value) and should approach 100 for reasonably reliable estimates (i.e. an 80% probability that the measured value is within 18% of the true value).

Overlap Averaging

The reference above to m samples, each of duration T, implies that they are mutually exclusive, as shown by Figure 3.25a . However, the computing capabilities of modern analysers mean that the DFT is calculated in an extremely short time and, consequently, that a new transform could be computed rather sooner than a new complete sample has been collected. In this case, it is sometimes convenient to perform a second transform as soon as possible, using the most recent N data points, even though some of these may have been used in the previous transform. This procedure is depicted in Figure 3.25b and it is clear that 100 averages performed in this way cannot have the same statistical properties as would 100 completely independent samples.

Nevertheless, the procedure is more effective than if all the data points are used only once and it manifests this extra processing by producing smoother spectra than would be obtained if each data sample were used only once.

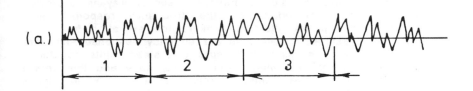

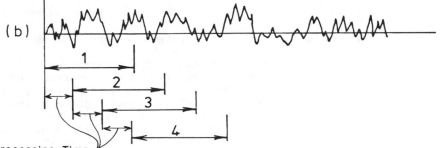

Processing Time

Fig 3.25   *Sequential and Overlap Averaging*
              (a)   Sequential
              (b)   Overlap

3.7 USE OF DIFFERENT EXCITATION TYPES

It is now appropriate to discuss the different types of excitation which can be used to drive the test structure so that measurements can be made of its response characteristics.   These excitations include:

–   stepped–sinusoidal
–   slow sine sweep
–   periodic
–   random
–   transient (chirp or impact)

and all are in widespread use, each having its own particular merits and drawbacks.

3.7.1 Stepped–Sine Testing

This is the name given to the classical method of measuring a frequency response function in which the command signal supplied to the exciter is a discrete sinusoid with a fixed amplitude and frequency.   In order to encompass a frequency range of interest, the command signal frequency is stepped from one discrete value to another in such a way as to provide the necessary density of points on the frequency response plot. Invariably driving through an attached shaker, the excitation force and response(s) are measured, usually with a Frequency Response Analyser. In this technique, it is necessary to ensure that steady-state conditions have been attained before the measurements are made and this entails delaying the start of the measurement process for a short while after a new frequency has been selected as there will be a transient response as well as the steady part. The extent of the unwanted transient response will depend on:

(i)   the proximity of the excitation frequency to a natural frequency of the structure;

(ii)   the abruptness of the changeover from the previous command signal to the new one; and

(iii)   the lightness of the damping of the nearby structural modes.

The more pronounced each of these features, the more serious is the transient effect and the longer must be the delay before measurements are made. In practice, it is only in the immediate vicinity of a lightly damped resonance that the necessary delay becomes significant when compared with the actual measurement time and at this condition, extra attention is usually required anyway because there is a tendency for the force signal to become very small and to require long measurement times in order to extract an accurate estimate of its true level.

One of the advantageous features of the discrete sine test method is the facility of taking measurements just where and as they are required. For example, the typical FRF curve has large regions of relatively slow changes of level with frequency (away from resonances and antiresonances) and in these it is sufficient to take measurements at relatively widely spaced frequency points. By contrast, near the resonance and antiresonant frequencies, the curve exhibits much more rapid changes and it is more appropriate to take measurements at more closely spaced frequencies. It is also more efficient to use less delay and measurement time away from these critical regions, partly because there are less problems there but also because these data are less likely to be required with great accuracy for the modal analysis phases later on. Thus, we have the possibility of optimising the measurement process when using discrete sinusoidal excitation, especially if the whole measurement is under the control of a computer or processor, as is increasingly the case. Figure 3.26 shows a typical FRF curve measured using discrete sine excitation, in which two sweeps have been made through the range of interest: one a rapid coarse sweep with a large frequency increment, followed by a set of small fine sweeps localised around the resonances of interest using a much finer frequency increment and taking more care with each measured point. Of course, accurate detail of a resonance peak will only be possible if a sufficiently small increment is used for the fine sweeps. As a guide to the required increment, the following table shows the largest error that might be incurred by taking the maximum FRF value as the true peak value for that resonance.

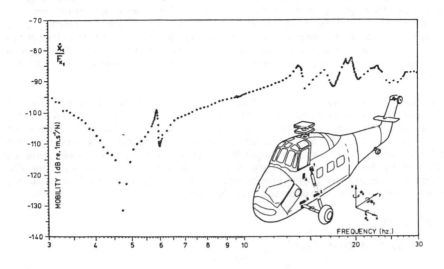

Fig 3. 26   Typical FRF Data from Stepped-Sine Test

Number of Frequency Intervals Between Half-Power Points*	Largest Error	
	%	dB
1	30	3
2	10	1
3	5	0. 5
5	2	0. 2
8	1	0. 1

* For definition, see Section 4. 2

3. 7. 2 Slow-Sine Sweep

This is the traditional method of mobility (or frequency response) measurement and involves the use of a sweep oscillator to provide a sinusoidal command signal, the frequency of which is varied slowly but continuously through the range of interest.   As before, it is necessary to check that progress through the frequency range is sufficiently slow to check that steady-state response conditions are attained before measurements are made.   If an excessive sweep rate is used, then distortions of the FRF plot are introduced, and these can be as severe as those illustrated in Figure 3.27a which shows the apparent FRF curves produced by different sweep rates, both increasing and decreasing in frequency through a resonance region. One way of checking the suitability of a sweep rate is to make the measurement twice, once sweeping up and the second time sweeping down through the frequency range. If the same curve results in the two cases, then there is a probability (though not an assurance) that the sweep rate is not excessive.

It is possible to prescribe a 'correct' or optimum sweep rate for a given structure, taking due account of its prevailing damping levels. In theory, any sweep rate is too fast to guarantee that the full steady-state response level will be attained, but in practice we can approach very close to this desired condition by using a logarithmic or similar type of sweep rate as indicated by the graphs in Figure 3.27b, c and d. Alternatively, the ISO Standard (Reference [10]) prescribes maximum linear and logarithmic sweep rates through a resonance as follows:

<u>Linear Sweep</u>

$$S_{max} < 54 \ (f_r)^2 \ (\eta_r)^2 \qquad \text{Hz/min}$$

$$\text{or} \quad < 216 \ (f_r)^2 \ (\zeta_r)^2$$

<u>Logarithmic Sweep</u>

$$S_{max} < 78 \ (f_r) \ (\eta_r)^2 \qquad \text{octaves/min}$$

$$\text{or} \ < 310 \ (f_r) \ (\zeta_r)^2$$

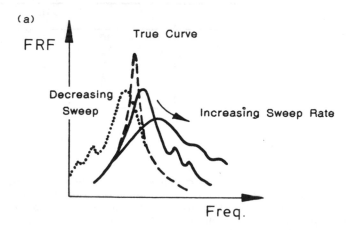

(a)

FRF

True Curve

Decreasing Sweep

Increasing Sweep Rate

Freq.

Fig 3.27   *FRF Measurement by Sine Sweep Test*
      (a) Distorting Effect of Sweep Rate

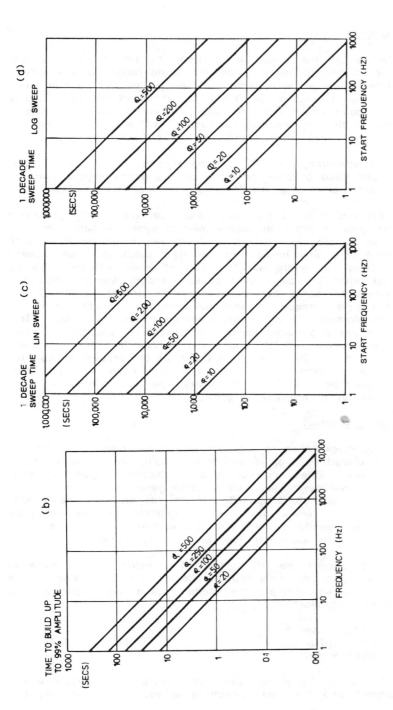

Fig 3.27   FRF Measurement by Sine Sweep Test
(b)   Time to build up to Resonance
(c), (d)   Recommended Sweep Rates

3.7.3 Periodic Excitation

With the facility of the spectrum analyser to provide simultaneous information on all the frequency bands in a given range, it is a natural extension of the sinewave test methods to use a complex periodic input signal which contains not one but all the frequencies of interest. This is nothing more complicated than a superposition of several sinusoids simultaneously, with the spectrum analyser capable of extracting the response to each of these components, again simultaneously.

The method of computing the FRF is quite simple: the discrete Fourier transform is computed of both the force and response signals and the ratio of these transforms gives the FRF, just as in equation 2.115.

Two types of periodic signal are used, and both are usually generated within the analyser in order to ensure perfect synchronisation with the analysis part of the process. One is a clearly systematic signal in which all the components are mixed with ordered amplitude and phase relationships (e.g. a square wave), some of which will inevitably be relatively weak, while the other is a pseudo-random type. This latter category involves the generation of a random mixture of amplitudes and phases for the various frequency components and may be adjusted to suit a particular requirement – such as equal energy at each frequency. This signal is generated and output repeatedly for several successive cycles (Note that one complete cycle must coincide exactly with a complete sample for the input to the analyser in order for the process to be truly periodic) and a satisfactory measurement is then made. A particular advantage of this type of excitation is its exact periodicity in the analyser bandwidth, resulting in zero leakage errors.

3.7.4 Random Excitation

For a truly random excitation, a different approach is required although it is possible to undertake such measurements using the same spectrum analyser as before. Often, the source of a random command signal is found in an external device such as a noise generator and not in the analyser itself, although some types do contain independent noise sources for this purpose. In either event, it is important that the signal be different from the 'pseudo-random' type just mentioned. It is usual for random excitation to be applied through an attached shaker.

The principle upon which the FRF is determined using random excitation has been explained in the theory chapter (Section 2.9) and relies on the following equations which relate the excitation and the response of a system in random vibration:

$$S_{xx}(\omega) = |H(\omega)|^2 . S_{ff}(\omega)$$
$$S_{fx}(\omega) = H(\omega) . S_{ff}(\omega) \qquad\qquad (3.6)$$
$$S_{xx}(\omega) = H(\omega) . S_{xf}(\omega)$$

where $S_{xx}(\omega)$, $S_{ff}(\omega)$, $S_{xf}(\omega)$ are the auto spectra of the response and excitation signals and the cross spectrum between these two signals, respectively, and $H(\omega)$ is the frequency response function linking the quantities x and f.

The spectrum analyser has the facility to <u>estimate</u> these various spectra, although it must be appreciated that such parameters can never be measured accurately with only a finite length of data. However, in this case we have the possibility of providing a cross check on the results by using more than one of the equations (3.6). We can obtain an estimate to the required FRF using the second equation in (3.6), for example, and we shall denote this estimate as $H_1(\omega)$:

$$H_1(\omega) = S_{fx}(\omega)/S_{ff}(\omega) \qquad (3.7a)$$

We can also compute a second estimate for the FRF using the third equation in (3.6) and this we shall denote as $H_2(\omega)$:

$$H_2(\omega) = S_{xx}(\omega)/S_{xf}(\omega) \qquad (3.7b)$$

Now, because we have used different quantities for these two estimates, we must be prepared for the eventuality that they are not identical as, according to theory, they should be and to this end we shall introduce a quantity γ^2, which is usually called the 'coherence' and which is defined as:

$$\gamma^2 = H_1(\omega)/H_2(\omega) \qquad (3.8)$$

The coherence can be shown to be always less than or equal to 1.0.

Clearly, if all is well with the measurement, the coherence should be unity and we shall be looking for this condition in our test to reassure us that the measurements have been well made. In the event that the coherence is not unity, it will be necessary to establish why not, and then to determine what is the correct value of the FRF. It should be noted at this stage that many commercial analysers provide only one of these two FRF estimates as standard and, because it is fractionally easier to compute, this is generally $H_1(\omega)$. Of course, given the coherence as well, it is a simple matter to deduce the other version, $H_2(\omega)$, from equation 3.8 and it is an interesting exercise to overlay the two estimates on the analyser screen.

There are several situations in which an imperfect measurement might be made, and a low coherence recorded. There may well be noise on one or other of the two signals which could degrade the measured spectra: near resonance this is likely to influence the force signal so that $S_{ff}(\omega)$ becomes vulnerable while at antiresonance it is the response signal which will suffer, making $S_{xx}(\omega)$ liable to errors. In the first of these cases, $H_1(\omega)$ will suffer most and so $H_2(\omega)$ might be a better indicator near resonance while the reverse applies at antiresonance, as shown in the following equations:

$$H_1(\omega) = \frac{S_{fx}(\omega)}{S_{ff}(\omega) + S_{nn}(\omega)} \qquad (3.9a)$$

$$H_2(\omega) = \frac{S_{xx}(\omega) + S_{mm}(\omega)}{S_{xf}(\omega)} \qquad (3.9b)$$

where $S_{mm}(\omega)$ and $S_{nn}(\omega)$ are the auto-spectra of the noise on the output and input, respectively.

A second possible problem area arises when more than one excitation is applied to the structure. In this case, the response measured cannot be directly attributed to the force which is measured and the cross checks afforded by the above procedure will not be satisfied. Such a situation can arise all too easily if the coupling between the shaker and the structure is too stiff and a lateral or rotational constraint is inadvertently applied to the testpiece, as discussed in Section 3.3.5.

Yet another possible source of low coherence arises when the structure is not completely linear. Here again, the measured response cannot be completely attributed to the measured excitation, and hence a less-than-unity coherence will result.

It is known that a low coherence can arise in a measurement where the frequency resolution of the analyser is not fine (small) enough to describe adequately the very rapidly changing functions such as are encountered near resonance and antiresonance on lightly-damped structures. This is known as a 'bias' error and it can be shown that when it occurs near resonance, the $H_2(\omega)$ estimate is always the more accurate of the two, although this can itself be seriously in error relative to the correct value. This is often the most likely source of low coherence on lightly-damped structures.

Figure 3.28a shows a typical measurement made using random excitation, presenting the standard FRF, $H_1(\omega)$ and the coherence γ^2. This shows the trend for a great many practical cases, demonstrating a good coherence everywhere except near resonance and antiresonance. Figure 3.28b shows a detail from the previous plot around one of the resonances, and included this time are both the FRF estimates, $H_1(\omega)$ and $H_2(\omega)$. Here it can be seen that the second alternative shows a larger and more distinct modal circle and is in fact a much more accurate representation of the true response function. When this situation is encountered (low coherence near resonance), the best solution is usually to make a zoom measurement. This is the procedure described in 3.6.6 whereby the standard number of lines available on the spectrum analyser may be applied to any frequency range, not just to a 'baseband' range of $0-f_{max}$ Hz. Thus, we can analyse in more detail between f_{min} and f_{max}, thereby improving the resolution and often removing one of the major sources of low coherence.

It is worth just illustrating this aspect of zoom measurements by means of a simple example. Suppose we have made a measurement, such as

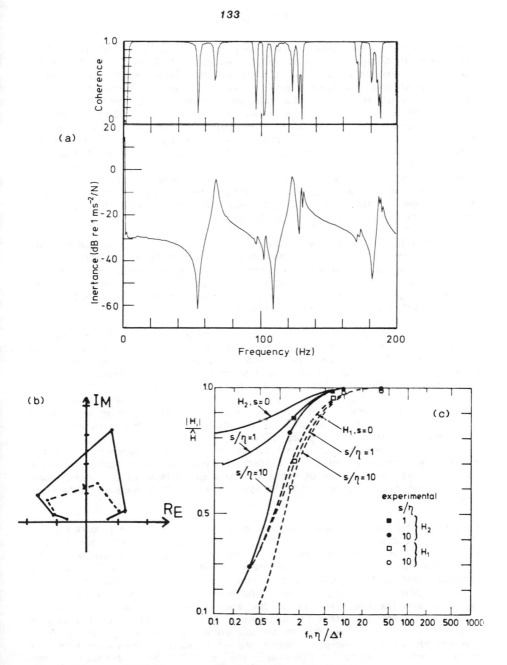

Fig 3.28   FRF Measurement by Random Excitation
        (a)   Modulus and Coherence Plots
        (b)   Nyquist Plots of Both FRF Estimates
        (c)   Maximum Error in Resonance Peak Estimates

that in Figure 3.28a, over a frequency range from 0 to 200 Hz. This measurement gives us a frequency resolution of 0.78 Hz (1024-point transform) which is clearly too coarse for the sharp resonance regions, especially around the lowest one where the frequency increment is a particularly large fraction of the natural frequency concerned. We can improve the resolution by, for example, 8 times by using a 25 Hz bandwidth zoom analysis with the analyser set to measure 25 Hz range between 113 and 138 Hz. By this device, we can greatly enhance the accuracy of the measurements around resonance as is illustrated by the sequence of plots in Figure 3.29. It must be remembered, however, that this extra accuracy is gained at the cost of a longer measurement time: the analyser is now working approximately 8 times slower than in the first measurement as the sample length (and thus data acquisition time) is linked to the overall frequency resolution.

Exactly how fine a frequency increment is required in order to reduce this source of error to a minimum depends on several factors, including the damping of the structure and the shaker/structure interaction discussed in Section 3.3. Figure 3.28c indicates the maximum error which might be incurred in assuming that the true peak value of FRF is indicated by the maximum value on the measured spectrum.

As a parting comment in this section on random excitation, we should mention the need to make several successive measurements and to accumulate a running average of the corresponding FRF estimates and coherence. It is sometimes thought that a poor coherence can be eliminated by taking a great many averages but this is only possible if the reason for the low coherence is random noise which can be averaged out over a period of time. If the reason is more systematic than that, such as the second and third possibilities mentioned above, then averaging will not help. A sequence of plots shown in Figure 3.30 helps to reinforce this point. However, for these cases or frequency ranges where the coherence genuinely reflects a statistical variation, then some guidance as to the required number of averages for a given level of confidence can be obtained from Figure 3.31, based on the ISO Standard (Reference [10]).

Lastly, mention should be made here of a type of excitation referred to as 'Periodic Random' which is, in fact, a combination of pseudo-random (Section 3.7.3) and 'true' random. In this process, a pseudo-random (or periodic) excitation is generated and after a few cycles, a measurement of the input and the now steady-state response is made. Then, a different pseudo-random sequence is generated, the procedure repeated and the result treated as the second sample in what will develop to be an ensemble of random samples. The advantage over the simple random excitation is that due to the essential periodic nature of each of the periodic random samples, there are no leakage or bias errors in any of the measurements. However, the cost is an increase in the measurement time since 2/3 or 3/4 of the data available is unused while steady response conditions are awaited for each new sample.

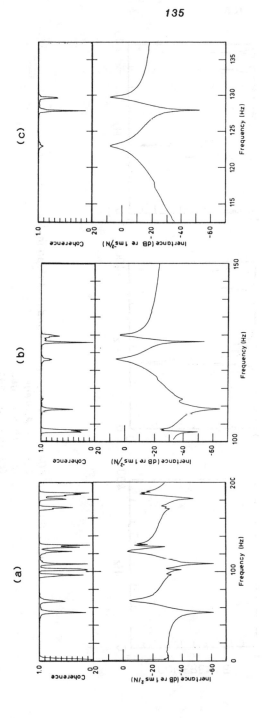

Fig 3.29 Use of Zoom Spectrum Analysis
          (a) 0-200 Hz
          (b) 100-150 Hz
          (c) 113-138 Hz

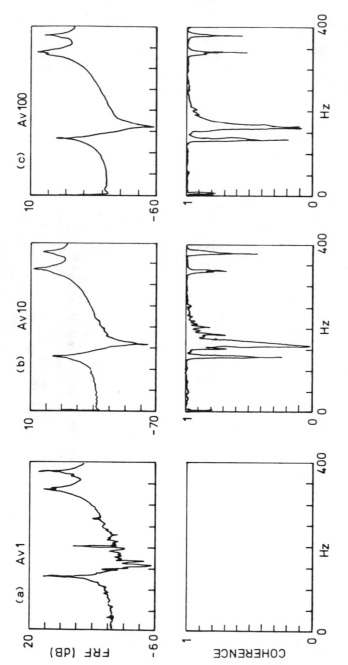

Fig 3.30   Effect of Averaging on Random Vibration Measurement
            (a)   1 Average
            (b)   10 Averages
            (c)   100 Averages

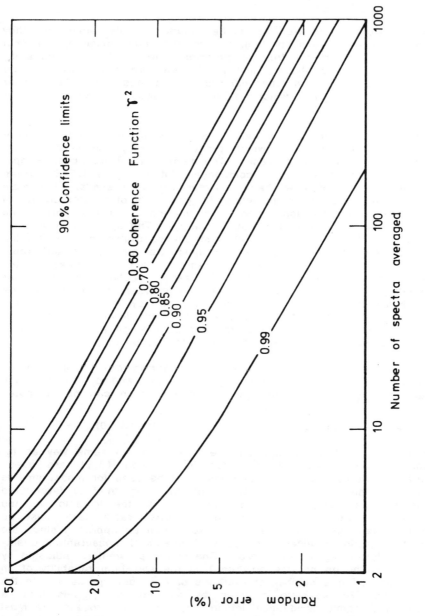

Fig 3.31   Interpretation of Coherence

3.7.5 Transient Excitation

There are two types of excitation to be included in this section and they are the rapid sine sweep (or 'chirp', after the sound made by the input signal), and the impact from a hammer blow. The first generally requires an attached shaker, just as do the previous sinusoidal and random methods, but the latter can be implemented with a hammer or similar impactor device which is not permanently attached to the structure.

The chirp consists of a short duration signal which has the form shown in Figure 3.32a and b and which produces a response such as that shown in the accompanying graph. The hammer blow produces an input and response as shown in the companion plot of Figure 3.32c. From the analysis point of view the two cases are very similar, the main difference being that the chirp offers the possibility of greater control of both amplitude and frequency content of the input and also permits the input of a greater amount of vibration energy. The spectrum of a chirp such as that shown in Figure 3.32 is strictly controlled to be within the range between the starting and finishing frequencies of the rapid sinusoidal sweep, while that of the hammer blow is dictated by the materials involved (as described in the earlier section) and is rather more difficult to control. However, it should be recorded that in the region below the first cut-off frequency induced by the elasticity of the hammer tip/structure contact, the spectrum of the force signal tends to be very flat whereas that for a chirp, applied through a shaker, suffers similar problems to those described earlier in Section 3.

In both these cases, a discrete Fourier series description can be obtained of both the input force signal, $F(\omega_k)$, and of the response signal, $X(\omega_k)$, and the frequency response function can be computed from:

$$H(\omega_k) = X(\omega_k)/F(\omega_k) \qquad\qquad (3.10)$$

Alternatively, the force signals can be treated in the same way as for random excitation, and the formulae in Equation (3.7) are used. Usually, therefore, a spectrum analyser must be used for measurements made by transient excitation. Users of the chirp tend to favour the former approach while those more familiar with the impactor method advocate the latter method. However, considerable care must be exercised when interpreting the results from such an approach since the coherence function – widely used as an indicator of measurement quality – has a different significance here. One of the parameters indicated by coherence (although not the only one) is the statistical reliability of an estimate based on a number of averages of a random process. In the case of an FRF estimate obtained by treating the signals from a succession of nominally-identical impacts as a random process, we must note that, strictly, each such sample is a deterministic, and not probabilistic, calculation and should contain no statistical uncertainty. Thus, the main source for low coherence in this instance can only be bias errors, non-linearity or high noise levels – not the same situation as for random excitation.

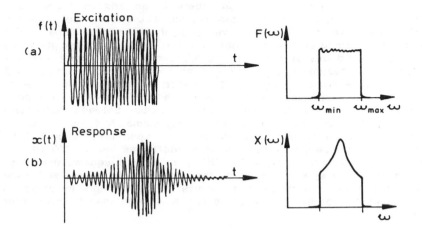

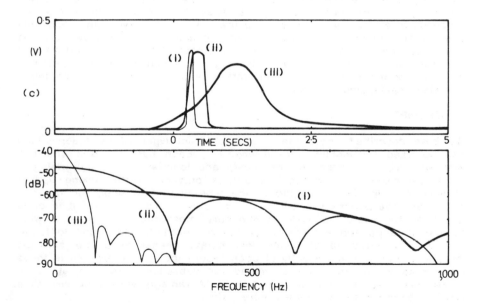

Fig 3.32   Signals and Spectra for Chirp and Impact Tests
(a)   Chirp Excitation
(b)   Chirp Response
(c)   Impact Excitations

In the case of a transient excitation, there is an additional constraint imposed by the requirement that the signals (in effect, the response signals) must have died away by the end of the sample time. For lightly-damped structures this may well result in rather long sample times being required and this in turn poses a problem because it has a direct influence on the frequency range that can be covered. For example, if it is decided that a sample length of 2 seconds is necessary in order to ensure that the response has died away, and we have a 512-point transform, then the minimum time interval possible between successive points on the digitised time histories will be approximately 4 ms. This, in turn, means that the frequency resolution of the spectrum will be 0.5 Hz and the highest frequency on that spectrum will be as low as 250 Hz and it will not be possible to measure the FRF at higher frequencies than this. Such a restriction may well clash with the demands of the test and quite elaborate action may be required to remove it, for example by using an exponential window or by using a zoom facility as explained in the earlier sections.

Another feature usually employed in transient testing is that of making a whole series of repeat measurements under nominally-identical conditions and then averaging the resulting FRF estimates. The idea behind this is that any one measurement is likely to be contaminated by noise, especially in the frequency regions away from resonance where the response levels are likely to be quite low. While this averaging technique does indeed enhance the resulting plots, it may well be that several tens of samples need to be acquired before a smooth FRF plot is obtained and this will diminish somewhat any advantage of speed which is a potential attraction of the method. Further details of both methods may be found in Reference[11] and Reference[12].

POSTSCRIPT

We have described above the various different types of excitation which can be used for mobility measurements. Each has its good and bad features and, of course, its advocates and followers. Not surprisingly, no single method is the 'best' and it is probably worth making use of several types in order to optimise the time and effort spent on the one hand, and the accuracy obtained on the other. To this end, it is often found to be useful to make preliminary measurements using a wide frequency range and a transient or random excitation type and to follow this up with accurate sinusoidal-test measurements at a few selected frequency points in the vicinity of each resonance of interest. It is these latter data which are then submitted for subsequent analysis, at which stage their greater accuracy is put to full advantage while excessive time has not been wasted on unnecessary points.

3.8 CALIBRATION

As with all measurement processes, it is necessary to calibrate the equipment which is used and in the case of mobility measurements, there are two levels of calibration which should be made. The first of these is a periodic 'absolute' calibration of individual transducers (of force and response) to check that their sensitivities are sensibly the same as those specified by the manufacturer. Any marked deviation could indicate internal damage which is insufficient to cause the device to fail completely, but which might nevertheless constitute a loss of linearity or repeatability which would not necessarily be detected immediately. The second type of calibration is one which can and should be carried out during each test, preferably twice – once at the outset and again at the end. This type of calibration is one which provides the overall sensitivity of the complete instrumentation system without examining the performance of the individual elements.

The first type of calibration is quite difficult to make accurately. As in all cases, the absolute calibration of a transducer or a complete system requires an independent measurement to be made of the quantity of interest, such as force or acceleration, and this can be quite difficult to achieve. The use of another transducer of the same type is seldom satisfactory as it is not strictly an independent measure, except in the case of using a reference transducer which has been produced to have very stable and reliable characteristics and which has previously been calibrated against an accepted standard under strictly controlled conditions. Other means of making independent measurements of displacements are generally confined to optical devices and these are not widely available, while independent methods of measuring force are even more difficult to obtain.

As a result, absolute calibration of transducers is generally undertaken only under special conditions and is most often performed using a reference or standard accelerometer, both for accelerometers and – with the aid of a simple mass – of force transducers.

One of the reasons why the absolute type of calibration has not been further developed for this particular application is the availability of a different type of calibration which is particularly attractive and convenient. With few exceptions, the parameters measured in a modal test are ratios between response and force levels, such as mobility or receptance, and so what is required is the ability to calibrate the whole measurement system. The quantities actually measured in the great majority of cases are two voltages, one from the force transducer and its associated electronics and the other from the response transducer. These voltages are related to the physical quantities being measured by the sensitivities of the respective transducers thus:

$$V_f = E_f \ f$$
$$V_{\ddot{x}} = E_{\ddot{x}} \ \ddot{x} \qquad\qquad (3.11)$$

As mentioned above, there is some difficulty in determining values for E_f and $E_{\ddot{x}}$ individually but we note that, in practice, we only ever use the measured voltages as a ratio, to obtain the frequency response function:

$$(\ddot{x}/f) = (V_{\ddot{x}}/V_f) \ (E_f/E_x) = E(V_x/V_f) \qquad\qquad (3.12)$$

and so what is required in the ratio of the two sensitivities, $(E_f/E_x) = E$.

This overall sensitivity can be more readily obtained by a calibration process because we can easily make an independent measurement of the quantity now being measured – the ratio of response to force. Suppose the response parameter is acceleration, then the FRF obtained is inertance (or accelerance) which has the units of (1/mass), a quantity which can readily be measured by other means. If we undertake a mobility or inertance measurement on a simple rigid mass-like structure, the result we should obtain is a constant magnitude over the frequency range at a level which is equal to the reciprocal of the mass of the calibration block, a quantity which can be accurately determined by weighing.

Figure 3.33 shows a typical calibration block in use together with the result from a calibration measurement indicating the overall system calibration factor which is then used to convert the measured values of (volts/volt) to those of (acceleration/force), or whatever frequency response quantity is to be produced. The scale factor thus obtained should be checked against a corresponding value computed using the manufacturers' stated sensitivities and amplifier gains to make sure that no major errors have been introduced and to see whether either of the transducers has changed its sensitivity markedly from its nominal value. In practice, this check need only be made occasionally as the approximate scale factor for any given pair of transducers will become known and so any marked deviations will be spotted quite quickly.

A calibration procedure of this type has the distinct advantages that it is very easy to perform and that it can be carried out in situ with all the measurement equipment in just the same state as is used for the mobility measurements proper. In view of this facility, and the possibility of occasional faults in various parts of the measurement chain, frequent checks on the calibration factors are strongly recommended: as mentioned at the outset, at the beginning and end of each test is ideal.

3.9 MASS CANCELLATION

It was shown earlier how it is important to ensure that the force is measured directly at the point at which it is applied to the structure, rather than deducing its magnitude from the current flowing in the shaker coil or other similar indirect processes. This is because near resonance the actual applied force becomes very small and is thus very prone to inaccuracy. This same argument applies on a lesser scale as we examine the detail around the attachment to the structure, as shown in Figure 3.34. Here we see part of the structure, an accelerometer and the force transducer and also shown is the plane at which the force is actually measured. Now, assuming that the extra material (shown by the cross hatching) behaves as a rigid mass, m^*, we can state that the force actually applied to the structure, f_t, is different from that measured by the transducer, f_m, by an amount dependent on the acceleration level at the drive point, $\ddot{x}$, according to:

$$f_t = f_m - m^*.\ddot{x} \qquad (3.13)$$

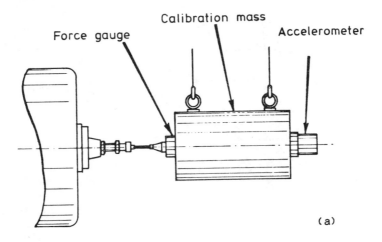

Force gauge

Calibration mass

Accelerometer

(a)

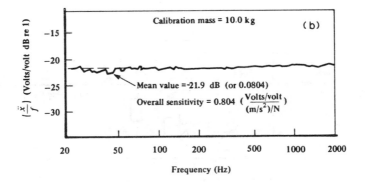

Calibration mass = 10.0 kg

(b)

Mean value = -21.9 dB (or 0.0804)

Overall sensitivity = 0.804 $\left(\frac{\text{Volts/volt}}{(\text{m/s}^2)/\text{N}} \right)$

$(\frac{\ddot{x}}{f})$ (Volts/volt dB re 1)

Frequency (Hz)

Fig 3. 33   Mass Calibration Procedure
               (a)   Test Setup
               (b)   Typical Measurement

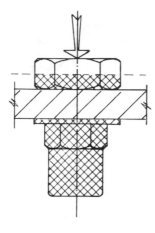

Fig 3.34   Mass Cancellation

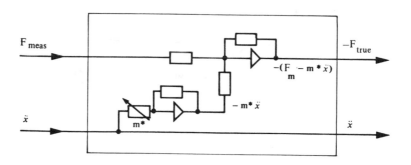

Fig   3.35   Mass Cancellation Circuit

Physically, what is happening is that some of the measured force is being 'used' to move the additional mass so that the force actually applied to the structure is the measured minus the inertia force of the extra mass.

Now, the frequency response quantity we actually require is $A_t (= \ddot{x}/f_t)$, although we have measurements of $\ddot{x}$ and f_m only, yielding an indicated inertance, A_m. This is a complex quantity and if we express it in its Real and Imaginary parts, we can obtain a relationship between A_m and A_t as follows:

$$Re(f_t) = Re(f_m) - m^* . Re(\ddot{x})$$
$$Im(f_t) = Im(f_m) - m^* . Im(\ddot{x}) \qquad (3.14a)$$

or

$$Re(1/A_t) = Re(1/A_m) - m^*$$
$$Im(1/A_t) = Im(1/A_m) \qquad (3.14b)$$

Equally, it is possible to perform this process of 'mass cancellation', or 'cancelling the mass below the force gauge', by using an electronic circuit which takes the two signals and carries out the vector addition of equation (3.11) before the signals are passed to the analyser. A suitable circuit using high-gain operational amplifiers is shown in Figure 3.35, containing a variable potentiometer whose setting is selected according to the magnitude of the mass to be cancelled, m^*. A straightforward way of determining the correct setting with a device of this type is to make a 'measurement' with the force transducer and accelerometer connected together but detached from the structure. Then, by adjusting the variable potentiometer until there is effectively zero corrected force signal, f_t, we can determine the appropriate setting for that particular combination of transducers.

Mass cancellation is important when the mass to be cancelled (m^*) is of the same order as the apparent mass of the modes of the structure under test, and this latter is a quantity which varies from point to point on the structure. If we are near an antinode of a particular mode, then the apparent mass (and stiffness) will tend to be relatively small – certainly, a fraction of the actual mass of the structure – and here mass cancellation may well be important. However, if we now move the same force and response transducers to another position which is near a nodal point of that same mode, we shall find that the apparent mass (and stiffness) is much greater so that the addition of m^* is less significant and the mass cancellation correction is less urgent. This phenomenon manifests itself by a given structure appearing to have different values for each of its natural frequencies as the excitation and/or response points are varied around the structure.

One important feature of mass cancellation is that it can only be applied to point measurements, where the excitation and response are both considered at the same point. This arises because the procedure described above corrects the measured force for the influence of the additional mass at the drive point. If the accelerometer is placed at another point then its inertia force cannot be subtracted from the measured force since it no longer acts at the same point. It is still possible to correct for that part of m* which is due to part of the force transducer mass but this is not the total effect. Also, it should be noted that the transducers' inertia is effective not only in the direction of the excitation but also laterally and in rotation. There are therefore several inertia forces and moments in play, only one of which can usually be compensated for. Nevertheless, there are many cases where this correction provides a valuable improvement to the measurement and should also be considered.

3. 10   ROTATIONAL MOBILITY MEASUREMENT

It is a fact that 50% of all coordinates are rotations (as opposed to translations) and 75% of all frequency response functions involve rotational coordinates. However, it is extremely rare to find any reference to methods for the measurement of rotational mobilities and this reflects the fact that virtually none are made. This situation arises from a considerable difficulty which is encountered when trying to measure either rotational responses or excitations and also when trying to apply rotational excitation, i. e. an excitation moment.

A number of methods have been tried, with limited success, but these are still in a development stage. However, it is believed that these FRF terms will be of increasing importance for future applications of modal testing and so it is appropriate to include here a brief discussion of some of the aspects of measuring rotational mobilities.

There are basically two problems to be tackled; the first is that of measuring rotational responses and the second is a companion one of generating and measuring the rotational excitations. The first of these is the less difficult and a number of techniques have been evaluated which use a pair of matched conventional accelerometers placed a short distance apart on the structure to be measured, or on a fixture attached to the structure. Both configurations are illustrated in Figure 3. 36 which also shows the coordinates of interest, x_0 and θ_0. The principle of operation of either arrangement is that by measuring both accelerometer signals, the responses x_0 and θ_0 can be deduced by taking the mean and difference of x_A and x_B:

$$x_o = 0.5(x_A + x_B)$$
$$\theta_o = (x_A - x_B)/l \qquad\qquad (3.15)$$

This approach permits us to measure half of the possible FRFs – all those which are of the x/F or θ/F type. The others can only be measured directly by applying a moment excitation and in the absence of any suitable rotational exciters it is necessary to resort to a similar device to the above. Figure 3. 37 shows an extension of the exciting block principle in which a single applied excitation force, F_1 say, can become the simultaneous application of a force F_0 $(=F_1)$ and a moment M_0 $(=-F_1.l_1)$. A second test with the same excitation device applied at position 2 gives a simultaneous excitation force F_0 $(= F_2)$ and moment $M_0(= F_2.l_2)$. By adding and differencing the responses produced by these two separate excitation conditions, we can deduce the translational and rotational responses to the translational force and the rotational moment separately, thus enabling the measurement of all four types of FRF:

x/F, θ/F, x/M and θ/M.

The same principle can be extended to more directions by the use of a multidimensional excitation fixture until the full 6x6 mobility matrix at any given point can be measured. However, it must be noted that the procedures involved are quite demanding, not least because they require the acquisition of subsequent processing of many different measurements made at different times.

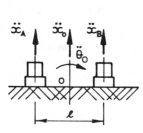
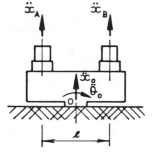

Fig 3.36   Measurement of Rotational Response

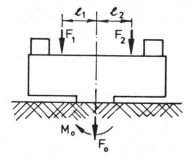

Fig 3.37   Application of Moment Excitation

Other methods for measuring rotational effects include specially developed rotational accelerometers and shakers but in all cases, there is a major problem that is encountered, which derives from the fact that the prevailing levels of output signal generated by the translational components of the structure's movement tend to overshadow those due to the rotational motions, a fact which makes the differencing operations above liable to serious errors. For example, the magnitude of the difference in equation 3.13 is often of the order of 1-2% of either of the two individual values. When the transducers have a transverse sensitivity of the order of 1-2%, the potential errors in the rotations are enormous. Nevertheless, several applications of these methods have been quite successful.

3.11 MEASUREMENTS ON NON-LINEAR STRUCTURES

Most of the theory upon which modal testing and mobility measurement is founded relies heavily on the assumption that the test structure's behaviour is linear. By this is meant that (i) if a given loading is doubled, the resulting deflections are doubled and (ii) the deflection due to two simultaneously applied loads is equal to the summation of the deflections caused when the loads are applied one at a time. In practice, real structures are seldom completely linear although for practical purposes many will closely approximate this state. However, there are many complex structures which do behave in a non-linear way and these can give rise to concerns and problems when they are being tested.

Signs of non-linear behaviour include:

- natural frequencies varying with position and strength of excitation;
- distorted frequency response plots;
- unstable or unrepeatable data.

Perhaps the most obvious way of checking for non-linearity is to repeat a particular mobility measurement a number of times using different levels of excitation (and hence response) each time. If the resulting curves differ from one such measurement to the next, especially around the resonances, as illustrated in Figure 3.38, then there is a strong possibility of non-linearity, and this is a check which will work with most types of excitation signal.

If signs of non-linear behaviour are thus detected, it is useful to have a strategy for how to proceed with the modal test because many of the basic relationships used in the analysis can no longer be relied upon. It turns out that most types of non-linearity are amplitude-dependent and so if it were possible to measure a mobility curve keeping the amplitude of response (specifically the displacement response) at a constant level, the structure would be linearised and would behave just as a linear system. Of course the data and the model obtained in this way would strictly only apply at that particular vibration level but the fact that the behaviour had been maintained as linear is an important achievement.

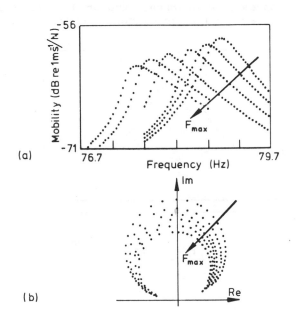

Fig 3. 38　　Example of Non-linear System Response for Different Excitation Levels
(a)　Mobility Modulus Plot
(b)　Receptance Nyquist Plot

While discussing the question of non-linearity, it is interesting to see what form is taken by a single mobility curve for a non-linear system when no response level control is imposed. The result depends markedly on the type of excitation signal used. Figure 3.39 shows some typical results from measurements made on an analogue computer circuit programmed to exhibit a cubic stiffness characteristic using sinusoidal, random and transient excitations. The sinusoidal (FRA) method clearly shows the distortion to the frequency response plots caused by the slight non-linearity. However, neither of the other two cases – both of which used the FFT spectrum analyser – is anything like as effective at detecting the presence of the non-linearity. It must be concluded from this result that when using a spectrum analyser, the appearance of a normal-looking FRF does not guarantee that the test system is indeed linear: there is some aspect of the signal processing which has the effect of linearising the structure's behaviour.

In fact, true random excitation applies a linearisation procedure to the structure's behaviour and is believed to provide an optimised linear model for the test structure. Other methods of excitation – sine, periodic, transient – each produce different results although that from a sinusoidal excitation can readily be related to the theoretical analysis used in Section 2.10.

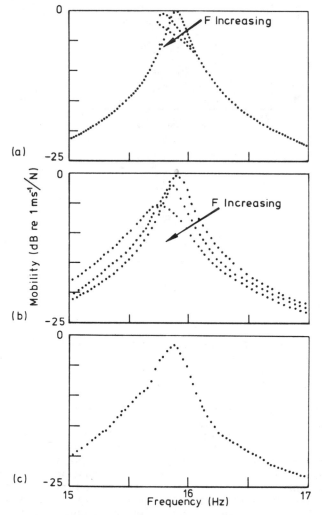

Fig 3.39   FRF Measurements on Nonlinear Analogue System Using
            Different Excitation Types and Different Levels
            (a)   Sinusoidal Excitation
            (b)   Random Excitation
            (c)   Transient Excitation

We shall discuss in the next chapter a means of detecting and identifying nonlinear behaviour from the modal analysis processing of measured FRF data. However, as it is important to detect these effects as early as possible in the test procedure, it is appropriate to consider every opportunity for this task. One recently-developed approach offers the possibility of identifying different types of structural non-linearity from a single FRF curve, always providing that this still contains the necessary evidence (see comments above regarding the use of the Fourier Transform methods for measuring FRF data). This method is based on the properties of the Hilbert Transform (related to the Fourier Transform but different in that it transforms within the frequency domain (or time domain) rather than between the two), which dictates that the Real Part of a frequency response function is related to the corresponding Imaginary Part by a direct Hilbert Transform.

Thus, if we have measurements of both parts (as is usually the case), we can perform a check on the data by using the measured Real Part to compute an estimate for the Imaginary Part and then comparing this with the actual measured values. A similar comparison can also be made in the other direction using the measured Imaginary Part to estimate the Real Part. Differences between estimated and measured curves are then taken as an indication of non-linearity and the nature of the differences used to identify which type. An example of the procedure is shown in Figure 3.40 and further details may be found in Reference [13]. It must be noted that this procedure will only work effectively if the FRF data have been measured using a sinusoidal excitation and care must be taken to avoid misleading results which may arise if the data relate only to a limited frequency range, thereby restricting the effectiveness of the Hilbert Transform.

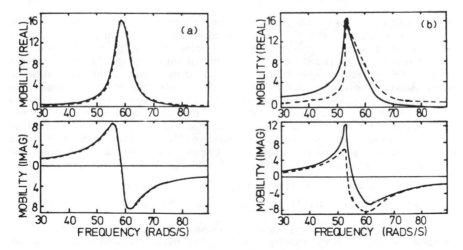

Fig 3.40   Use of Hilbert Transform to Detect Non-linearity
            (a)   Effectively Linear System
            (b)   Non-linear System

3. 12 MULTI-POINT EXCITATION METHODS

Although the great majority of modal tests are performed using a single-point excitation procedure, it should be noted that there are other approaches possible which make use of several simultaneously-applied excitations. A detailed description of these alternative methods lies outside the scope of this work although it is recognised that they may be highly suitable for certain specific applications, such as large aerospace type structures. The theory upon which such multi-point excitation methods are based has been presented in Chapter 2 and we shall briefly discuss here the practical implementation of two rather different methods. A more detailed account of these methods, and others of the same type, may be found in Reference [29].

It was shown earlier (equations (2.67) to (2.69)) that it is theoretically possible to generate a monophased response vector by a multi-point, monophased harmonic force vector, and furthermore that these two vectors would be exactly 90° out of phase when the excitation frequency is equal to one of the undamped system's natural frequencies. If we satisfy the conditions posed in Equations (2.67) to (2.69) where the force and response vectors are exactly in quadrature with each other, then (2.63) may be written as:

$$\{x\} = [\alpha_{RE}(\omega) + i \ \alpha_{IM}(\omega)] \ \{f\} \qquad (3.16)$$

It follows that this equation is valid only if $det |\alpha_{RE}(\omega)| = 0$ and this condition provides the basis of a method to locate the undamped system natural frequencies from measured FRF data. A second stage – to find the appropriate force vector – then follows by substitution of the specific frequencies back into Equation (3.16).

In the case of the multi-point random approach, the purpose of the method is to obtain the FRF data required for modal analysis but in a more optimal way. Specifically, the aim of using several exciters simultaneously is to reduce the probability of introducing systematic errors to the FRF measurements, such as can arise when using conventional single shaker methods. Once again, the underlying theory is presented in Chapter 2, this time in Equation (2.131). We shall consider the simplest form of a multiple excitation as that of a system excited by two simultaneous forces, f_1 and f_2, where the response x_i is of particular interest. Assuming that we have measured the various auto and cross spectral densities of and between the (three) parameters of interest, we can derive expressions for the required FRF parameters, α_{i1} and α_{i2}:

$$\alpha_{i1} = (S_{1i} \ S_{22} - S_{2i} \ S_{12}) \ / \ (S_{11} \ S_{22} - S_{12} \ S_{21})$$

$$\alpha_{i2} = (S_{2i} \ S_{11} - S_{1i} \ S_{21}) \ / \ (S_{11} \ S_{22} - S_{12} \ S_{21}) \qquad (3.17)$$

These expressions can be used provided that $S_{11} \ S_{22} \neq |S_{12}|^2$, a condition which is more readily described by the requirement that the two excitation forces must not be fully correlated. Care must be taken in practice to ensure satisfaction of this condition, noting that it is the applied forces, and not the signal sources, which must meet the requirement.

CHAPTER 4
Modal Parameter
Extraction Methods

4.0 INTRODUCTION

Having dealt with the first phase of any modal test – that of measuring the raw data from which the desired mathematical model is to be derived – we now turn our attention to the various stages of analysis which must be undertaken in order to achieve the objectives.   A major part of this analysis consists of curve-fitting a theoretical expression for an individual FRF (as developed in Chapter 2) to the actual measured data obtained by one of the methods discussed in Chapter 3.   The present chapter describes some of the many procedures which are available for this task and attempts to explain their various advantages and limitations: as with all other aspects of the subject, no single method is 'best' for all cases.

In increasing complexity, the methods discussed involve the analysis, or curve-fitting, first of part of a single FRF curve, then of a complete curve encompassing several resonances and, finally, of a set of many FRF plots all on the same structure.   In every case, however, the task undertaken is basically the same: to find the coefficients in a theoretical expression for the frequency response function which then most closely matches the measured data.   This task is most readily tackled by using the series form for the FRF, as developed in Sections 2.3 to 2.6 for different types of system.   The particular advantage of this approach is that the coefficients thus determined are directly related to the modal properties of the system under test, and these are generally the very parameters that are sought.

This phase of the modal test procedure is often referred to as 'modal analysis', or 'experimental modal analysis' because it is the corresponding stage in an experimental study to that called modal analysis in a theoretical study.   In both cases, modal analysis leads to a derivation of the system's modal properties.   However, it should be noted that the two processes themselves are quite different: one is a curve-fitting procedure while the other is a root-finding or eigensolution exercise.   The various methods used for experimental modal analysis tend to divide into two philosophies, one in which the analysis is essentially automatic – FRF data are supplied as input data and modal parameters are extracted without further involvement of the user – and a second one which is much more interactive, in which the user is expected to participate in various decisions throughout the analysis. Although, theoretically, there should be no need for this latter course of action, it is often found expedient in the light of the imperfect and incomplete data which are inevitably obtained in practical situations with real and complicated engineering structures.

A great many of the current curve-fitting methods operate on the response characteristics in the frequency domain – i.e. on the frequency response functions themselves – but there are other procedures which perform a curve-fit in the time domain. These latter methods use the fact that the Inverse Fourier Transform of the FRF is itself another characteristic function of the system – the Impulse Response Function – which represents the response of the system to a single unit impulse as excitation (analogous to the single unit sinusoid for the FRF). The majority of the following sections are concerned with modal analysis performed directly on the FRF curves but in later sections of this chapter we shall discuss this alternative approach to the problem using the impulse response properties.

4.1   PRELIMINARY CHECKS OF FRF DATA

Before commencing the modal analysis of any measured FRF data, it is always prudent to undertake a few preliminary and simple checks in order to ensure that time is not wasted on what subsequently turn out to be obviously bad data. It is not always possible to ascertain from visual inspection of a mobility plot whether it is a valid measurement, but there are certain characteristics which should be observed and these should be checked as soon as possible after the measurement has been made.

Most of the checks are made using a log-log plot of the modulus of the measured FRF, whether that be receptance, mobility or – as is usually the format of the raw measurements – inertance. The first feature to be examined is the characteristic at very low frequencies – below the first resonance, if data extend down that far – since in this region we should be able to see the behaviour corresponding to the support conditions chosen for the test. If the structure is grounded (see Chapter 3), then we should clearly see a stiffness-like characteristic at low frequencies, appearing as asymptotic to a stiffness line at the lowest frequencies, and the magnitude of this should correspond to that of the static stiffness of the structure at the point in question. Conversely, if the structure has been tested in a free condition, then we should expect to see a mass-line asymptote in this low frequency range and, here again, its magnitude may be deduced from purely rigid-body considerations. Deviations from this expected behaviour may be caused by the frequency range of measurements not extending low enough to see the asymptotic trend, or they may indicate that the required support conditions have not in fact been achieved. In the case of a freely-supported structure, there will generally be some rigid body modes at very low frequencies (i.e. considerably lower than the first flexural mode) and this will tend to interrupt the mass-like asymptotic trend.

A second similar check can be made towards the upper end of the frequency range where it is sometimes found, especially on point mobility measurements, that the curve becomes asymptotic to a mass line or, more usually, to a stiffness line. Such a tendency can result in considerable difficulties for the modal analysis process and reflects a situation where the excitation is being applied at a point of very high mass or flexibility. Although not incorrect, the data thus obtained will often prove difficult to analyse because the various modal parameters to be extracted are overwhelmed by the dominant local effects. Such a situation suggests the use of a different excitation point.

Another set of checks can be made for systems with relatively clear resonance and antiresonance characteristics. The first of these is a check to satisfy the expected incidence of antiresonances (as opposed to minima) occurring between adjacent resonances. For a point mobility, there must be an antiresonance after each resonance while for transfer mobilities between two points well-separated on the structure, we should expect more minima than antiresonances. A second check to be made at the same time, is that the resonance peaks and the antiresonance 'troughs' exhibit the same sharpness (on a log-log plot). Failure to do so may well reflect poor measurement quality, either because of a spectrum analyser frequency resolution limitation (see Section 3.7) causing blunt resonances, or because of inadequate vibration levels resulting in poor definition of the antiresonance regions.

There is another technique which will be described more fully in the next chapter that enables an overall check to be made on the relative positions of the resonances, antiresonances and ambient levels of the FRF curve. Essentially, it is found that the relative spacing of the resonance frequencies (R) and the antiresonance frequencies (A) is related to the general level of the FRF curve, characterised by its magnitude at points roughly halfway between these two types of frequency. Figure 4.1 shows two example mobility plots, one of which (Figure 4.1a) is mass-dominated and tends to drift downwards with antiresonances occuring immediately before resonances, while the other (Figure 4.1b) is of a stiffness-dominated characterstic which generally drifts upwards and has antiresonances immediately above resonances. There is a procedure for sketching a simple skeleton of mass-lines and stiffness-lines through a FRF curve which confirms whether or not the R and A frequencies are consistent with the general level of the curve: the skeleton should pass through the 'middle' of the actual FRF plot. Figure 4.1c shows a sketch of an apparently plausible FRF which does not satisfy the skeleton check. This may be because of poor data or because the parameter plotted is not in fact that expected (mobility, in this case) but a different format.

Finally, at a more detailed level, we can assess the quality of the measured data again at the stage of plotting the FRF data in a Nyquist format. Here, each resonance region is expected to trace out at least part of a circular arc, the extent depending largely on the interaction between adjacent modes. For a system with well-separated modes, it is to be expected that each resonance will generate the major part of a circle but as the modal interference increases, with closer modes or greater damping levels, it is to be expected that only small segments – perhaps 45° or 60° – will be identifiable. However, within these bounds, the Nyquist plot should ideally exhibit a smooth curve and failure to do so may indicate a poor measurement technique, often related to the use of the analyser.

(a)

(b)

(c)

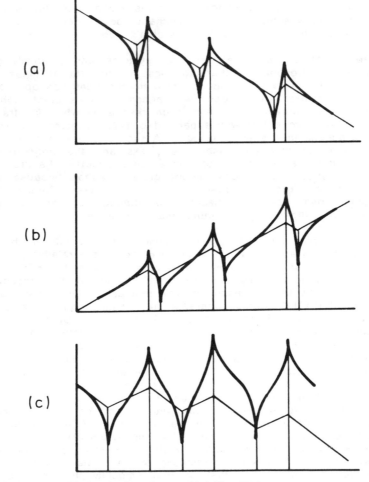

Fig 4.1   Skeleton Checks on Mobility Plots
(a)   Mass-Dominated
(b)   Stiffness-Dominated
(c)   Incorrect Plot

4.2 SDOF MODAL ANALYSIS I – PEAK-AMPLITUDE

We shall begin our study of the various methods available for analysing measured FRF data to obtain the described mathematical models of our test structure by examining the simplest approaches.   There exist a number of modal analysis methods which, although different in their detail, all share the same basic assumption: namely, that in the vicinity of a resonance the total response is dominated by the contribution of the mode whose natural frequency is closest.   The methods vary as to whether they assume that *all* the response is attributed to that single mode or whether the other modes' contributions are represented by a simple approximation.

Perhaps the simplest of these methods is one which has been used for a long time and which is sometimes referred to as the 'peak-amplitude' or 'peak-picking' method.   This is a method which works adequately for structures whose FRF exhibit well-separated modes which are not so lightly-damped that accurate measurements at resonance are difficult to obtain but which, on the other hand, are not so heavily damped that the response at a resonance is strongly influenced by more than one mode. Although this appears to limit the applicability of the method, it should be noted that in the more difficult cases, such an approach can be useful in obtaining initial estimates to the parameters required, thereby speeding up the more general curve-fitting procedures described later.   The method is applied as follows:

(i)   first, individual resonance peaks are detected on the FRF plot (Figure 4.2a), and the frequency of maximum response taken as the natural frequency of that mode (ω_r);

(ii)   second, the maximum value of the FRF is noted ($|\hat{\alpha}|$) and the frequency bandwidth of the function for a response level of $|\hat{\alpha}|/\sqrt{2}$ is determined $(\Delta\omega)$.   The two points thus identified as ω_b and ω_a are the 'half-power points': see Figure 4.2b.

(iii)   The damping of the mode in question can now be estimated from one of the following formulae (whose derivation is given below in (4.13)):

$$\eta_r = (\omega_a{}^2-\omega_b{}^2)/\omega_r{}^2 \triangleq \Delta\omega/\omega_r$$

$$\zeta_r = 2\eta_r \qquad\qquad (4.1)$$

(iv)   Last, we may now obtain an estimate for the modal constant of the mode being analysed by assuming that the total response in this resonant region is attributed to a single term in the general FRF series (Equation (2.65)).   This can be found from the equation

$$|\hat{\alpha}| = A_r/(\omega_r{}^2\eta_r)$$
or

$$A_r = |\hat{\alpha}|\omega_r{}^2\eta_r \qquad\qquad (4.2a)$$

It is appropriate now to consider the possible limitations to this method. First, it must be noted that the estimates of both damping and modal constant depend heavily on the accuracy of the maximum FRF level, $|\hat{\alpha}|$, and as we have seen in the previous chapter on measurement techniques, this is not a quantity which is readily measured with great accuracy. Most of the errors in measurements are concentrated around the resonance region and particular care must be taken with lightly-damped structures where the peak value may rely entirely on the validity of a single point in the FRF spectrum. Also, it is clear that only real modal constants – and that means real modes, or proportionally damped structures – can be deduced by this method.

The second most serious limitation will generally arise because the single-mode assumption is not strictly applicable. Even with clearly-separated modes, it is often found that the neighbouring modes do contribute a noticeable amount to the total response at the resonance of the mode being analysed. It is to deal with this problem that the more general circle-fit method, described in the next section, was developed as a refinement of this current approach. The problem is illustrated in Figure 4.2c and 4.2d where a Nyquist type of plot is used to show two possible FRF characteristics which might equally well give the modulus plot shown in Figure 4.2b. The limitation of the method described above becomes evident and it will, in the second example, produce an overestimate of the damping level and an erroneous modal constant.

However, it is possible to adapt the above procedure slightly, without involving the curve-fitting processes to be discussed next, by working with a plot of the Real part of the receptance FRF, instead of the modulus plot as shown in Figure 4.2a and b. Figure 4.2e and f show plots of the Real part of the receptance detail previously illustrated in Figure 4.2c and d. From these it can be seen that the positions and values of the maximum and minimum values of the plot yield good estimates of the locations of the half-power points and of the diameter of the circle in the Nyquist plot. This last quantity is a better indicator of the maximum magnitude of the single term in the FRF series upon which the estimate of the modal constant is based, equation (4.2a). Furthermore, a more refined estimate of the natural frequency itself can be derived from the midway point between the maximum and minimum on the Imaginary plot: see Figures 4.2c and d. Thus we use

$$A_r = (|MX| + |MN|) \, \omega_r^2 \eta_r \qquad\qquad (4.2b)$$

4.3   SDOF MODAL ANALYSIS II – CIRCLE-FIT METHOD

4.3.1   General

We shall now examine the slightly more detailed SDOF analysis method based on circle-fitting FRF plots in the vicinity of resonance. It was shown in Chapter 2 that for the general SDOF system, a Nyquist plot of frequency response properties produced circle-like curves and that, if the appropriate parameter was chosen for the type of damping model, this

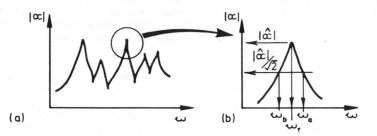

(a)

(b)

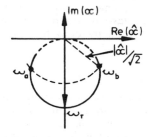

(c)

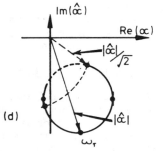

(d)

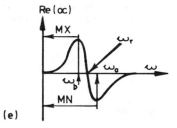

(e)

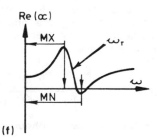

(f)

Fig 4.2   Peak Amplitude Method of Modal Analysis
             (a)   Overall FRF
             (b)   Resonance Detail
             (c)   Nyquist Plot of Resonance – Possibility 1
             (d)   Nyquist Plot of Resonance – Possibility 2
             (e)   Real vs Freq Plot for (c)
             (f)   Real vs Freq Plot for (d)

would produce an exact circle. Further, we saw in the later sections concerned with MDOF systems that these also produce Nyquist plots of FRF data which include sections of near-circular arcs corresponding to the regions near the natural frequencies. This characteristic provides the basis of one of the most important types of modal anaysis, that known widely as 'the SDOF circle-fit method'.

We shall base our treatment in this section on a system with structural damping and thus shall be using the receptance form of FRF data as it is this parameter which produces an exact circle in a Nyquist plot for the properties of a simple oscillator (see section 2.2). However, if it is required to use a model incorporating viscous damping, then it is the mobility version of the FRF data which should be used. Although this gives a different general appearance to the diagrams – as they are rotated by 90° on the complex plane – most of the following analysis and comments apply equally to that choice. Some of the more discriminating modal analysis packages offer the choice between the two types of damping and simply take receptance or mobility data for the circle-fitting according to the selection.

4.3.2   The SDOF Assumption

Before detailing the actual steps involved in the circle-fitting procedure, it is necessary to examine the assumptions which will be made and the basis on which the method is founded. As the name implies, the method exploits the fact that in the vicinity of a resonance, the behaviour of most systems is dominated by a single mode. Algebraically, this means that the magnitude of the FRF is effectively controlled by one of the terms in the series, that being the one relating to the mode whose resonance is being observed. We can express the assumption as follows. From Chapter 2, we have:

$$\alpha_{jk}(\omega) = \sum_{s=1}^{N} \frac{{}_sA_{jk}}{\omega_s^2 - \omega^2 + i\eta_s\omega_s^2} \qquad (4.3a)$$

This can be rewritten, without simplification, as

$$\alpha_{jk}(\omega) = \frac{{}_rA_{jk}}{\omega_r^2 - \omega^2 + i\eta_r\omega_r^2} + \sum_{\substack{s=1 \\ \neq r}}^{N} \frac{{}_sA_{jk}}{\omega_s^2 - \omega^2 + i\eta_s\omega_s^2} \qquad (4.3b)$$

Now, the SDOF assumption is that for a small range of frequency in the vicinity of the natural frequency of mode r, the second of the two terms in (4.3b) is approximately independent of frequency ω and the expression for the receptance may be written as:

$$\alpha_{jk}(\omega) \Big|_{\omega=\omega_r} \simeq \frac{{}_rA_{jk}}{\omega_r^2 - \omega^2 + i\eta_r\omega_r^2} + {}_rB_{jk} \qquad (4.4)$$

This can be illustrated by a specific example, shown in Figure 4.3. Using a 4DOF system, the receptance properties have been computed in the immediate vicinity of the second mode and each of the two terms in equation (4.3b) has been plotted separately, in Figures 4.3a and 4.3b. Also shown, in Figure 4.3c, is the corresponding plot of the total receptance over the same frequency range. What is clear in this example is the fact that the first term (that relating to the mode under examination) varies considerably through the resonance region, sweeping out the expected circular arc, while the second term, which includes the combined effects of all the other modes, is effectively constant through the narrow frequency range covered. Thus we see from the total receptance plot in Figure 4.3c that this may, in effect, be treated as a

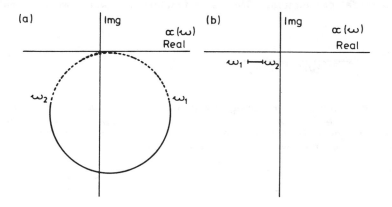

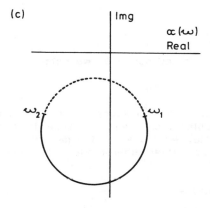

Fig 4.3　　　*Nyquist Plot of* 4DOF *Receptance Data*
　　　　　　(a)　First Term
　　　　　　(b)　Second Term
　　　　　　(c)　Total

circle with the same properties as the modal circle for the specific mode in question but which is displaced from the origin of the Argand plane by an amount determined by the contribution of all the other modes. Note that this is not to say that the other modes are unimportant or negligible – quite the reverse, their influence can be considerable – but rather that their combined effect can be represented as a constant term around this resonance.

4.3.3 Properties of Modal Circle

Having established the plausibility of observing an individual modal circle from a (measured) FRF plot, we shall now explore some of the properties of the modal circle since these provide the means of extracting the required modal parameters. The basic function with which we are dealing is:

$$\alpha = \frac{1}{\omega_r{}^2(1-(\omega/\omega_r)^2 + i\eta_r)} \qquad (4.5)$$

since the only effect of including the modal constant $_rA_{jk}$ is to scale the size of the circle (by $|_rA_{jk}|$) and to rotate it (by $\angle_rA_{jk}$). A plot of the quantity α is given in Figure 4.4. Now, it may be seen that for any frequency, ω, we may write the following relationships:

$$\tan \gamma = \eta_r/(1-(\omega/\omega_r)^2) \qquad (4.6a)$$

$$\tan(90^o-\gamma) = \tan(\theta/2) = (1-(\omega/\omega_r)^2)/\eta_r \qquad (4.6b)$$

from which we obtain:

$$\omega^2 = \omega_r{}^2 (1-\eta_r \tan(\theta/2)) \qquad (4.6c)$$

If we differentiate equation (4.6c) with respect to θ, we obtain:

$$d\omega^2/d\theta = (-\omega_r{}^2\eta_r/2)\{1 + (1-(\omega/\omega_r)^2)^2/\eta_r\} \qquad (4.7)$$

The reciprocal of this quantity – which is a measure of the rate at which the locus sweeps around the circular arc – may be seen to reach a maximum value (maximum sweep rate) when $\omega = \omega_r$, the natural frequency of the oscillator. This is shown by further differentation, this time with respect to frequency:

$$d/d\omega(d\omega^2/d\theta) = 0 \text{ when } (\omega_r{}^2-\omega^2) = 0 \qquad (4.8)$$

It may also be seen from this analysis that an estimate of the damping is provided by the sweep rate parameter since:

$$(d\theta/d\omega^2)_{\omega=\omega_r} = -2/(\omega_r{}^2\eta_r) \qquad (4.9)$$

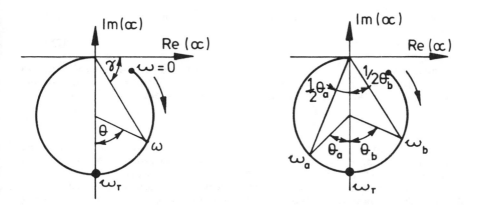

Fig 4.4   Properties of Modal Circle

The above property proves useful in analysing MDOF system data since, in general, it is not known exactly where is the natural frequency, but if we can examine the relative spacing of the measured data points around the circular arc near each resonance, then we should be able to determine its value.

Another valuable result can be obtained by further inspection of this basic modal circle. Suppose we have two specific points on the circle, one corresponding to a frequency (ω_b) below the natural frequency, and the other to one (ω_a) above the natural frequency. Referring to Figure 4.4, we can write:

$$\tan(\theta_b/2) = (1-(\omega_b/\omega_r)^2)/\eta_r$$

$$(4.10)$$

$$\tan(\theta_a/2) = ((\omega_a/\omega_r)^2-1)/\eta_r$$

and from these two equations we can obtain an expression for the damping of the mode:

$$\eta_r = (\omega_a^2-\omega_b^2)/(\omega_r^2(\tan(\theta_a/2)+\tan(\theta_b/2))) \qquad (4.11)$$

This is an exact expression, and applies for all levels of damping. If we are concerned with light damping (say, loss factors of less than 2-3%), the expression above simplifies to:

$$\eta_r \simeq 2(\omega_a-\omega_b)/(\omega_r(\tan(\theta_a/2)+\tan\theta_b/2))) \qquad (4.12)$$

and if we further restrict our interest, this time to the two points for which $\theta_a = \theta_b = 90°$ (the half-power points), we obtain the familiar formula:

$$\eta_r = (\omega_2-\omega_1)/\omega_r \qquad (4.13a)$$

or if the damping is not light, to:

$$\eta_r = (\omega_2{}^2 - \omega_1{}^2)/\omega_r{}^2 \qquad\qquad (4.13b)$$

The final property relates to the diameter of the circle which, for the quantity specified in equation (4.5), is given by $1/\omega_r{}^2\eta_r$. When scaled by a modal constant added in the numerator, the diameter will be

$$_rD_{jk} = |_rA_{jk}|/(\omega_r{}^2\eta_r)$$

and, as mentioned earlier, the whole circle will be rotated so that the principal diameter – the one passing through the natural frequency point – is oriented at an angle arg $(_rA_{jk})$ to the negative imaginary axis. (Note that this means that the circle will be in the upper half of the plane if A is effectively negative, a situation which cannot arise for a point measurement but which can for transfer data.)

Viscous Damping

We shall complete this section by deriving corresponding formulae to (4.11)–(4.13) for the case of a SDOF system with viscous, rather than structural, damping. Recalling that in this case we should use mobility in place of receptance, we can write

$$Y(\omega) = \frac{i\omega}{(k-\omega^2m)+i(\omega c)}$$

$$\qquad\qquad (4.14)$$

or

$$Re(Y) = \omega^2c/((k-\omega^2m)^2 + (\omega c)^2)$$

$$Im(Y) = i\omega(k-\omega^2m)/((k-\omega^2m)^2 + (\omega c)^2)$$

From there, we have

$$\tan(\theta/2) = \omega(k-\omega^2m)/\omega^2c = (1-(\omega/\omega_0)^2)/(2\zeta\omega/\omega_0) \qquad (4.15)$$

and using the same procedure as before for ω_b and ω_a (points before and after ω_0, respectively):

$$\tan(\theta_b/2) = (1-(\omega_b/\omega_0)^2)/(2\zeta\omega_b/\omega_0)$$

$$\tan(\theta_a/2) = ((\omega_a/\omega_0)^2-1)/(2\zeta\omega_a/\omega_0)$$

These yield:

$$\zeta = (\omega_a{}^2-\omega_b{}^2)/(2\omega_0(\omega_a\tan(\theta_a/2) + \omega_b\tan(\theta_b/2)) \qquad (4.16a)$$

or, for light damping,

$$\zeta \approx (\omega_a-\omega_b)/(\omega_0(\tan(\theta_a/2)+\tan(\theta_b/2))) \qquad (4.16b)$$

Finally, selecting the half-power points as those frequencies for which $\theta_a = \theta_b = 90^{\circ}$, we have

$$\zeta = (\omega_2 - \omega_1)/(2\omega_0)$$

(4.16c)

and this is EXACT for any level of damping.

4.3.4   Circle-Fit Analysis Procedure

Armed with the above insight into the structure of a FRF plot near resonance, it is a relatively straightforward matter to devise an analysis procedure to extract the necessary coefficients in equation (4.3a), and thence the modal parameters themselves.   Basing the following comments on the case for structural damping, the sequence is:

(i)   select points to be used;
(ii)   fit circle, calculate quality of fit;
(iii)   locate natural frequency, obtain damping estimate;
(iv)   calculate multiple damping estimates, and scatter;
(v)   determine modal constant.

Step (i) can be made automatic by selecting a fixed number of points on either side of any identified maximum in the response modulus or it can be effected by the operator whose judgement may be better able to discern true modes from spurious perturbations on the plot and to reject certain suspect data points.   The points chosen should not be influenced to any great extent by the neighbouring modes and, whenever possible without violating that first rule, should encompass some 270° of the circle.   This is often not possible and a span of less than 180° is more usual, although care should be taken not to limit the range excessively as this becomes highly sensitive to the accuracy of the few points used.   Not less than 6 points should be used.

The second step, (ii), can be performed by one of numerous curve-fitting routines and consists simply of finding a circle which gives a least-squares deviation for the points included.   Note that there are two possible criteria which can be applied here: one is that which minimises the deviations of points from the nearest point on the circle and the other, which is more accurate, minimises the deviations of the measured points from where they ought to be on the circle.   This latter condition is more difficult to apply and so it is the former which is more common.   At the end of this process, we have specified the centre and radius of the circle and have produced a quality factor which is the mean square deviation of the chosen points from the circle.   'Errors' of the order of 1-2% are commonplace and an example of the process is shown in Figure 4.5a.

Step (iii) can be implemented by constructing (here used metaphorically as the whole process is performed numerically) radial lines from the circle centre to a succession of points around the resonance and by noting the angles they subtend with each other.   Then, the rate of sweep through the region can be estimated and the frequency at which it reaches a maximum can be deduced. If, as is usually the case, the frequencies of the points used in this analysis are spaced at regular intervals (i.e. a linear frequency increment), then this process can be effected using a finite difference method. Such a procedure enables one to pinpoint the natural frequency with a precision of about 10% of the frequency increments between the points. At the same time, an estimate for the damping is derived although this will be somewhat less accurate than that for the natural frequency. Figure 4.5b shows the results from a typical calculation.

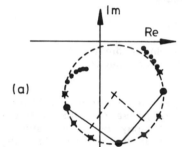

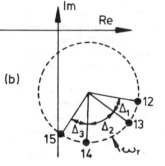

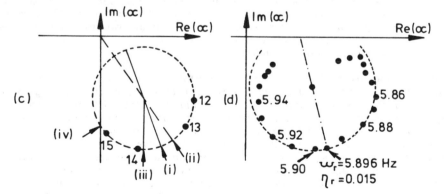

Fig 4.5   Example of Circle-Fit to FRF Data
           (a)   Circle-Fit
           (b)   Natural Frequency Location
           (c)   Alternative Definitions of Natural Frequency
           (d)   Typical Application

It is interesting to note at this point that other definitions of the natural frequency are sometimes used, including:

(a)   the frequency of maximum response;
(b)   the frequency of maximum imaginary receptance;
(c)   the frequency of zero real receptance.

These are all indicated on the figure and while they seldom make a significant difference to the value of the natural frequency itself, selecting the wrong one can have implications for the values found for the damping factor and for the modal constant (and thus the mode shapes).

Next, for step (iv), we are able to compute a set of damping estimates using every possible combination from our selected data points of one point below resonance with one above resonance using equation (4.11). With all these estimates we can either compute the mean value or we can choose to examine them individually to see whether there are any particular trends.   Ideally, they should all be identical and so an indication   not only of the mean but also of the deviation of the estimates is useful.   If the deviation is less than 4-5%, then we have generally succeeded in making a good analysis.   If, however, the scatter is 20 or 30%, there is something unsatisfactory.   If the variations in damping estimate are random, then the scatter is probably due to measurement errors but if it is systematic, then it could be caused by various effects (such as poor experimental setup, interference from neighbouring modes, non-linear behaviour, etc.), none of which should, strictly, be averaged out.   Thus, if a large scatter of damping estimates is indicated, a plot of their values such as that shown in Figure 4.6 should be examined.

Lastly, step (v) is a relatively simple one in that it remains to determine the magnitude and argument of the modal constant from the diameter of the circle, and from its orientation relative to the Real and Imaginary axes.   This calculation is straightforward once the natural frequency has been located and the damping estimates obtained.

Finally, if it is desired to construct a theoretically-regenerated FRF plot against which to compare the original measured data, it will be necessary to determine the contribution to this resonance of the other modes and that requires simply measuring the distance from the 'top' of the principal diameter to the origin, this quantity being the value of $_rB_{jk}$ in equation (4.4).   Then, using that equation together with the modal parameters extracted from the circle-fit, it is possible to plot a curve based on the 'model' obtained.

NOTE   If previous estimates for ω_r and η_r are available, steps (iii) and (iv) can be omitted, and only the modal constant derived.

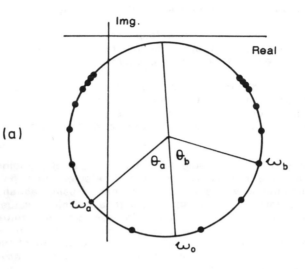

(a)

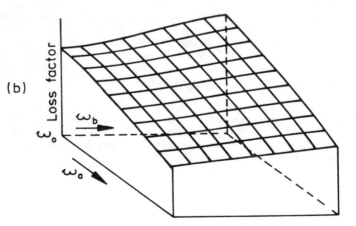

(b)

Fig 4. 6   *Multiple Damping Estimates from Circle-Fit*
           (a)   Circle-Fit in Nyquist Plane
           (b)   Plot of Damping Estimates

4.4 SDOF MODAL ANALYSIS III – INVERSE METHOD

Although the circle-fit method is very widely used, there are alternative procedures available which work within the same general confines and assumptions. We shall briefly discuss one here: a direct alternative to the circle-fit called the 'Inverse Method'.

This method uses the fact that a function which generates a circle when plotted in the complex (Nyquist) plane will, when plotted as a reciprocal, trace out a straight line. Thus, if we were to plot the reciprocal of receptance (not dynamic stiffness in the strict sense) of a SDOF system with structural damping, we would find that in the Argand diagram it produces a straight line as can be seen from inspection of the appropriate expressions for a SDOF system:

$$\alpha(\omega) = \frac{(k-\omega^2 m) - i(h)}{(k-\omega^2 m)^2 + h^2} \qquad (4.17a)$$

and

$$\frac{1}{\alpha(\omega)} = (k-\omega^2 m) + i(h) \qquad (4.17b)$$

Sketches of these two forms of the FRF are shown in Figure 4.7 and the procedure which may be used to determine the modal parameters using the inverse FRF is as follows. First, a least-squares best-fit straight line

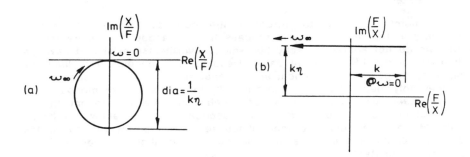

Fig 4.7   *Nyquist Plots of Receptance and Inverse Receptance*
            (a)   Receptance
            (b)   Inverse Receptance

is constructed through the data points and an estimate for the damping parameter is immediately available from the intercept of the line with the imaginary axis. Furthermore, an indication of the reliability of that estimate may be gained from the nature of the deviations of the data points from the line itself : if these are randomly scattered above and below the line, then we probably have typical experimental errors, but if they deviate in a systematic fashion – such as by being closer to a curve than a straight line, or to a line of other than zero slope – then there is a source of bias in the data which should be investigated before making further use of the results.

Then, a second and independent least-squares operation is performed, this time on the deviation between the Real part of the measured data points and that of the theoretical model. Resulting from this, we obtain estimates for the mass and stiffness parameters in the theoretical model to complete the description.

It should be noted that this approach is best suited to systems with real modes (effectively assumed in the analysis) and to relatively well-separated modes as corrective action is required in the event that the FRF is not locally dominated by a single mode. However, the method is relatively insensitive to whether or not data are measured exactly at the natural frequency (at which point the Real part of the inverse receptance is zero) as the straight line can readily be obtained with data points which are well away from resonance.

As in the previous cases, the approach described here for structural damping can equally be applied to viscous damping simply by using mobility data instead of receptances. In this case, the Nyquist diagrams are rotated by 90° but are otherwise very similar in appearance.

4.5   RESIDUALS

At this point we need to introduce the concept of residual terms, necessary in the modal analysis process to take account of those modes which we do not analyse directly but which nevertheless exist and have an influence on the FRF data we use. Usually, it is necessary to limit the frequency range of measurement and/or analysis for practical reasons and this inevitably means that we cannot identify the properties of modes which exist outside this range. However, their influence is present in the measured FRF data and we must take account of it somehow. (NOTE. It should be noted that the topic discussed here is not related to the 'residue' quantities used in some analyses as an alternative definition to our 'modal constant'.)

The first occasion on which the residual problem is encountered is generally at the end of the analysis of a single FRF curve, such as by the repeated application of an SDOF curve-fit to each of the resonances in turn until all modes visible on the plot have been identified. At this point, it is often desired to construct a 'theoretical' curve, based on the modal parameters extracted from the measured data, and to overlay this

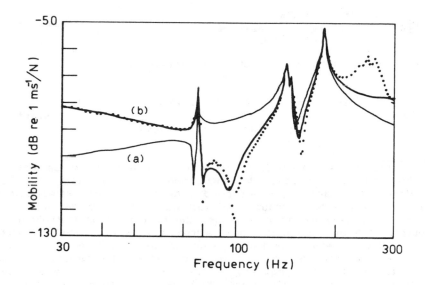

Fig 4. 8   *Effect of Residual Terms on Regenerated Mobility Curve*
           (a)   Without Residuals
           (b)   With Residuals Added

on the original measured curve to assess the success of the curve–fit process.   (A more appropriate description of the calculated curve is 'theoretically–regenerated', since it does not come from a purely theoretical analysis of the system, and we shall use this terminology subsequently.)   When the regenerated curve is compared with the original measurements, the result is often disappointing, as illustrated in Figure 4.8a.   However, by the inclusion of two simple extra terms – the 'residuals' – the modified regenerated curve is seen to correlate very well with the original experimental data, as shown in Figure 4.8b.   The origin of these residual terms may be explained as follows.

If we regenerate a FRF curve from the modal parameters we have extracted from the measured data, we shall use a formula of the type:

$$Y_{jk}(\omega) = \sum_{r=m_1}^{m_2} \frac{i\omega \, _rA_{jk}}{\omega_r^2 - \omega^2 + i\eta_r\omega_r^2} \qquad (4.18)$$

in which we have shown the limits in the modal series as m_1 and m_2 to reflect the fact that, in general, we do not always start below the first mode (r = 1) and we seldom continue to the highest mode (r = N). However, just because we choose to limit our frequency range of measurement and analysis does not mean that the measured FRF data are unaffected by modes which lie outside this range.   Indeed, the equation which most closely represents the measured data is:

$$Y_{jk}(\omega) = \sum_{r=1}^{N} \frac{i\omega \; _rA_{jk}}{\omega_r^2 - \omega^2 + i\eta_r\omega_r^2} \tag{4.19a}$$

which may be rewritten, without loss of generality, as:

$$Y_{jk}(\omega) = \sum_{r=1}^{m_1-1} + \sum_{r=m_1}^{m_2} + \sum_{r=m_2+1}^{N} \left(\frac{i\omega \; _rA_{jk}}{\omega_r^2 - \omega^2 + i\eta_r\omega_r^2} \right) \tag{4.19b}$$

In this equation, we shall refer to the first of the three terms as that of the 'low-frequency' modes; to the third term as that of the 'high-frequency' modes while the second term is that which relates to the modes actually identified. Figure 4.9 illustrates plots of typical values for each of the three terms individually, and the middle one is that which is computed using only the modal data extracted from the modal analysis process, such as demonstrated in a particular case in Figure 4.8. Now, it is usually the case that we are seeking a model of the structure which is accurate within the frequency range of our tests (it would be unreasonable to expect to derive one which was representative beyond the measured frequency range) and so we need to find a way of correcting the regenerated plot within the central frequency range to take account of the low-frequency and high-frequency modes. From the sketch, it may be seen that within the frequency range of interest, the first term tends to approximate to a mass-like behaviour, while the third term, for the high-frequency modes, approximates to a stiffness effect. Thus, we have a basis for the residual terms and shall rewrite equation (4.19b):

$$Y_{jk}(\omega) \simeq - \frac{i\omega}{\omega^2 M^R_{jk}} + \sum_{r=m_1}^{m_2} \left(\frac{i\omega \; _rA_{jk}}{\omega_r^2 - \omega^2 + i\eta_r\omega_r^2} \right) + \frac{i\omega}{K^R_{jk}} \tag{4.20}$$

where the quantities M^R_{jk} and K^R_{jk} are the residual mass and stiffness for that particular FRF and, it should be noted, for that particular frequency range (if we extend or limit the range of analysis, the residual terms will also change).

The way in which residual terms are calculated is relatively straightforward and involves an examination of the FRF curve at either end of the frequency range of interest. First, we compute a few values of the regenerated FRF curve at the lowest frequencies covered by the tests, using only the identified modal parameters. Then, by comparing these values with those from actual measurements, we estimate a mass residual constant which, when added to the regenerated curve, brings this closely into line with the measured data. Then, the process is repeated at the top end of the frequency range, this time seeking a stiffness residual. Often, the process is more effective if there is an antiresonance near either end of the frequency range and this is used as the point of adjustment. The procedure outlined here may need to be repeated iteratively in case the addition of the stiffness residual term then upsets the effectiveness of the mass term, and so on, but if the frequency range encompassed is a decade or greater, such interaction is generally minor.

Finally, it should be noted that often there is a physical significance to the residual terms. If the test structure is freely-supported, and its rigid body modes are well below the minimum frequency of measurement, then the low-frequency or mass residual term will be a direct measure of the rigid body mass and inertia properties of the structure and, as such, is

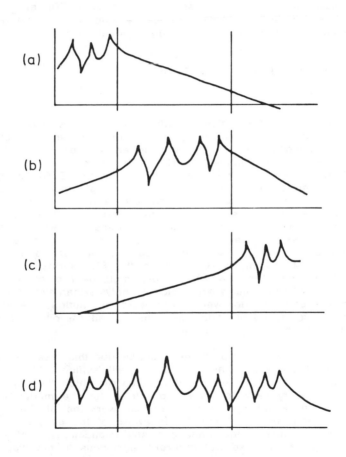

Fig 4.9   Contributions of Various Terms in Modal Series for FRF
(a)   Low-Frequency Modes
(b)   Identified Modes
(c)   High-Frequency Modes
(d)   All Modes

amenable to direct computation using simple dynamics. At the other extreme, the high-frequency residual can represent the local flexibility at the drive point. It can be seen, from inspection of the expression (4.19b), that the magnitude of this stiffness residual will vary according to the type of frequency response function considered. If we are concerned with a point measurement, then all the modal constants in the series $r = m_2$ to N will be positive, and as the denominator will always have the same sign, all the contributions from the high-frequency modes will be additive, resulting in the maximum possible magnitude for the residual. On the other hand, for a transfer FRF, we find that the terms in the series will be of varied sign, as well as magnitude, and so the total expression will tend to be less than for a point FRF and, in some cases, will tend to be very small, if not negligible. This characteristic should be borne in mind when computing residual terms.

4.6 MDOF CURVE-FITTING PROCEDURES

4.6.1 General

There are a number of situations in which the SDOF approach to modal analysis is inadequate or inappropriate and for these there exist several alternative methods which may generally be classified as multi-degree-of-freedom curve-fits. The particular cases which demand a more elaborate treatment than that afforded by the SDOF concept are those with closely-coupled modes, where the single mode approximation is inappropriate, and those with extremely light damping, for which measurements at resonance are inaccurate and difficult to obtain. By closely-coupled modes we mean those systems for which either the natural frequencies are very closely spaced, or which have relatively heavy damping, or both, in which the response even at resonance is not dominated by just one mode (or term in the FRF series). For these cases, and for all others where a very high degree of accuracy is demanded, we look to a more exact modal analysis than that described in the previous sections. However, as a word of caution: we should be wary of using overrefined numerical analysis procedures on measured data which themselves have a finite accuracy.

There are many individual algorithms available for this task and we shall not attempt to describe them all in detail. It will suffice to distinguish the different approaches and to explain the bases on which they operate. It is seldom necessary (and is often impossible) for the modal analyst to have an intimate knowledge of the detailed workings of the numerical processes but it is important that he is aware of the assumptions which have been made, and of the limitations and implications. Also, in the happy event that he has several different algorithms at his disposal, he must always be able to select the most appropriate for each application.

We shall first outline three different methods of frequency-domain MDOF curve-fitting and shall, as before, use the hysteretically-damped system as our example. However, as we engage the more sophisticated techniques of numerical analysis, we need be less concerned with the detailed differences between viscous and hysteretic damping models. Mathematically, the difference is simply that in one version the imaginary parts of the FRF expression are constant while in the other (viscous) they are frequency-dependent. The various methods all share the feature of permitting a curve-fit to the entire FRF measurement in one step and the three approaches considered here are:

(i)   an extension of the SDOF method outlined in 4.2;
(ii)   a general approach to multi-mode curve-fitting; and
(iii)   a method particularly suited to very lightly-damped structures.

One final note before we examine the details: the comments in Section 4.5 concerning residuals apply in exactly the same way to these cases for MDOF analysis. Indeed, as we are proposing to consider the entire curve in one step, rather than an isolated mode, it is necessary to incorporate the residual terms from the outset. If we do not do so, then the modal parameters which would result from the modal analysis would be distorted in order to compensate for the influence of the out-of-range modes in the measured data.

4.6.2   Method 1: Extension of SDOF Method

In the circle-fit and associated SDOF modal analysis methods discussed above, an assumption was made that near the resonance under analysis, the effect of all the other modes could be represented by a constant. By building on the results thus obtained, we can relax that restriction and thereby make a more precise analysis of the data.

We can write the following expression for the receptance FRF in the frequency range of interest:

$$\alpha_{jk}(\omega) = \sum_{s=m_1}^{m_2} \frac{{}_sA_{jk}}{\omega_s^2-\omega^2+i\eta_s\omega_s^2} + \frac{1}{{}^KR_{jk}} - \frac{1}{\omega^2{}^MR_{jk}} \qquad (4.21a)$$

which we can arrange into two terms as:

$$\alpha_{jk}(\omega) = \frac{{}_rA_{jk}}{\omega_r^2-\omega^2+i\eta_r\omega_r^2} + \sum_{\substack{s=m_1 \\ \neq r}}^{m_2} \frac{{}_sA_{jk}}{\omega_s^2-\omega^2+i\eta_s\omega_s^2} + \frac{1}{{}^KR_{jk}} - \frac{1}{\omega^2{}^MR_{jk}}$$

$$(4.21b)$$

In the previous methods, the second term was assumed to be a constant throughout the curve-fit procedure to find the modal parameters for mode r. However, if we have some (good) estimates for the coefficients which constitute the second term, for example by having already completed a SDOF analysis, we may remove the restriction on the analysis. Suppose we take a set of measured data points around the resonance at ω_r and denote these as:

$\alpha^m{}_{jk}(\omega)$

then at each frequency for which we have a measured FRF value, we can compute the magnitude of the second term in (4.21b) and subtract this from the measurement. The resulting adjusted data points should then conform to a true single-degree-of-freedom behaviour as demonstrated by:

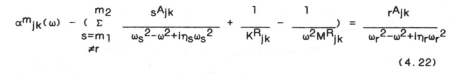

$$\alpha^m{}_{jk}(\omega) - (\sum_{\substack{s=m_1 \\ \neq r}}^{m_2} \frac{{}_sA_{jk}}{\omega_s{}^2-\omega^2+i\eta_s\omega_s{}^2} + \frac{1}{K^R{}_{jk}} - \frac{1}{\omega^2M^R{}_{jk}}) = \frac{{}_rA_{jk}}{\omega_r{}^2-\omega^2+i\eta_r\omega_r{}^2}$$

$$(4.22)$$

and we can use the same technique as before to obtain better estimates to the modal parameters for mode r. This procedure can be repeated iteratively for all the modes in the range of interest as many times as is necessary to obtain convergence to acceptable answers. It is often found that on 'normal' FRF data, where most of the modes are relatively weakly coupled, the improvement in the modal parameters is quite small – see Figure 4.10 for an example – but in cases where there is stronger coupling, the enhancement can be significant.

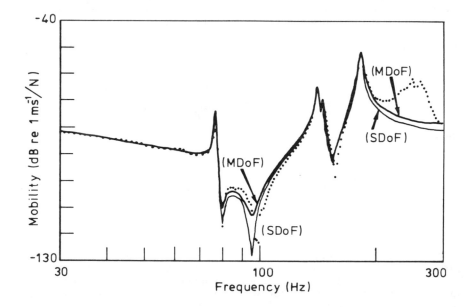

Fig 4.10   Comparison of SDOF and MDOF Curve-Fits

4.6.3   Method 2:   General Curve-Fit Approach

The previous method was presented as it forms a natural development of the earlier SDOF analysis method but it paves the way for more general methods of MDOF curve-fitting.   Many of the longer-established modal analysis techniques were devised in the days of less powerful computation facilities, and may, as a result, seem somewhat pedestrian by current numerical analysis standards.   However, they often have the advantage thay they permit the user to retain rather more direct contact with the processes being used than would be the case in a more powerful, and automatic algorithm.   The secret is to maintain a balance between computational sophistication on the one hand (which might just be thwarted by the relatively poor quality of the input data), and the lengthy and often tedious practices which involve the user in many of the decisions.

However, we can describe the basics of a general MDOF curve-fit philosophy, detailed implementation of which has been perfected by many workers and made widely available.   We shall denote the individual FRF measured data as:

$$\alpha^m_{jk}(\Omega_l) = \alpha^m_l \qquad (4.23a)$$

while the corresponding 'theoretical' values are denoted by

$$\alpha_{jk}(\Omega_l) = \alpha_l = \sum_{s=m_1}^{m_2} \frac{{}_sA_{jk}}{\omega_s^2 - \Omega_l^2 + i\eta_s\omega_s^2} + \frac{1}{K_{jk}^R} - \frac{1}{\Omega_l^2 M_{jk}^R} \qquad (4.23b)$$

where the coefficients ${}_1A_{jk}, {}_2A_{jk} \ldots \omega_1, \omega_2 \ldots \eta_1, \eta_2 \ldots . K_{jk}^R$ and M_{jk}^R are all to be determined.   We can define an individual error as ϵ_l where:

$$\epsilon_l = (\alpha^m_l - \alpha_l) \qquad (4.24)$$

and express this as a scalar quantity:

$$E_l = |\epsilon_l^2| \qquad (4.25)$$

If we further increase the generality by attaching a weighting factor w_l to each frequency point of interest, then the curve-fit process has to determine the values of the unknown coefficients in (4.23) such that the total error:

$$E = \sum_{l=1}^{p} w_l E_l \qquad (4.26)$$

is minimised.   This is achieved by differentiating the expression in (4.26) with respect to each unknown in turn, thus generating a set of as many equations as there are unknowns, each of the form:

$$(dE/dq) = 0; \quad q = {}_1A_{jk}, \; {}_2A_{jk}, \; \ldots \; \text{etc} \qquad (4.27)$$

Unfortunately, the set of equations thus formed are not linear in many of the coefficients (all the ω_s and η_s parameters) and thus cannot be solved directly. It is from this point that the differing algorithms choose their individual procedures, making various simplifications and assumptions in order to contain the otherwise very large computational task to within reasonable proportions. Most use some form of iterative solution, some linearise the expressions in order to simplify the problem and almost all rely heavily on good starting estimates. For further details the reader is referred to various papers such as [14] and [15].

4.6.4 Method 3: Lightly–Damped Structures

It is found that some structures do not provide FRF data which respond very well to the above modal analysis procedures mainly because of difficulties encountered in acquiring good measurements near resonance. This problem is met on very lightly–damped structures, such as is the case for many components of engineering structures when treated individually. For such structures, also, it is often the case that interest is confined to an undamped model of the test structure since the damping in a complete structural assembly is provided mostly from the joints and not from the components themselves. Thus, there is scope for an alternative method of modal analysis which is capable of providing the required modal properties – in this case, natural frequencies and (real) modal constants only – using data measured away from the resonance regions. Such a method, which is very simple to implement, is described below.

The requirements for the analysis are as follows:

(i)   measure the FRF over the frequency range of interest;
(ii)   locate the resonances (obvious for this type of structure) and note the corresponding natural frequencies (which will thus be measured with an accuracy equal to the frequency resolution of the analyser);
(iii)   select individual FRF measurement data points from as many frequencies as there are modes, confining the selection to points away from resonance;
(iv)   using the data thus gathered, compute the modal constants (as described below);
(v)   construct a regenerated curve and compare with the full set of measured data points.

The theory behind the method is quite simple and will be presented for the ideal case of all modes being included in the analysis. If, as discussed earlier, the frequency range chosen excludes some modes, these are represented as two additional modes with natural frequencies supposed to be at zero and at a very high frequency respectively and two additional FRF data points are taken, usually one from close to either end of the frequency range covered.

For an effectively undamped system, we may write:

$$\alpha_{jk}(\omega) = \sum_{r=1}^{N} \frac{{}_sA_{jk}}{\omega_r^2 - \omega^2} \qquad (4.28)$$

which, for a specific value, measured at frequency Ω_l, can be rewritten in the form:

$$\alpha_{jk}(\Omega_l) = \{(\omega_1^2 - \Omega_l^2)^{-1} \ (\omega_2^2 - \Omega_l^2)^{-1} \ . \ . \ .\} \begin{Bmatrix} {}_1A_{jk} \\ {}_2A_{jk} \\ \cdot \\ \cdot \\ \cdot \end{Bmatrix} \qquad (4.29)$$

If we collect a total of N such individual measurements, these can be expressed by a single equation:

$$\begin{Bmatrix} \alpha_{jk}(\Omega_1) \\ \alpha_{jk}(\Omega_2) \\ \cdot \\ \cdot \end{Bmatrix} = \begin{bmatrix} (\omega_1^2 - \Omega_1^2)^{-1} & (\omega_2^2 - \Omega_1^2)^{-1} & \cdot \cdot \\ (\omega_1^2 - \Omega_2^2)^{-1} & (\omega_2^2 - \Omega_2^2)^{-1} & \cdot \cdot \\ \cdot & & \cdot \cdot \\ \cdot & \cdot & \cdot \cdot \end{bmatrix} \begin{Bmatrix} {}_1A_{jk} \\ {}_2A_{jk} \\ \cdot \\ \cdot \end{Bmatrix} \qquad (4.30a)$$

or

$$\{\alpha_{jk}(\Omega)\} = [R] \ \{A_{jk}\} \qquad (4.30b)$$

from which a solution for the unknown modal constants $_rA_{jk}$ in terms of the measured FRF data points $\alpha_{jk}(\Omega_l)$ and the previously identified natural frequencies ω_r may be obtained:

$$\{A_{jk}\} = [R]^{-1} \ \{\alpha_{jk}(\Omega)\} \qquad (4.31)$$

An example of the application of the method is shown in Figure 4.11 for

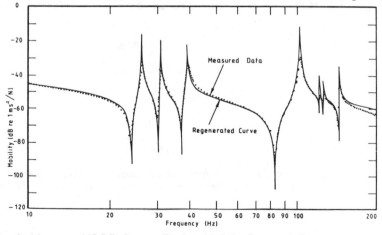

Fig 4.11   MDOF Curve-Fit for Lightly Damped Structure

an aerospace structure while further details of its finer points are presented in Reference [16]. The performance of the method is found to depend upon the points chosen for the individual FRF measurements, and these should generally be distributed throughout the frequency range and, wherever possible, should include as many antiresonances as are available. This last feature has the particular advantage that at an antiresonance, the theoretical model will exhibit a zero response: hence it is possible to supply such a nil value for the appropriate data in equation (4.31). In the limit, this means that only one FRF data point may be required from the measurements, all the others being set to be identically zero, even though from the measurements on a real structure their values would be extremely small, but finite.

4.7 MDOF CURVE-FITTING IN THE TIME DOMAIN

4.7.1 Complex Exponential Method

As mentioned earlier in this Chapter, there are a number of alternative modal analysis methods which work on measured data in a time domain format, rather than the more familiar frequency domain versions. Most of the available methods derive from a technique known as the 'complex exponential' method, although there are several variants and refinements which have been introduced in order to make the numerical procedures more efficient and suitable for small computers. The basis of the method, whose principal advantage is that it does not rely on initial estimates of the modal parameters, is outlined below.

As the method uses the time domain version of system response data, in the form of the Impulse Response Function, its present application is limited to models incorporating viscous damping only. (It will be recalled that the hysteretic damping model presents difficulties for a time domain analysis.) Our starting point is the expression for the receptance FRF of a general MDOF system with viscous damping, which may be written as:

$$\alpha_{jk}(\omega) = \sum_{r=1}^{N} \frac{{}_rA_{jk}}{\omega_r\zeta_r + i(\omega - \omega_r\sqrt{1-\zeta_r^2})} + \frac{{}_rA^*_{jk}}{\omega_r\zeta_r + i(\omega + \omega_r\sqrt{1-\zeta_r^2})} \qquad (4.32a)$$

or

$$\alpha_{jk}(\omega) = \sum_{r=1}^{2N} \frac{{}_rA_{jk}}{\omega_r\zeta_r + i(\omega - \omega_r')} \quad ; \quad \begin{array}{l} \omega_r' = \omega_r\sqrt{1-\zeta_r^2} \\ \omega'_{r+N} = -\omega_r' \\ {}_{(r+N)}A_{jk} = {}_rA^*_{jk} \end{array} \qquad (4.32b)$$

From classical theory, we can obtain the corresponding Impulse Response Function (IRF) by taking the Inverse Fourier Transform of the receptance:

$$h_{jk}(t) = \sum_{r=1}^{2N} {}_rA_{jk}e^{s_rt} \; ; \; s_r = -\omega_r\zeta_r + i\omega_r' \tag{4.33}$$

If the original FRF has been measured, or obtained, in a digital form, and is thus described at each of a number of equally-spaced frequencies, the resulting IRF (found via the Inverse Fourier Transform of the FRF) will similarly be described at a corresponding number of equally-spaced time intervals ($\Delta t = 1/\Delta f$) and we may conveniently define this data set as follows:

$$h_0, \; h_1, \; h_2, \; . \; . \; . \; = h(0), \; h(\Delta t), \; h(2\Delta t), \; . \; . \; . \tag{4.34}$$
$$. \; . \; h_q \qquad\qquad\qquad . \; . \; h(q\Delta t)$$

From this point, it is convenient to omit the jk subscript and to use an abbreviated notation, as follows:

$${}_rA_{jk} \rightarrow A_r \; ; \quad e^{s_r\Delta t} \rightarrow V_r \tag{4.35}$$

so that equation (4.33) becomes:

$$h(t) = \sum_{r=1}^{2N} A_r e^{s_rt} \tag{4.36}$$

Thus, for the lth sample, we have:

$$h_l = \sum_{r=1}^{2N} A_r V_r^l \tag{4.37a}$$

which, when extended to the full data set of q samples, gives:

$$
\begin{array}{llllll}
h_0 & = & A_1 & + & A_2 \; . \; . \; . \; + & A_{2N} \\
h_1 & = & V_1A_1 & + & V_2A_2 \; . \; . \; . \; + & V_{2N}A_{2N} \\
h_2 & = & V_1^2A_1 & + & V_2^2A_2 \; . \; . \; . \; + & V_{2N}^2A_{2N} \\
\vdots & & \vdots & & \vdots & \vdots \\
h_q & = & V_1^qA_1 & + & V_2^qA_2 \; . \; . \; . \; + & V_{2N}^qA_{2N}
\end{array}
\tag{4.37b}
$$

Provided that the number of sample points q exceeds 4N, this equation can be used to set up an eigenvalue problem, the solution to which yields the complex natural frequencies contained in the parameters V_1, V_2 etc., via a solution using the Prony method.

Taking (4.37), we now multiply each equation by a coefficient, β_i, to form the following set of equations:

$$\beta_0 \ h_0 \ = \ \beta_0 \ A_1 \ + \ \beta_0 \ A_2 \ + \ . \ . \ . \ \beta_0 \ A_{2N}$$

$$\beta_1 \ h_1 \ = \ \beta_1 \ A_1 \ V_1 \ + \ \beta_1 \ A_2 \ V_2 \ + \ . \ . \ . \ \beta_1 \ A_{2N} \ V_{2N}$$

$$\beta_2 \ h_2 \ = \ \beta_2 \ A_1 \ V_1^2 \ + \ \beta_2 \ A_2 \ V_2^2 \ + \ . \ . \ . \ \beta_2 \ A_{2N} \ V_{2N}^2$$

$$.$$
$$.$$
$$.$$

$$\beta_q \ h_q \ = \ \beta_q \ A_1 \ V_1^q \ + \ \beta_q \ A_2 \ V_2^q \ + \ . \ . \ . \ \beta_q \ A_{2N} \ V_{2N}^q \tag{4.38}$$

Adding all these equations gives

$$\sum_{i=0}^{q} \beta_i \ h_i \ = \ \sum_{j=1}^{2N} (A_j \sum_{i=0}^{q} \beta_i \ V_j^i) \tag{4.39}$$

What are the coefficients, β_i? These are taken to be the coefficients in the equation

$$\beta_0 + \beta_1 \ V + \beta_2 \ V^2 + \ . \ . \ . \ \beta_q \ V^q = 0 \tag{4.40}$$

for which the roots are V_1, V_2, . . . V_q.

We shall seek to find values of the β coefficients in order to determine the roots of (4.40) – values of V_r – and hence the system natural frequencies. Now, recall that q is the number of data points from the Impulse Response Function, while 2N is the number of degrees of freedom of the system's model (constituting N conjugate pairs of 'modes'). It is now convenient to set these two parameters to the same value, i.e. to let q = 2N.

Then from (4.40) we can see that

$$\sum_{i=0}^{2N} \beta_i \ V_r^i = 0 \qquad \text{for } r = 1, \ 2N \tag{4.41}$$

and thus that every term on the RHS of (4.39) is zero so that

$$\sum_{i=0}^{2N} \beta_i \ h_i = 0 \tag{4.42}$$

thus we shall rearrange (4.42) so that

$$\sum_{i=0}^{2N-1} \beta_i \ h_i = -h_{2N} \qquad \text{by setting } \beta_{2N}=1 \tag{4.43}$$

and this may be written as:

$$\{h_0 \ h_1 \ h_2 \ \ldots \ h_{2N-1}\} \begin{Bmatrix} \beta_0 \\ \beta_1 \\ \cdot \\ \cdot \end{Bmatrix} = -h_{2N} \qquad (4.44)$$

Now, we may repeat the entire process from equation (4.34) to (4.44) using a different set of IRF data points and, further, we may choose the new data set to overlap considerably with the first set – in fact, for all but one item – as follows

$$\{h_1 \ h_2 \ h_3 \ \ldots \ h_{2N}\} \begin{Bmatrix} \beta_0 \\ \beta_1 \\ \cdot \\ \cdot \end{Bmatrix} = -h_{2N+1} \qquad (4.45)$$

Successive applications of this procedure lead to a full set of 2N equations:

$$\begin{bmatrix} h_0 & h_1 & h_2 & \ldots & h_{2N-1} \\ h_1 & h_2 & h_3 & \ldots & h_{2N} \\ \cdot & \cdot & \cdot & \ldots & \cdot \\ \cdot & \cdot & \cdot & \ldots & \cdot \\ h_{2N-1} & h_{2N} & h_{2N+1} & \ldots & h_{4N-2} \end{bmatrix} \begin{Bmatrix} \beta_0 \\ \beta_1 \\ \cdot \\ \cdot \\ \beta_{2N-1} \end{Bmatrix} = - \begin{Bmatrix} h_{2N} \\ h_{2N+1} \\ \cdot \\ \cdot \\ h_{4N-1} \end{Bmatrix}$$

or

$$\underset{2N\times2N}{[h]} \quad \underset{2N\times1}{\{\beta\}} \quad = \quad \underset{2N\times1}{-\{\widetilde{h}\}} \qquad (4.46a)$$

from which we can obtain the unknown coefficients:

$$\{\beta\} = -[h]^{-1} \{\widetilde{h}\} \qquad (4.46b)$$

With these coefficients, we can now use (4.40) to determine the values $V_1, V_2 \ldots V_{2N}$ from which we obtain the system natural frequencies, using the relationship

$$V_r = e^{s_r \Delta t}$$

We may now complete the solution by deriving the corresponding modal constants, $A_1, A_2, \ldots A_{2N}$ using equation (4.37). This may be written as

$$\begin{bmatrix} 1 & 1 & \cdot & \cdot & \cdot & 1 \\ V_1 & V_2 & \cdot & \cdot & \cdot & V_{2N} \\ V_1^2 & V_2^2 & \cdot & \cdot & \cdot & V_{2N}^2 \\ \cdot & \cdot & & & & \cdot \\ V_1^{2N-1} & V_2^{2N-1} & \cdot & \cdot & & V_{2N}^{2N-1} \end{bmatrix} \begin{Bmatrix} A_1 \\ A_2 \\ A_3 \\ \cdot \\ A_{2N} \end{Bmatrix} = \begin{Bmatrix} h_0 \\ h_1 \\ h_2 \\ \cdot \\ h_{2N-1} \end{Bmatrix}$$

or

$$[V] \ \{A\} = \{h\} \qquad (4.47)$$

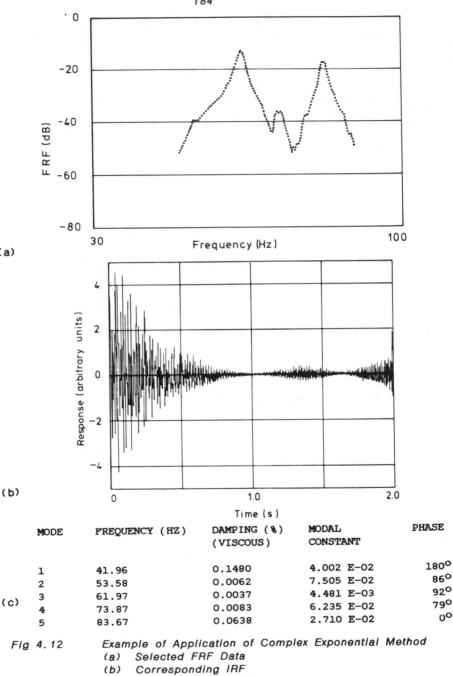

MODE	FREQUENCY (HZ)	DAMPING (%) (VISCOUS)	MODAL CONSTANT	PHASE
1	41.96	0.1480	4.002 E-02	180°
2	53.58	0.0062	7.505 E-02	86°
3	61.97	0.0037	4.481 E-03	92°
4	73.87	0.0083	6.235 E-02	79°
5	83.67	0.0638	2.710 E-02	0°

Fig 4.12   Example of Application of Complex Exponential Method
            (a)   Selected FRF Data
            (b)   Corresponding IRF
            (c)   Results of Curve-Fit

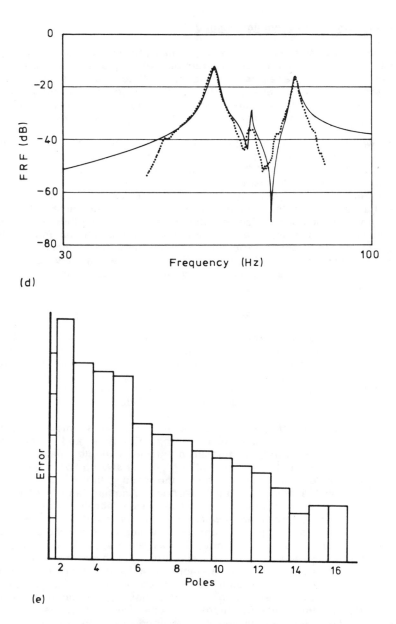

(d)

(e)

Fig 4.12   Example of Application of Complex Exponential Method
(d)   Regenerated Curves (5 modes)
(e)   Error Plot to Determine Number of Modes

Use of Complex Exponential Method

The foregoing method is generally employed in the following way. An initial estimate is made for the number of degrees of freedom and the above mentioned analysis is made. When completed, the modal properties thus found are used in (4.32) to compute a regenerated FRF curve which is then compared with the original measured data. At this stage, the deviation or error between the two curves can be computed.

The whole procedure is then repeated using a different number of assumed degrees of freedom (2N) and this error again computed. A plot of error vs number of DOF will generally produce a result of the form shown in Figure 4.12 in which there should be a clearly-defined reduction in the error as the 'correct' number of degrees of freedom is attained. The inclusion of a larger number than this critical value will cause the creation of a number of 'computational' modes in addition to the genuine 'physical' modes which are of interest. Such additional modes serve to account for the slight imperfection inevitably present in measured data and are generally easily identified from the complete list of V_r and A_r modal properties by their unusually high damping factors and/or small modal constants.

4.7.2 Ibrahim Time Domain Method

Directly following the previous section on the complex exponential method, it is appropriate now to introduce the Ibrahim Time Domain (ITD) technique. Although the ITD method is not strictly a curve-fitting procedure in the sense that all the preceding ones are and, indeed, it would fit more readily into the next section, we shall present it here as a logical extension of the complex exponential idea.

The basic concept of the ITD method is to obtain a unique set of modal parameters – natural frequencies, damping factors and mode shapes – from a set of free vibration measurements in a single analysis. In other words, we shall not be curve-fitting or analysing a single FRF (or equivalent) at a time, as has been the case hitherto, but we shall be processing all the measured data at once. Another feature of the method is that it can be used with any measured free vibration data, whether or not the excitation forces are available. In the event that these data are known, then it is possible to derive fully scaled eigenvector properties, otherwise only the unscaled mode shapes will be available along with the modal frequency and damping parameters. Perhaps the most likely way in which the method will be applied in a modal testing context is by measuring a set of FRF properties – based on a selection as prescribed in the next chapter – and then by using these to obtain a corresponding set of Impulse Response Functions. These may then be used as the free response data required by the ITD method with the knowledge that the magnitude of the excitation which produced them (a unit impulse) is implicit.

The theory of the method is as follows. As before, it is based on the free vibration solution of a viscously-damped MDOF system and takes as

Its starting point the assumption that we may write any individual response as:

$$x_i(t_j) = \sum_{r=1}^{2m} {}_r\psi_i \; e^{s_r t_j} \qquad\qquad (4.48)$$

where i represents the coordinate and j the specific time increment at which the response is measured; s_r is the rth root or complex eigenvalue of the system's characteristic equation (see Equation 2.73) and $\{\psi\}_r$ is the corresponding eigenvector, with ${}_r\psi_i$ being the ith element in that vector. At this point, the eigenvectors are unscaled. Also, we are assuming that the total number of degrees of freedom available in our model is m. In fact, this is not necessarily the same as the number of degrees of freedom of the system (N): m is the number of degrees of freedom which are necessary to represent the measured data and this may be possible with many less than the full set if, for example, the response is confined to a limited frequency range, as will usually be the case in practice.

Now, if we measure the response at several points on the structure − i=1, n − and at several instants in time − i=1, q − then we can construct a matrix equation of the form:

$$\begin{bmatrix} x_1(t_1) & x_1(t_2) & .. & x_1(t_q) \\ x_2(t_1) & x_2(t_2) & .. & x_2(t_q) \\ . & . & & . \\ x_n(t_1) & x_n(t_2) & .. & x_n(t_q) \end{bmatrix} = \begin{bmatrix} {}_1\psi_1 & {}_2\psi_1 & .. & {}_{2m}\psi_1 \\ {}_1\psi_2 & {}_2\psi_2 & .. & {}_{2m}\psi_2 \\ . & . & & . \\ {}_1\psi_n & {}_2\psi_n & .. & {}_{2m}\psi_n \end{bmatrix} \begin{bmatrix} e^{s_1 t_1} & ... & e^{s_1 t_q} \\ e^{s_2 t_1} & ... & e^{s_2 t_q} \\ . & & . \\ e^{s_{2m} t_1} & ... & e^{s_{2m} t_q} \end{bmatrix}$$

$$(4.49a)$$

or, in simpler form:

$$[x] = [\psi] \; [\Lambda] \qquad\qquad (4.49b)$$

Here, [x] is an n x q matrix of free response measurements from the structure, and is known;
[ψ] is an n x 2m matrix of unknown eigenvector elements; and
[Λ] is a 2m x q matrix depending on the complex eigenvalues (as yet unknown) and the response measurement times (which are known).

A second, similar, equation is then formed by using a second set of measured response data, each item of which relates to a time which is exactly Δt later than for the first set. Thus we have:

$$x_i(t_j+\Delta t) = \sum_{r=1}^{2m} {}_r\psi_i \; e^{s_r(t_j+\Delta t)} \qquad\qquad (4.50a)$$

or:

$$\hat{x}_i(t_j) = \sum {}_r\hat{\psi}_i \; e^{s_r(t_j)} ; \quad {}_r\hat{\psi}_i = {}_r\psi_i \; e^{s_r\Delta t} \qquad (4.50b)$$

which leads to a second set of equations:

$$[\hat{x}] = [\hat{\Psi}] \ [\Lambda] \tag{4.51}$$

Next, remembering that the number of assumed modes (m) is a variable (we do not yet know how many modes are required to describe the observed motion), we can arrange that $n = 2m$, so that the matrices $[\Psi]$ and $[\hat{\Psi}]$ are square. It may be seen that these two matrices are closely related and we can define a matrix [A], often referred to as the 'system matrix', as:

$$[A] \ [\Psi] = [\hat{\Psi}] \tag{4.52}$$

From (4.49b) and (4.51), we find

$$[A] \ [x] = [\hat{x}] \tag{4.53}$$

and this provides us with a means of obtaining [A] from the measured data contained in [x] and [$\hat{x}$]. If we have selected the number of time samples (q) to be identical to the number of measurement points (n), (which we have now set to be equal to 2m), then [A] can be obtained directly from Equation (4.53). However, it is customary to use more data than the minimum required by setting q to a value greater than 2m. In this case, use of Equation (4.53) to determine [A] will be via the pseudo-inverse process which yields a least-squares solution for the matrix, using all the data available. In this case, an expression for [A] is:

$$[A] = [\hat{x}] \ [x]^T \ ([\hat{x}] \ [x]^T)^{-1} \tag{4.54}$$

Returning now to Equation (4.50), we can see that individual columns in $\{\psi\}_r$ are simply related to the corresponding ones in $\{\hat{\psi}\}_r$ by the relationship:

$$\{\hat{\psi}\}_r = \{\psi\}_r e^{s_r \Delta t} \tag{4.55}$$

Thus, using (4.52) we can write:

$$[A] \ \{\psi\}_r = (e^{s_r \Delta t}) \ \{\psi\}_r \tag{4.56}$$

which will be recognised as a standard form of a set of equations whose solution is obtained by determining the eigenvalues of the matrix [A]. It must be noted immediately that these eigenvalues are NOT the same as those of the original equations of motion (since equation (4.56) is not an equation of motion) but they are closely related and we shall see that it is a straightforward process to extract the system's natural frequencies, damping factors and mode shapes from the solution to Equation (4.56). The eigenvalues of [A] are the particular values of $(e^{s_r \Delta t})$ and so if we have λ_r as one of these eigenvalues, then we can determine the corresponding complex natural frequency of the system (s_r) from:

$$e^{s_r \Delta t} = \lambda_r = a_r + ib_r = e^{-\omega_r \zeta_r \Delta t} \, e^{i\omega_r' \Delta t} = c_r \, e^{i\theta_r}$$

$$c_r = (a_r^2 + b_r^2)^{1/2}; \qquad \theta_r = \tan^{-1}(-b_r/a_r) \qquad\qquad (4.57a)$$

from which we can derive the natural frequency (ω_r) and viscous damping factor (ζ_r) using

$$\omega_r \, \zeta_r = -\ln (a_r^2 + b_r^2) \, / \, (2\Delta t)$$

$$\omega_r' = \omega_r \sqrt{1 - \zeta_r^2} = \tan^{-1} (b_r/a_r) \, / \, \Delta t \qquad\qquad (4.57b)$$

Corresponding to each eigenvalue there is an eigenvector and this can be seen to be identical to the mode shape vector for that mode. No further processing is required in this case. It should, however, be noted that the mode shapes thus obtained are generally unscaled and, as such, are inadequate for regenerating FRF curves. Only if the original free vibration response data were derived from a FRF-IRF procedure can scaled (mass-normalised) eigenvectors be obtained.

Use of the ITD Method

As with other similar procedures, the ITD method requires the user to make some decisions and judgements concerning which of his measurements to use for the calculation (there will generally be an excess of measured data). For example, there will often be more response points than there are genuine modes to be identified, but the method will always produce one mode per two response points. Examination of the set of modal properties, and especially the modal damping factors, will generally indicate which are genuine structural modes and which are 'fictitious' modes caused by noise or other irregularities in the measured data. Various techniques are proposed for a systematic examination of the results as the number of assumed degrees of freedom is increased. Generally, these methods look for a 'settling down' of the dominant modes of vibration, or for a marked reduction in the least-squares error between the original measured data and that regenerated on the basis of the identified modal properties. Further details of the method, and its sensitivity to various parameters are provided in reference [18].

4.8 MULTI-CURVE FITS

In the next chapter we shall be discussing how results from the modal analysis of several FRF plots for a given structure may be further processed in order to yield the full modal model. At the present time, having performed modal analysis on each of the individual frequency responses, we have found the natural frequencies and damping factors but we do not yet have the mode shapes explicitly – only combinations of the individual eigenvector elements as modal constants. A further stage of processing is required – here referred to as 'modelling' – in order to combine the various individual results obtained thus far. However, that phase is somewhat anticipated by some of the more recent curve-fitting procedures which are not confined to working with individual curves but which are capable of performing a multi-curve fit. In other words, they fit several FRF curves simultaneously, taking due account of the fact that the properties of all the individual curves are related by being from the same structure. In simple terms, all FRF plots on a given testpiece should indicate the same values for natural frequency and damping factor of each mode. In practice, this does not happen exactly, unless they are constrained to be identical, and in the next chapter we discuss ways of dealing with this apparently unsatisfactory result. However, in a multi-curve fit, the constraints are imposed ab initio and such methods have the advantage of producing a unique and consistent model as direct output. One of the first published methods was that by Goyder [19], using an extension of the frequency domain method. Other methods, such as the Ibrahim Time Domain and one referred to as 'Polyreference' [20] are also available.

Another way in which a set of measured FRF curves may be used collectively, rather than singly, is by the construction of a single composite Response Function. We recall that

$$\alpha_{jk}(\omega) = \sum_{r=1}^{n} {}_rA_{jk}/(\omega_r^2-\omega^2+i\omega_r^2\eta_r) \qquad (4.58)$$

and note that if we simply add several such FRFs, thus:

$$\sum_j \sum_k \alpha_{jk}(\omega) = \sum_j \sum_k \left(\sum_{r=1}^{N} (\ldots) \right) = HH(\omega) \qquad (4.59)$$

The resulting function $HH(\omega)$ will have the frequency and damping characteristics of the structure appearing explicitly, just as does any individual FRF, although the coefficients Σ_r (which replace the modal constants) are now very complicated combinations of the mode shape elements which depend heavily upon which FRFs have been used for the summation. Nevertheless, the composite function $HH(\omega)$ can provide a useful means of determining a single (average) value for the natural frequency and damping factor for each mode where the individual functions would each indicate slightly different values.

As an example, a set of mobilities measured in a practical structure are shown individually in Figure 4.13a and their summation shown as a single composite curve in Figure 4.13b. The results from analysis of the separate curves produce estimates for the natural frequency and damping factor for each mode, and these can be used to derive a mean value for each modal parameter. Also available are the unique values for each parameter produced by analysis of the single composite curve.

A similar property applies to the impulse response functions for use with time domain, rather than frequency domain, analysis methods.

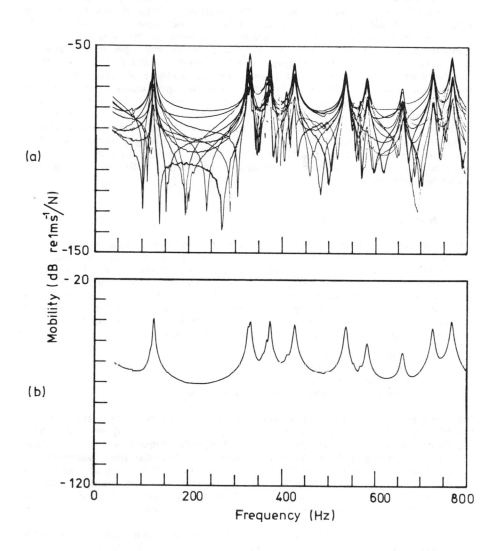

Fig 4.13   Curve-Fitting Several FRF Curves
               (a)   Individual Curves
               (b)   Composite Curve

Both frequency domain and time domain methods are amenable to the expansion to multi-curve analysis. The techniques are simply quantitative extensions of their single curve counterparts and have as disadvantages first, the computation power required is unlikely to be available in an on-line mini-computer, and secondly that there may be valid reasons why the various FRF curves exhibit slight differences in their characteristics and it may not always be appropriate to average out all the variations. Throughout the whole procedure of mobility measurements and modal analysis, we invoke the averaging process many times – to smooth rough FRF curves, to reduce the effects of measurement noise, to remove discrepancies and anomalies between different modal properties – and we should always remember that averaging is a valid means of removing random variations but it is not an appropriate way of treating systematic variations. We do not always make that distinction.

4.9 NON-LINEAR SYSTEMS

We have seen in earlier chapters that slight non-linearities in the system behaviour can result in distortions in the measured FRF curves, and that the results produced by sinusoidal, random and transient excitations are all different. At this stage, it is interesting to investigate the consequences of these effects on the modal analysis process and this can effectively be achieved by using the SDOF circle fit method described in Section 4.3. We shall use this method, and in particular the graphical display of the damping estimates it produces, to examine

   (a) theoretically-generated FRF data;
   (b) data measured on an analogue computer circuit with controlled non-linear effects; and
   (c) tests on a practical built-up structure.

For the first case, using theoretical data, we show some results for a system with cubic stiffness non-linearity, Figure 4.14a, and one with coulomb friction (as well as viscous) damping, Figure 4.14b. In both cases, a striking and systematic variation in the damping estimates is seen, with a different trend for each of the two cases. It is clear from these results that taking the average of several such damping estimates is pointless – the resulting mean value being heavily dependent upon which estimates are included rather than on how many.

Turning next to some measured data obtained using the standard analysis instrumentation (FRA and FFT) but from measurements made on an analogue computer programmed to behave as a SDOF system with an added cubic stiffness non-linearity, Figure 4.15a shows a typical result obtained from a sinusoidal excitation measurement while Figure 4.15b gives the corresponding result for narrow band random excitation set to generate approximately the same vibration level. The first result clearly demonstrates the trend predicted by theory while the second one shows no signs of such effects and, indeed, does not suggest the existence of any non-linearity in the tested system. However, this result is not unexpected in view of the processing to which the measured data have

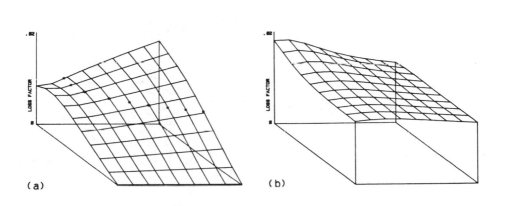

Fig 4.14   *Identification of Nonlinearity Via Modal Analysis*
                  (a)   Theoretical System with Cubic Stiffness
                  (b)   Theoretical System with Coulomb Damping

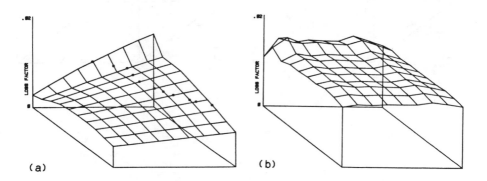

Fig 4.15   *Modal Analysis of Analogue Computer Measurements*
                  (a)   Sinusoidal Excitation
                  (b)   Narrow-band Random Excitation

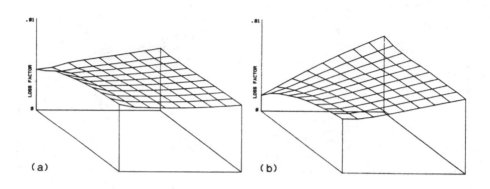

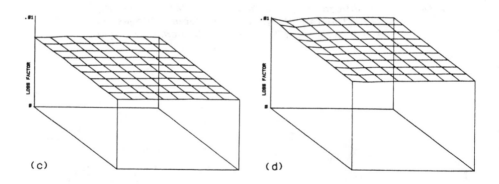

Fig 4.16   Modal Analysis of FRF Data Measured by Sinusoidal Excitation
(a)   Constant Force – Low Level
(b)   Constant Force – High Level
(c)   Constant Response – Low Level
(d)   Constant Response – High Level

been subjected – the formulae used to compute the FRF assume and rely on superposition – and it is found that the function produced by DFT analysis is that for a linearisation of the actual tested system.

The last results are taken from a series of measurements on a complete built-up structure and refer to a specific mode and to a specific FRF – mode 3 in mobility $Y_{7,12}$ – measured using sinusoidal excitation. The first two plots, in Figure 4.16(a) and (b) result from measurements made during two different constant-excitation level tests and show clear signs of systematic non-linearity (although for a more complex form than the specific cubic stiffness type examined above). The second two examples, in Figures 4.16(c) and (d) refer to exactly the same resonance but this time result from tests made at two different constant-response levels. Here, the data from either measurement are clearly very linear although the numerical values of the modal parameters differ for the two different cases. In this test, the behaviour of the structure has been consciously linearised, under known conditions, along the lines proposed in the discussion on measurement techniques, Chapter 3.11.

Large Structure Undergoing Modal Test

CHAPTER 5
Derivation of
Mathematical Models

5.0   INTRODUCTION

At this stage we have described all the main tools available to the modal
analyst.   Now we consider how these may be marshalled in order to
achieve the original objective, namely that of deriving a mathematical
model of the test structure.   It will be recalled from the earlier parts of
the book that we found it convenient to classify the various types of model
which can be constructed and also to consider the many different
applications for which these models might be required.   The subject is
sufficiently broad that no single model is suitable for all cases and so the
particular combination of measurement and analysis steps will vary
according to the application.   Thus we arrive at a most important aspect
of the modelling process: the need to decide exactly which type of model
we should seek before setting out on the acquisition and processing of
experimental data.

It will be recalled that three main categories of system model were
identified, these being the Spatial Model (of mass, stiffness and damping
properties), the Modal Model (comprising the natural frequencies and
mode shapes) and the Response Model (in our case, consisting of a set
of frequency response functions).   In addition to this grouping, we have
also seen that there exist Complete Models of each type (a theoretical
ideal) and the more realistic Incomplete Models, which consist of
something less than a full description of the structure.   In almost all
practical cases, we are obliged to consider these incomplete models.

While the relative sequence of these three types of model has previously
been stated as Spatial-Modal-Response for a theoretical analysis and,
conversely, Response-Modal-Spatial for an experimental study, we now
view them in a different order, according to the facility with which each
may be derived from the test data.   This viewpoint ranks the models:
Modal, Response and then Spatial and directly reflects the quantity of the
completeness of data required in each case.

A modal model (albeit an incomplete one) can be constructed using just
one single mode, and including only a handful of coordinates, even

though the structure has many modes and coordinates. Such a model can be built up by adding data from more modes but it is not a requirement that all the modes should be included nor even that all the modes in the frequency range of interest must be taken into account. Thus such a model may be derived with relatively few, or equally, with many data.

The response type of model in the form of a FRF matrix, such as the mobility matrix, also need only include information concerning a limited number of points of interest – not all the coordinates must be considered. However, in this case it is generally required that the model be valid over a specified frequency range and here it is necessary that all the modes in that range be included, and moreover, that some account be taken of those modes whose natural frequencies lie outside the range of interest. Thus, the response type of model demands more data to be collected from the tests.

Lastly, a representative spatial model can only really be obtained from experimental data if we have measured most of the modes of the structure and if we have made measurements at a great many of the coordinates it possesses. This is generally a very difficult requirement to meet and, as a result, the derivation of a spatial model is very difficult to achieve successfully.

5.1 MODAL MODELS

A modal model of a structure is one which consists of two matrices: one containing the natural frequencies and damping factors of the modes included, and a second one which describes the shapes of the corresponding modes. Thus, we can construct such a model with just a single mode and, indeed, a more complete model of this type is assembled simply by adding together a set of these single-mode descriptions.

The basic method of deriving a modal model is as follows. First, we note that from a single FRF curve, Y_{jk}, it is possible to extract certain modal properties for the rth mode by curve-fitting so that we can determine

$$Y_{jk}(\omega) \rightarrow \omega_r, \ \eta_r, \ _rA_{jk} \ ; \ r = 1, \ m \qquad (5.1)$$

Now, although this gives us the natural frequency and damping properties directly, it does not explicitly yield the mode shape: only a modal constant which is formed from the mode shape data. In order to extract the 'individual' elements of the mode shape matrix, [Φ], it is necessary to make a series of measurements of specific frequency response functions including, especially, the point mobility at the excitation position. If we measure Y_{kk}, then using (5.1) we see that analysis of this curve will yield not only the natural frequency properties, but also the specific elements in the mode shape matrix corresponding to the excitation point via:

$$Y_{kk}(\omega) \rightarrow \omega_r, \; \eta_r, \; _rA_{kk} \rightarrow _r\phi_k \; ; \; r = 1, \; m \tag{5.2}$$

If we then measure any transfer FRF using the same excitation position, such as Y_{jk}, we are able to deduce the mode shape element corresponding to the new response point using the fact that the relevant modal constants may be combined with those from the point measurement:

$$_r\phi_j = _rA_{jk}/_r\phi_k \tag{5.3}$$

Hence we find that in order to derive a modal model referred to a particular set of n coordinates, we need to measure and analyse a set of n FRF curves, all sharing the same excitation point (or the same response point, in the event that it is the excitation which is varied) and thus constituting one point and (n−1) transfer FRFs. In terms of the complete FRF matrix, this corresponds to a requirement to measure one column (or one row, since the FRF matrix is generally symmetric), see Figure 5.1a. In practice, however, this requirement is the barest minimum of data which will provide the necessary model and it is prudent to measure rather more than a single column. Often, several additional elements from the FRF matrix would be measured to provide a check, or to replace poor data, and sometimes a complete second column or row might be advised in order to ensure that one or more modes have not been completely missed by an unfortunate choice of exciter location, see Figure 5.1b.

Once all the selected FRF curves have been measured and individually analysed, using the most appropriate methods from Chapters 3 and 4, there remains a further stage of processing to be done. Using any of the single-curve modal analysis methods outlined in Chapter 4, we shall find ourselves in possession of a set of tables of modal properties containing rather more data than we are seeking. In particular, we shall have determined many separate estimates for the natural frequency and damping factor of each mode of interest as these parameters are extracted from each FRF curve in the measured set. In theory, all such estimates should be identical but in practice they seldom are, even allowing for experimental errors, and we must find a way to reduce them to the single value for each property which theory demands. A similar situation arises for the mode shape parameters also in the event that we have measured more than the minimum FRF data, i.e. if we have measured more than one row or column from the FRF matrix.

The simplest procedure is simply to average all the individual estimates to obtain mean values, ω_r and η_r. In practice, not all the estimates would carry equal weight because some would probably derive from much more satisfactory curve-fits than others and so a more refined procedure would be to calculate a weighted mean of all the estimates, taking some account of the reliability of each. In fact, it is possible to attach a quality factor to each curve-fit parameter extraction in most of the methods described in Chapter 4 and these quality factors serve well as weighting functions for an averaging process such as that just suggested.

$$\begin{bmatrix} \alpha_{11} & \alpha_{12} & \cdots & \alpha_{1i} & \cdots & \alpha_{1j} & \cdots & \alpha_{1N} \\ \alpha_{21} & \alpha_{22} & \cdots & \alpha_{2i} & \cdots & \alpha_{2j} & \cdots & \alpha_{2N} \\ \cdot & \cdot & & \cdot & & \cdot & & \cdot \\ \cdot & \cdot & & \cdot & & \cdot & & \cdot \\ \alpha_{i1} & \alpha_{i2} & \cdots & \alpha_{ii} & \cdots & \alpha_{ij} & \cdots & \alpha_{iN} \\ \cdot & \cdot & & \cdot & & \cdot & & \cdot \\ \cdot & \cdot & & \cdot & & \cdot & & \cdot \\ \alpha_{j1} & \alpha_{j2} & \cdots & \alpha_{ji} & \cdots & \alpha_{jj} & \cdots & \alpha_{jN} \\ \cdot & \cdot & & \cdot & & \cdot & & \cdot \\ \cdot & \cdot & & \cdot & & \cdot & & \cdot \\ \alpha_{N1} & \alpha_{N2} & \cdots & \alpha_{Ni} & \cdots & \alpha_{Nj} & \cdots & \alpha_{NN} \end{bmatrix}$$

(a)   Minimum Data Requirement

$$\begin{bmatrix} \alpha_{11} & \alpha_{12} & \cdots & \alpha_{1i} & \cdots & \alpha_{1j} & \cdots & \alpha_{1N} \\ \alpha_{21} & \alpha_{22} & \cdots & \alpha_{2i} & \cdots & \alpha_{2j} & \cdots & \alpha_{2N} \\ \cdot & \cdot & & \cdot & & \cdot & & \cdot \\ \cdot & \cdot & & \cdot & & \cdot & & \cdot \\ \alpha_{i1} & \alpha_{i2} & \cdots & \alpha_{ii} & \cdots & \alpha_{ij} & \cdots & \alpha_{iN} \\ \cdot & \cdot & & \cdot & & \cdot & & \cdot \\ \cdot & \cdot & & \cdot & & \cdot & & \cdot \\ \alpha_{j1} & \alpha_{j2} & \cdots & \alpha_{ji} & \cdots & \alpha_{jj} & \cdots & \alpha_{jN} \\ \cdot & \cdot & & \cdot & & \cdot & & \cdot \\ \cdot & \cdot & & \cdot & & \cdot & & \cdot \\ \alpha_{N1} & \alpha_{N2} & \cdots & \alpha_{Ni} & \cdots & \alpha_{Nj} & \cdots & \alpha_{NN} \end{bmatrix}$$

(b)   Typical Data Selection

Fig 5.1   Frequency Response Function Matrix

It is important to note that if we choose to accept a mean or otherwise revised value for the natural frequency and damping factor of a particular mode, then in some cases the values assumed for the modal constants should be revised accordingly. For example, we noted in the circle-fitting procedure that the diameter of the modal circle is given by:

$$_rD_{jk} = {_rA_{jk}}/(\omega_r^2\eta_r) \qquad\qquad (5.4)$$

and so if we redefine ω_r and η_r then we should revise the value of $_rA_{jk}$ since there is no reason to modify the circle diameter itself. Thus, we obtain a corrected set of modal constants, and so mode shape elements for each curve analysed using:

$$_r\tilde{A}_{jk} = {_rA_{jk}}\ \omega_r^2\eta_r/(\tilde{\omega}_r^2\tilde{\eta}_r) \qquad\qquad (5.5)$$

where the $\sim$ indicates a revised value.

As mentioned towards the end of Chapter 4, there now exist a number of advanced curve-fitting methods which obviate the need for the above stage of the process by the simple device of making their analysis of the complete set of FRF curves in a single step. Whatever method is used to reduce the analysed data to their final form, this must consist of the two matrices which constitute a modal model, namely:

$$\lceil\ \omega_r^2(1+i\eta_r)\ \rfloor_{mxm}\ ,\ [\Phi]_{nxm}$$

Finally, mention should be made of a simplified form of the modal model which can be obtained rather more quickly than by following the above procedure. This alternative approach requires first the measurement and full analysis of one FRF, preferably the point mobility, in order to determine values for the natural frequencies and damping factors. But then the analysis of the subsequent FRF curves consists simply of measuring the diameters of the modal circles, omitting the stages which yield further natural frequency and damping estimates. Such a procedure is acceptable in those cases where one has total confidence in the first or reference FRF measurement, or where accuracy is not of paramount concern.

5.2 DISPLAY OF MODAL MODEL

One of the attractions of the modal model is the possibility of obtaining a graphic display of its form by plotting the mode shapes, thereby giving some visual insight into the way in which the structure is vibrating. As there are a number of alternatives for this phase, and a number of important features, it is worth discussing them briefly.

Once the modal model has been determined and tabulated according to the description given in the previous section, there are basically two choices for its graphical display: a static plot or a dynamic (animated) display. While the former is far less demanding than the latter in respect of the material necessary to produce the display, it does have serious limitations in its ability to illustrate some of the special features of complex modes. In cases where the modes have significant complexity and individual displacements have phase angles which are not simply 0° or 180° from the others, only an animated display is really capable of presenting a realistic image.

Static Display

However, a static display is often adequate for depicting relatively simple mode shapes and, in any case, is the only format suitable for permanent documentation in reports. The procedure is to draw first an outline of the test structure using a viewpoint which permits visibility of all important points on the structure. Usually, this drawing is formed of a frame linking the various coordinates included in the modal survey, such as that shown in Figure 5.2a for a stiffened plate, and often this datum grid is drawn in faint or broken lines. Then, the grid of measured coordinate points is redrawn on the same plot but this time displaced in each direction (x, y and z) by an amount proportional to the corresponding element in the mode shape matrix. The elements in the matrix are scaled according to the normalisation process used – and are usually mass-normalised – and their absolute magnitudes have no particular significance in the present process. It is customary to select the largest eigenvector element and to scale the whole vector by an amount that makes that displacement on the plot a viable amount. It is not possible to dictate how large a deflection is 'viable' as this depends on the particular mode shape as well as on the complexity of the structural form itself. It is necessary to be able to see how the whole structure deforms but the displacements drawn on the plot must not be so large that the basic geometry of the structure appears to be violated. Figure 5.2b shows a suitable plot for a mode of the plate previously illustrated in 5.2a.

In this process, it will be necessary to assign a positive or negative phase to each element in the mode shape vector. Only phase angles which are effectively 0° or 180° with respect to the norm can be accommodated on this type of plot even though the results from the modal test may indicate marked deviations from such a pattern. Thus, it is often necessary to perform a 'whitewashing' exercise on the modal data and sometimes this requires making difficult judgements and decisions, such as how to incorporate an eigenvector element whose phase angle is closer to 90° than to 0° or 180°. Fortunately, this dilemma is most often encountered on modal deflections which are relatively small so that they do not influence the overall shape of the plot very much. However, the selection of positive or negative phase for such a point usually has the effect of determining the location of a nodal point or line, and this in itself may be important.

Dynamic Display

The above-mentioned difficulties are avoided by the alternative display, that of the animated mode shape. Using a suitable VDU and

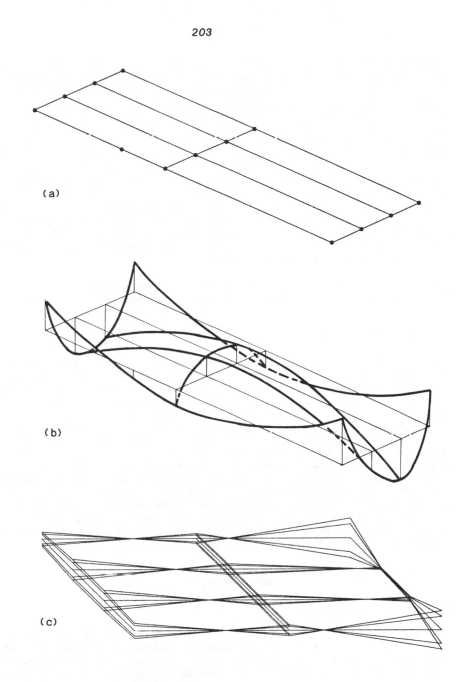

Fig 5.2   Mode Shape Plots
           (a)   Basic Grid
           (b)   Deformed Mode Shape
           (c)   Freeze-Frame of Animated Mode Shape

computation facilities, it is possible to display on the screen a plot of the type just described, and to update this picture at regular and frequent intervals of time so that a simulation of the vibration is displayed in slow motion. Usually what is done is that the coordinates for the basic picture are computed and stored, as are a corresponding set for a fraction of a vibration cycle later, and then for a further fraction of a cycle later, and so on. Each of these sets of data constitutes one 'frame' and some 10-20 frames are used for a complete cycle, i.e. at intervals of some 20° to 40° in angular frequency. Once this data set has been constructed, successive frames are displayed with an update rate which is suitable to give a clear picture of the distortion of the structure during vibration; a rate which can be adjusted to accommodate the varying phase angles of complex modes. Another advantage of most animated mode shape displays is the additional facility of changing the viewpoint from which the picture is drawn, often necessary as different modes can be best viewed from different orientations.

A static plot can be obtained from a dynamic display simply by 'freezing' the animation (i.e. by requesting a zero update rate) : see Fig. 5.2c.

5.3 RESPONSE MODELS

There are two main requirements in the form of a response model, the first being that of regenerating 'theoretical' curves for the frequency response functions actually measured and analysed and the second being that of synthesising the other functions which were not measured. In general, the form of response model with which we are concerned is a FRF matrix whose order is dictated by the number of coordinates included in the test. (Note that this is not necessarily equal to the number of modes studied.) Also, as explained in Section 5.1, it is not normal practice to measure and analyse all the elements in the FRF matrix but rather to select a small fraction of these, usually based on one column or row with a few additional elements included as a backup. Thus, if we are to construct an acceptable response model it will be necessary to synthesise those elements which have not been directly measured. However, in principle this need present no major problem as it is always possible to compute the FRF matrix from a modal model using:

$$[\alpha] = [\Phi] \ulcorner (\lambda_r^2 - \omega^2) \lrcorner^{-1} [\Phi]^T \qquad (5.6)$$
$$\text{nxn} \qquad \text{nxm} \qquad \text{mxm} \qquad \text{mxn}$$

Regenerated FRF Curves

It is usual practice to regenerate a FRF curve using the results from the modal analysis as a means of checking the success of that analysis, as described in Chapter 4. However, if the collected results from several FRF curves are subjected to an averaging process, such as that described in Section 5.1, then a new regenerated curve should be produced and, if necessary, a new set of residuals computed (see Section 4.5.). It should be noted at this stage that in order to construct an acceptable response model, it is essential that all the modes in the frequency range of interest be included, as also are suitable residual terms to take account of out-of-range modes. In this respect, the demands of the response model are more stringent than those of the modal model.

Synthesis of FRF Curves

One of the implications of equation (5.6) is that it is possible to synthesise the FRF curves which were not measured. In simple terms, this arises because if we measure three individual mobilities such as $Y_{ik}(\omega)$, $Y_{jk}(\omega)$ and $Y_{kk}(\omega)$, then modal analysis of these yields the modal parameters from which it is possible to generate, or 'synthesise' the mobilities $Y_{ij}(\omega)$, $Y_{jj}(\omega)$ etc. Indeed, application of this principle is sometimes suggested as a means of checking the overall performance of a modal analysis exercise.

However, it must be noted that there is an important limitation to this procedure which can sometimes jeopardise the success of the whole exercise. This limitation derives from the fact that only that part of the relevant FRF which is due to the modes whose properties are available can be computed. The remaining part, due to the out-of-range modes – the residual part – is NOT available by this method of synthesis and, as a result, a response model thus formed is liable to error unless values for the relevant residual terms are available.

As an example, the result of applying this synthesis procedure to measurements made on a turbine rotor are shown in Figure 5.3. Mobility data Y_{11} and Y_{21}, at and between the ends of the rotor, were measured and analysed and the resulting modal parameters used to predict or 'synthesise' the other mobility Y_{22}, initially unmeasured. This predicted curve was then compared with measurements, producing the result shown in Figure 5.3a. Clearly, the agreement is poor and would tend to indicate that the measurement/analysis process had not been successful. However, the 'predicted' curve contained only those terms (in the complete modal series) relating to the modes which had actually been studied from Y_{11} and Y_{21} and this set of modes (as is often the case) did not include all the modes of the structure. Thus our predicted curve, Y_{22}, omitted the influence of out-of-range modes or, in other words, lacked the residual terms. The inclusion of these two additional terms (obtained here only after measuring and analysing Y_{22} itself) resulted in the greatly improved predicted vs measured comparison shown in Figure 5.3b

The appropriate expression for a 'correct' response model, derived via a set of modal properties, is thus:

$$[\alpha] = [\Phi] \ulcorner (\lambda_r^2 - \omega^2) \lrcorner^{-1} [\Phi]^T + [R] \qquad (5.7)$$

In order to obtain all the data necessary to form such a model, we must first derive the modal model on which it is based (as described in 5.1) and then find some means of determining or estimating the elements in the residual matrix, [R]. This latter task may be most accurately

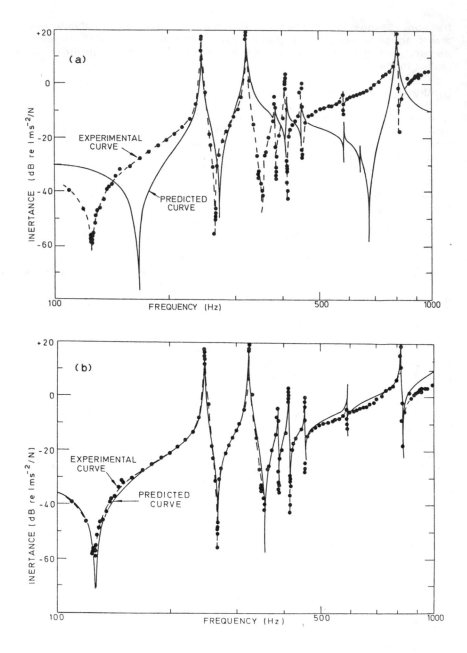

Fig 5.3   Synthesised FRF Plot
               (a)   Using Measured Modal Data Only
               (b)   After Addition of Residual Terms

achieved by measuring all (or at least something over half) of the elements in the FRF matrix, but this would constitute a major escalation in the quantity of data to be measured and analysed. A second possibility, and a reasonably practical one, is to extend the frequency range of the modal test beyond that over which the model is eventually required. In this way, much of the contents of the residual terms is included in separate modes and their actual magnitudes are reduced to relatively unimportant dimensions. The main problem with this approach is that one does not generally know when this last condition has been achieved although a detailed examination of the regenerated curves using all the modes obtained and then again less the highest one(s) will give some indications in this direction.

A third possibility is to try to assess which of the many FRF elements are liable to need large residual terms and to make sure that these are included in the list of those which are measured and analysed. We noted earlier that it is the point mobilities which are expected to have the highest-valued residuals and the remote transfers which will have the smallest. Thus, the significant terms in the [R] matrix will generally be grouped close to the leading diagonal, and this suggests making measurements of most of the point mobility parameters. Such a procedure will seldom be practical unless analysis indicates that the response model is ineffective without such data, in which case it may be the only option.

Direct Measurement

Finally on this topic, it should be noted that it is quite possible to develop a response model by measuring and analysing all the elements in one half of the FRF matrix (this being symmetric, only one half is essential) and by storing the results of this process without constructing a modal model, or 'modal data base' as this is sometimes called. Such a procedure clearly solves the residual problem discussed above but it is likely to present another one by introducing inconsistencies into the model. Unless the structural behaviour, the measurements and the analysis are all of a remarkable calibre, the small differences described in Section 5.1 will be locked into the response model thus formed and will undoubtedly cause serious difficulties when that model is put to use. At the very least, the natural frequencies and damping factors of the individual modes should be rationalised throughout the model but even that is insufficient to ensure a satisfactory model.

Many of the same comments apply to the very crude method of obtaining a response model by simply storing the raw measurements made of each of the elements in the FRF matrix, a technique which bypasses the data reduction and smoothing facilities afforded by modal analysis. Although there are some instances where this is a viable procedure, they are rare and rather special.

5.4   SPATIAL MODELS

It would appear from the basic orthogonality properties of the modal model that there exists a simple means of constructing a spatial model from the modal model, but this is not so.   From Section 2.3 we have that:

$$[\Phi]^T [M] [\Phi] = \lceil I \rfloor$$

$$[\Phi]^T [K] [\Phi] = \lceil \lambda_r^2 \rfloor \tag{5.8}$$

from which it would appear that we can write:

$$[M] = [\Phi]^{-T} [\Phi]^{-1}$$

$$[K] = [\Phi]^{-T} \lceil \lambda_r^2 \rfloor [\Phi]^{-1} \tag{5.9}$$

Indeed, we can, but this latter equation is only applicable when we have available the complete NxN modal model.   This is seldom the case and it is much more usual to have an incomplete model in which the eigenvector matrix is rectangular and, as such, is non-invertible.   Even if we constrain the number of modes to be the same as the number of coordinates (an artificial and often impractical restriction) so that the matrix is square, the mass and stiffness matrices produced by equation (5.9) are mathematical abstractions only and carry very little physical significance, unless n is almost equal to N.

One step which can be made using the incomplete data is the construction of 'pseudo' flexibility and inverse-mass matrices.   This is accomplished using the above equations in the form:

$$\underset{nxn}{[K]^{-1}} = \underset{nxm}{[\Phi]} \underset{mxm}{\lceil \lambda_r^2 \rfloor^{-1}} \underset{mxn}{[\Phi]^T}$$

$$\underset{nxn}{[M]^{-1}} = \underset{nxm}{[\Phi]} \underset{mxn}{[\Phi]^T} \tag{5.10}$$

It is clear that a pair of pseudo matrices can be computed using the properties of just a single mode.   Further, it can be seen that the corresponding matrices are simply the arithmetic sums of those for each mode individually.   Because the rank of each pseudo matrix is less than its order, it cannot be inverted and so we are unable to construct stiffness or mass matrices from this approach.

Further discussion on the construction of spatial models may be found in the section concerned with the correlation of theory and experiment, Section 6.2.

5.5   MOBILITY SKELETONS AND SYSTEM MODELS

We have seen earlier how mobility and other FRF plots tend towards mass-like or stiffness-like behaviour at frequencies well away from resonance (and antiresonance). We have also suggested (in Section 4.1), that a 'skeleton' of mass and stiffness lines can be constructed based on the FRF curve and that this can be used to check the overall quality of the measured curve. We shall now examine these skeletons in rather more detail and show how they may be used to construct simple spatial models of a test structure.

We shall establish the basic features of the skeleton using a very simple mass-spring-mass 2DOF system, shown in Figure 5.4a and for which the point mobility Y_{11} has the form shown in Figure 5.4b.

Certain basic features of this plot may be predicted from knowledge of the system, without necessarily computing the FRF in detail. These features are that:

(i) there will be an antiresonance at $\omega_A{}^2 = k_1/m_2$ (note that this frequency is independent of the value of m_1 and would still apply if m_1 were doubled, or trebled or replaced by any combination of masses and stiffnesses):

(ii) there will be a resonance at $\omega_R{}^2 = k(1/m_1+1/m_2)$;

(iii) at very low frequencies ($\omega \ll \omega_A$) the FRF will be dominated by the rigid body motion of the system, since it is ungrounded, and will approximate to

$$Y_{11} \ (\omega \ll \omega_A) \simeq -i/\omega(m_1+m_2);$$

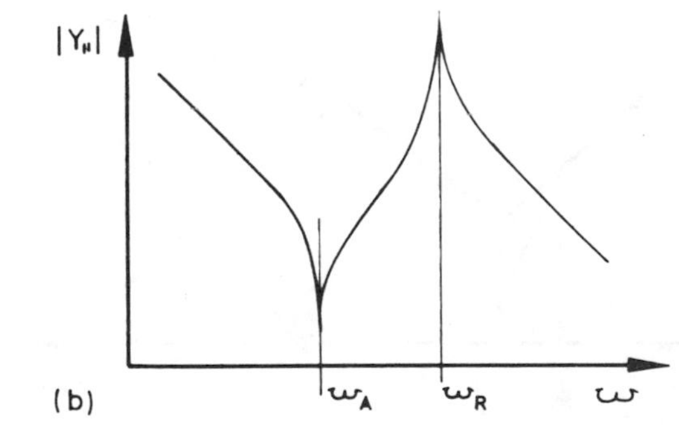

(a)

(b)

Fig 5.4   Basic Mass-Spring-Mass System and Mobility Plot

(iv)   similarly, at high frequencies, the FRF will be dominated by the mass of the drive point, so

$$Y_{11} \; (\omega > \omega_R) \simeq -i/(\omega m_1)$$

Now, it is possible to draw a skeleton of mass and stiffness lines on this FRF plot, changing from stiffness to mass at each resonance and from mass back to stiffness at each antiresonance, as sketched in Figure 5.5a.

The question is raised as to whether, when we construct such a skeleton starting from the low frequency asymptote of the FRF curve, the final arm (above ω_r) will also be asymptotic to the mobility curve as in 5.5b, or not (as in 5.5a). If it can be shown that the former case applies,

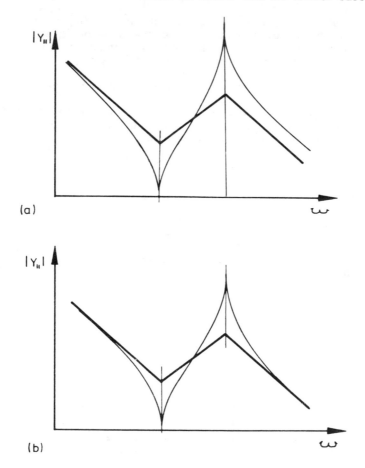

(a)

(b)

Fig 5.5   Concept of the Mobility Skeleton

then it is likely that a more general rule obtains which, in effect, requires the skeleton to 'follow' the FRF curve. The proof of such a property may be made using the 2DOF system, and referring to Figure 5.6a, as follows.

Suppose we define the skeleton as consisting of an initial mass line (m_1') for a mass of ($m_1 + m_2$) plus a final mass line (m_2') corresponding to the mass m_1, connected by a stiffness line (k_1') which meets the first

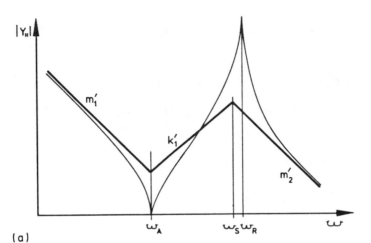

(a)

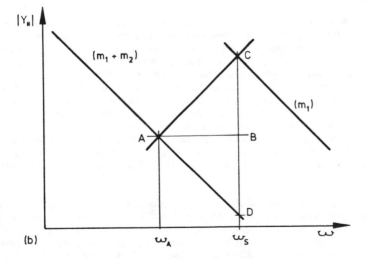

(b)

Fig 5.6   *Geometry of the Mobility Skeleton*

branch at the known antiresonance, ω_A. This skeleton satisfies the overall requirement that it 'follows' the FRF away from resonance and antiresonance but we have not yet imposed or met the condition that the change from stiffness (k_1') to mass (m_2') occurs at the resonant frequency, ω_R. Suppose these two branches meet at ω_S. Using the geometry of the skeleton shown in Figure 5.6b , we see that

$$AB = BC = BD = CD/2$$

Now

$$AB = \beta(\log \omega_S - \log \omega_A) = \beta \log (\omega_S/\omega_A)$$

Also:

$$CD = \beta (\log|Ym_2'(\omega_S)| - \log|Ym_1'(\omega_S)|)$$

$$= \beta \log (|Ym_2'(\omega_S)|/|Ym_1'(\omega_S)|) = \beta \log((m_1+m_2)/m_1)$$

So:

$$2\beta \log (\omega_S/\omega_A) = \beta \log ((m_1+m_2)/m_1)$$

or:

$$\omega_S^2 = \omega_A^2 ((m_1+m_2)/m_1) = k(m_1+m_2)/m_1 m_2$$

$$= \omega_R^2$$

Hence, the skeleton connecting the extreme asymptotic behaviour of the FRF changes from mass-like to stiffness-like and back to mass-like elements at antiresonance and resonance respectively.

This basic idea can be extended to more complex systems and the general rule for constructing skeletons is that the first will be mass-like (slope = −1 on mobility or alternate values for other FRF forms) or stiffness-like (mobility slope = +1) depending upon whether the structure is freely supported or grounded, respectively. Thereafter, the slope of the skeleton changes by +2 at each antiresonance and by −2 at each resonance. Thus, for a point mobility the skeleton branches are all of slope +1 or −1 but for a transfer mobility the slopes will be +1, −1, −3, −5, . . . and so on as the absence of an antiresonance between two resonances will cause a general downward drift of the skeleton (and, of course, of the FRF curve itself). By way of example, two of the set of FRF curves shown in Figure 2.16 are repeated in Figure 5.7 together with their skeletons.

It will be noted from the first example above, Figure 5.4a , that the physical system has three components, two masses and a spring (m_1, m_2 and k_1) and that the corresponding skeleton has two mass lines and one spring line (m_1', m_2' and k_1'). While it must be acknowledged that there is no direct correspondence between the two similar sets of parameters, they are related and each set may be derived from the

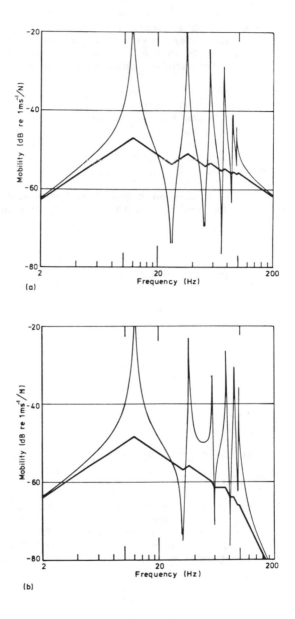

Fig 5. 7   *Mobility Skeletons for 6DOF System*

other. Indeed, this is a general rule that the skeleton for the point FRF contains just as many mass and stiffness links as there are corresponding elements in the physical system. This fact provides us with a mechanism for deriving spatial models from measured data.

It must be observed at the outset that it is left to the user to decide upon the configuration of the suitable model: analysis of the skeleton will then furnish the values for the model parameters. Consider the FRF indicated in Figure 5.8a.

Clearly, this relates to a 2DOF system such as that shown in Figure 5.8b or the one shown in Figure 5.8c.

In the first case, it can be shown that the model parameters may be determined from the skeleton parameters using the following formulae:

$$m_1 = m_2'$$

$$k_1 = m_2' \, (\omega_1^2 + \omega_2^2 - \omega_A^2) = m_2' \, (\frac{k_1'}{m_1'} + \frac{k_2'}{m_2'} - \frac{k_2'}{m_1'})$$

$$k_2 = (k_1) \, k_1' \, / \, ((k_1) - k_1')$$

$$m_2 = (k_1) + (k_2)/\omega_A^2$$

Alternatively, if the second configuration was the correct one, then the model parameters would be

$$k_1 = k_1'$$

$$m_1 = m_2'$$

$$k_2 = (m_2) \, (\omega_1^2 + \omega_2^2 - \omega_A^2) - (k_1)$$

$$m_2 = (k_2)/\omega_A^2$$

Hence the solution obtained is not unique and additional data would be required in the example above in order to establish which of the two configurations was the more representative. The additional data could be provided by other FRF plots. In his book, Salter [3] develops the skeleton idea in greater detail, presenting a useful additional tool to the modal analyst.

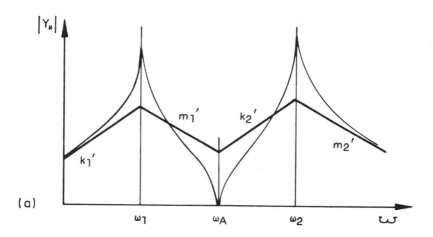

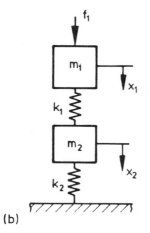

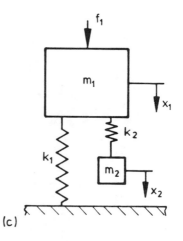

Fig 5.8   Mobility Skeleton of a 2DOF System
             (a) Mobility Curve and Skeleton
             (b) Possible System Configuration
             (c) Possible System Configuration

CHAPTER 6
Applications

6.0   INTRODUCTION

We turn our attention now to the destination of the final results from conducting a modal test: namely, the problem which we set out to resolve.   As mentioned in the first chapter, there are many possible application areas for modal tests and the major ones were described there.   We shall now consider these in turn and examine in more detail the specific procedures and methods which are available for each.

It should be noted at the outset, however, that the application of the techniques described below to practical engineering structures is often found to be more difficult or more onerous than at first expected.   This is due to many factors, not least the considerable volume of data usually required for real cases (by comparison with that used in simpler illustrative examples) and the inevitable incompleteness of the data which can be acquired under typical practical testing conditions and constraints. Nevertheless, this 'fact of life' should not be permitted to provide a deterrent to the ambitious or the tentative application of any of the procedures listed below.   The techniques can be used with great effect, especially if the user is fully aware of the extent or limitations of his data. Furthermore, dramatic advances are being made in measurement and analysis techniques which will reduce the limitations and enhance both the availability and quality of good data, thus enabling the modal analyst to make even more precise and confident assessments of structural dynamic behaviour.

6.1   COMPARISON OF EXPERIMENT AND PREDICTION

6.1.1   Different Methods of Comparison

Probably the single most popular application of modal testing is to provide a direct comparison between predictions for the dynamic behaviour of a structure and those actually observed in practice.   Sometimes this process is referred to as 'validating' a theoretical model although to do this effectively several steps must be taken.   The first of these is to make a direct and objective comparison of specific dynamic properties, measured vs predicted. The second (or, perhaps still part of the first) is to quantify the extent of the differences (or similarities) between the two sets of data. Then, third, to make adjustments or modifications to one or other set of results in order to bring them closer into line with each other. When this is achieved, the theoretical model can be said to have been validated and is then fit to be used for further analysis. In this section we shall be concerned with the first (and, to some extent, the second) of these stages, dealing with the others later.

In most cases, a great deal of effort and expense goes into the processes which lead to the production of an experimentally-derived model on the one hand (subsequently referred to as the 'experimental' model or data) and a theoretically-derived (or 'predicted') model on the other. This being so, it is appropriate to make as many different types or levels of comparison between the two sets of data as possible. As discussed much earlier in the work, we have identified three types of dynamic model, loosely called 'Spatial', 'Modal' and 'Response'. It is now convenient to return to this classification and to try to make comparisons between experiment and prediction at each (or at least more than one) of these. Thus we shall discuss comparisons of response characteristics and of modal properties, as both of these provide many opportunities for useful correlation between experiment and theory. Comparisons of spatial properties are more difficult, however, and we shall leave discussion of this aspect until the next Section (6.2).

Whichever medium is used for comparison purposes, either one or the other model will have to be developed fairly extensively from its original form and what is the most convenient format for one case will be the least accessible for the other. This situation derives from the different routes taken by theoretical and experimental approaches to structural vibration analysis, as shown in Figures 2.1 and 2.2. However, in closing these general remarks, it is appropriate to reinforce the recommendation to make as many different types of comparison as possible and not just to rely on one, usually the first one that comes to hand, or mind.

6.1.2 Comparison of Response Properties

If we start with the experimental model, we find that the raw data available in this case are those describing the response properties of the test structure since these are the only parameters we are able to measure directly. For the predicted model, the response properties are those most removed from the basic description of the structure and thus that require the most effort to produce. However, there are fewer uncertainties introduced in the process of computing the frequency response properties from the basic spatial model than arise in the alternative process (of deriving a spatial model of the structure from test data) and so this is the most appropriate form of comparison to be made in the first instance.

In Figure 6.1a we show the comparison between direct measurement and

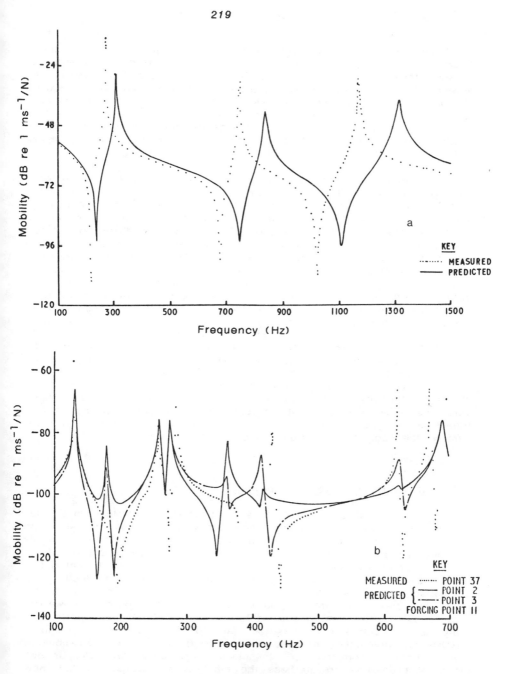

Fig 6.1   Comparison Between Measured and Predicted Mobility Data
            (a)   Point Mobility for Beam Structure
            (b)   Transfer Mobility for Plate Structure

prediction (via a finite element model) of a point FRF for a simple beam-like structure. The plot clearly shows a systematic discrepancy between the two sets of data (resulting in a steady frequency shift between the two curves) while at the same time indicating a high degree of correlation in the amplitude axis. Also of interest are the relative values of the frequencies of resonance and of antiresonance, close examination of which can indicate whether the discrepancies are due to localised errors (loss of stiffness at joints etc) or to more general factors (such as incorrect values of elastic modulus or material density etc).

A second example is shown in Figure 6.1b where a transfer mobility for a different structure is illustrated, again for both experimental and predicted data. However, in this case the location of the response point used in the modal test does not coincide exactly with any of the mesh of grid points used in the analytical model, thereby making a direct comparison impossible. In order to proceed, the predicted curves relating the two grid points closest to the test position (and these were only a few mm away, on a platelike structure of some 1m x 2m) are used and are displayed in Figure 6.1b. In this example, it is clear that not only are there marked differences between the two models (albeit of a different type to the previous case), but also there are striking differences between the two predicted curves which relate to two points very close to each other on the structure. This last observation is very useful when we consider how to assess the degree of correlation between the experimental and predicted models. Because the particular parameter being measured (a FRF) can be very sensitive to the exact location of the response point (and, possibly, to the excitation point, although that does not suffer from the same difficulty as does the response in the example cited), major differences may be apparent at the comparison stage which do not directly reflect on the quality of the model, but on something much more basic – namely, the coordinate geometry used in both instances.

6.1.3 Comparison of Modal Properties

Although the response data are those most directly available from test for comparison purposes, some theoretical analysis packages are less than convenient when it comes to predicting FRF plots. This is largely because of the requirement that all (or at least a large proportion) of the modes must be included in the calculation of a response characteristic. By contrast, modal properties can be predicted individually and comparisons can be confined to specific frequencies or to specific frequency ranges with much greater facility for the analyst. However, such a comparison does place additional demands on the experimental route as it requires the measured data to be subjected to a modal analysis or curve-fitting procedure in order to extract the corresponding modal properties from the test. In spite of this requirement, comparisons of modal properties are perhaps the most common and we shall now describe a number of methods which may be employed to that end.

Comparisons of Natural Frequencies

The most obvious comparison to make is of the measured vs the predicted natural frequencies. This is often done by a simple tabulation of the two sets of results but a more useful format is by plotting the experimental value against the predicted one for each of the modes included in the comparison, as shown in Figure 6.2. In this way it is possible to see not only the degree of correlation between the two sets of results, but also the nature (and possible cause) of any discrepancies which do exist. The points plotted should lie on or close to a straight line of slope 1. If they lie close to a line of different slope then almost certainly the cause of the discrepancy is an erroneous material property used in the predictions. If the points lie scattered widely about a straight line then there is a serious failure of the model to represent the test structure and a fundamental re-evaluation is called for. If the scatter is small and randomly distributed about a 45° line then this may be expected from a normal modelling and measurement process. However, a case of particular interest is where the points deviate slightly from the ideal line but in a systematic rather than a random fashion as this situation suggests that there is a specific characteristic responsible for the deviation and that this cannot simply be attributed to experimental errors.

There is an inclination to quantify the deviation of the plotted points from the ideal straight line as a means of assessing the quality of the comparison. Although this is indeed useful, it cannot replace the benefit gained from the plot itself as (without employing complicated functions) it is generally insensitive to the randomness or otherwise of the deviations and this is an important feature.

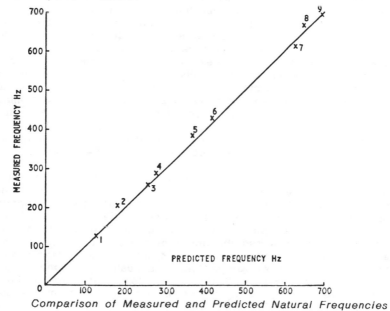

Fig 6.2   *Comparison of Measured and Predicted Natural Frequencies*

Comparisons of Mode Shapes - Graphical

If the above procedure is applied in practical cases, it will often be found more difficult than first anticipated because each of the plotted (or otherwise compared) points implies that the experimental and the predicted frequencies relate to the same mode of vibration. Whereas on simple structures with well-separated modes this presents no difficulty, on more complex structures - perhaps with closely spaced natural frequencies - ensuring that the comparisons are correctly made becomes more difficult and requires the additional information in each case of the mode shape as well as the natural frequency. Hence it is appropriate to make comparisons of mode shapes at the same time as those of natural frequencies.

In this case, we have rather more data to handle for each mode and one possible way of performing the comparison is by plotting the deformed shape for each model - experimental and predicted - along the lines described in Chapter 5, and overlaying one plot on the other. The disadvantage of this approach is that although differences are shown up, they are difficult to interpret and often the resulting plots become very confusing because there is so much information included. A more convenient approach is available by making a plot along similar lines to that used for the natural frequencies in which each element in the mode shape vector is plotted, experimental vs predicted, on an x-y plot such as is shown in Figure 6.3. The individual points on this plot relate to specific coordinates on the models (and so the caution mentioned in the previous section concerning the importance of using the same coordinates for the experimental work as for the theoretical model applies here also) and it is to be expected that they should lie close to a straight line passing through the origin. If, as is often the case, both sets of mode shape data consist of mass-normalised eigenvectors, then the straight line to which the points should be close will have a slope of ±1. Once again, the pattern of any deviation from this requirement can indicate quite clearly the cause of the discrepancy: if the points lie close to a straight line of slope other than ±1, then either one or other mode shape is not mass-normalised or there is some other form of scaling error in the data. If the points are widely scattered about a line, then there is considerable inaccuracy in one or other set and if the scatter is excessive, then it may be the case that the two eigenvectors whose elements are being compared do not relate to the same mode.

This form of presentation has particular value when the deviations of the points from the expected line are systematic in some way, such as is the case in Figure 6.3a . In this event it can be useful to superimpose the plots for several modes so that the basis of the comparison is broadened, and this has been done in Figure 6.3b for the first three modes of the structure. We now see that three of the points on the structure (4, 5 and 6) systematically produce a poor correlation between experiment and prediction although we are not yet in a position to identify which set are in error. From Figure 6.3b it is clear that most of the points for coordinates 4, 5 and 6 do in fact lie close to a straight line but one with a slope considerably different from 45°. If the discrepancy is due to

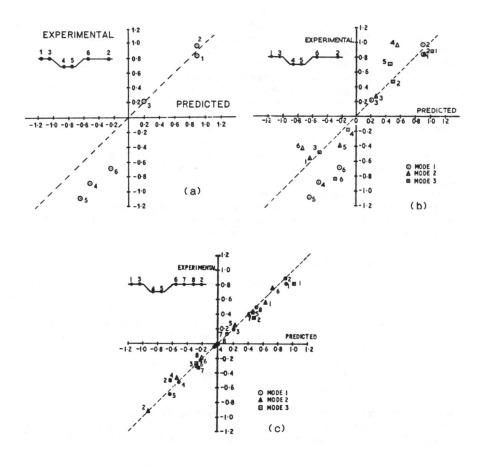

Fig 6.3   *Comparison of Measured and Predicted Mode Shapes*
      (a)   Single Mode   (b)   Three Modes
      (c)   Revised Analysis

poor analytical modelling (the natural assumption of the experimentalist!),
then it might reasonably be expected to differ in extent from one mode to
the next.   However, this is not the case here and it can be seen that the
deviations are consistent with the result which would follow from an
incorrect scaling factor on the FRF plots pertaining to points 4, 5 and 6
(since all modes would be equally affected by such an error).   A repeat
of the measurement (and modal analysis) phase in this case, together
with the inclusion of some additional coordinates, resulted in the revised
plot shown in Figure 6.3c: clearly a much more satisfactory comparison
and one achieved using the original analytical model.

At this juncture, it must be observed that the above method assumes implicitly that the mode shapes in both cases are real (as opposed to complex) and while it is highly likely that the results from a theoretical analysis will indeed comply with this assumption, those from an experimental source will, in general, not be so simple. Although it is possible to envisage a complex version of the type of plot discussed above, by using a third axis to display the imaginary part of each eigenvector element, this is not recommended as it tends to disguise the essential conflict which is inherent in comparing complex (experimental) data with real (predicted) values. It is necessary to make a conscious decision on how to handle this particular problem and that usually adopted is to 'whitewash' the measured data by taking the magnitude of each eigenvector element together with a + or − sign depending on the proximity of the phase angle to 0° or 180°. In many cases this is adequate but it is not satisfactory for highly complex modes. However, no form of comparison between these modes and the real data produced by a typically undamped theoretical model will be effective.

Comparison of Mode Shapes − Numerical

Several workers have developed techniques for quantifying the comparison between measured and predicted mode shapes (in fact, these methods are useful for all sorts of comparisons − not just experiment vs theory − and can be used for comparing any pair of mode shape estimates). As an alternative to the above graphical approach, we can compute some simple statistical properties for a pair of modes under scrutiny. The formulae given below assume that the mode shape data may be complex, and are based on a comparison between an experimentally-measured mode shape $\{\phi_x\}$ and a theoretically predicted one, $\{\phi_p\}$.

The first formula is for a quantity sometimes referred to as the 'Modal Scale Factor' (MSF) and it represents the 'slope' of the best straight line through the points as plotted in Figure 6.3. This quantity is defined as:

$$MSF(x,p) = \sum_{j=1}^{n} (\phi_x)_j \, (\phi_p)_j^* \; / \; \sum_{j=1}^{n} (\phi_p)_j \, (\phi_p)_j^* \qquad (6.1a)$$

and there are two possible expressions relating the two mode shapes, depending upon which is taken as the reference one:

$$MSF(p,x) = \sum_{j=1}^{n} (\phi_p)_j \, (\phi_x)_j^* \; / \; \sum_{j=1}^{n} (\phi_x)_j \, (\phi_x)_j^* \qquad (6.1b)$$

It should be noted that this parameter gives no indication as to the quality of the fit of the points to the straight line; simply its slope.

The second parameter is referred to as a Mode Shape Correlation Coefficient (MSCC) or Modal Assurance Criterion (MAC) and this provides a measure of the least squares deviation of the points from the straight line correlation. This is defined by:

$$MAC(p,x) = |\sum_{j=1}^{n} (\phi_x)_j (\phi_p)_j^*|^2 / (\sum_{j=1}^{n} (\phi_x)_j (\phi_x)_j^*) . (\Sigma(\phi_p)_j(\phi_p)_j^*)$$

(6.2)

and is clearly a scalar quantity, even if the mode shape data are complex. In the same way that the Modal Scale Factor does not indicate the degree of correlation, neither does the Modal Assurance Criterion discriminate between random scatter being reponsible for the deviations or systematic deviations, as described earlier. Thus, whereas these parameters are useful means of quantifying the comparison between two sets of mode shape data, they do not present the whole picture and should preferably be considered in conjunction with the plots of the form shown in Figure 6.3.

It is worth considering two special cases: (i) that where the two mode shapes are identical and (ii) where they differ by a simple scalar multiplier. Thus in case (i), we have:

$$\{\phi_x\} \equiv \{\phi_p\}$$

for which it can be seen that

$$MSF(x,p) - MSF(p,x) = 1$$

and also that:

$$MAC(x,b) = 1$$

In the second case, (ii), we have $\{\phi_x\} = A\{\phi_p\}$ and we find that

$$MSF(x,p) = A \qquad while \qquad MSF(p,x) = 1/A$$

although, since the two modes are still almost perfectly correlated, we still have:

$$MAC(x,p) = 1$$

In practice, typical data will be less ideal than this and what is expected is that if the experimental and theoretical mode shapes used are in fact from the same mode, then a value of the Assurance Criterion of close to 1.0 is expected, whereas if they actually relate to two different modes, then a value close to 0.0 should be obtained. Given a set of m_x experimental modes and a set of m_p predicted modes, wo can compute a matrix of $m_x \times m_p$ Modal Assurance Criteria and present these in a matrix which should indicate clearly which experimental mode relates to which predicted one. It is difficult to provide precise values which the Assurance Criterion should take in order to guarantee good results. However, it is generally found that a value in excess of 0.9 should be attained for correlated modes and a value of less than 0.05 for uncorrelated modes. However, the significance of these quantities depends considerably on the subsequent use planned for the model: some are much more demanding than others.

It is worth noting some of the causes of less-than-perfect results from these calculations. Besides the obvious reason – that the model is incorrect – values of the MAC of less than unity can be caused by:

(i)   nonlinerarities in the test structure;
(ii)   noise on the measured data; and
(iii)   poor modal analysis of the measured data.

6.2   CORRECTION OR ADJUSTMENT OF MODELS

6.2.1   Rationale of Model Adjustment

The next step to be considered is the possibility of extending any of the comparison methods we now have available in order to correct or adjust one or other model. This procedure might set out to produce a refined or optimised set of measured properties (by making certain assumptions as to which set are the more valid) or, alternatively, to adjust the theoretical model in the light of the measurements.

The first step must be to make a rational decision as to which of the two sets of data are to be taken as the reference (ie. the more correct) set. This decision will depend on several factors but will probably include considerations based on the various comments above.

We shall describe four particular approaches which can be undertaken, although the detailed procedures for each can vary. First, we shall examine the possibility of assessing the validity of measured mode shapes by checking their orthogonality through the theoretical mass matrix. The second is a method for refining a measured set of mode shapes, again using the theoretical model mass matrix. The third (which is in effect a sequel to the second) is a method for adjusting the theoretical model stiffness matrix, once a refined set of mode shapes are available. The fourth approach is for a method of locating the regions in the mass and stiffness matrices which harbour the greatest 'errors'. Although in theory these methods could not only locate such errors but also quantify them, the limitations imposed by the inevitable incompleteness of the measured data mean that such an aspiration would be over-ambitious at present.

6.2.2   Orthogonality Requirements

In this process, we extend the basic concept introduced above by performing a calculation with the measured mode shapes and the theoretical mass matrix. If we compute:

$$[\Phi_x]^T \ [M_p] \ [\Phi_x] \ = \ [\delta_x] \qquad\qquad\qquad (6.3)$$

we should obtain a unit matrix if the measured modes are indeed mass-normalised and orthogonal with respect to the mass matrix. In practice, it would be necessary to have ensured the measurement of every coordinate of the system and with a typical finite element model, this may well be quite impractical. It is clear from the simple equation above that if even only a few mode shape elements are omitted, the resulting orthogonality check is invalidated.

It is generally necessary, therefore, to obtain a reduced or condensed mass matrix $[M_p{}^R]$ with which to perform the orthogonality check. The mass matrix must be condensed down to the same coordinate set as has been used in the modal test. Then, we can expect to find values of the diagonal elements of the matrix produced by equation (6.3) in excess of 0.9 together with off-diagonal terms which are smaller than 0.05.

(NOTE: However, it should be noted that this procedure assumes that if we take a condensed mass and stiffness matrix pair and compute their eigenvalues and vectors, we shall find elements in the latter which are identical to those for the corresponding coordinates in the eigenvectors for the complete system model. It is not obvious that this will indeed be the case and so some caution should be used when drawing conclusions from orthogonality checks of this type, especially where a significant condensation or reduction has been carried out on the theoretical model matrices.)

An alternative approach to the question of orthogonality check and one which acknowledges the inevitable restriction on the number of elements available in the measured eigenvector, involves both the theoretical mass matrix and the corresponding stiffness matrix.

The basic equation:

$$([K] \ - \ \omega_r{}^2[M]) \ \{\phi\}_r \ = \ 0$$

is partitioned according to the measured elements (n) and the remainder (s):

$$\left(\begin{bmatrix} K_{nn} & K_{ns} \\ K_{sn} & K_{ss} \end{bmatrix} -\omega_r{}^2 \begin{bmatrix} M_{nn} & M_{ns} \\ M_{sn} & M_{ss} \end{bmatrix} \right) \begin{Bmatrix} \phi_n \\ \phi_s \end{Bmatrix}_r = \ \{0\} \qquad (6.4)$$

from which we have

$$\{\phi_s\}_r \ = \ - \ ([K_{ss}] \ - \ \omega_r{}^2[M_{ss}])^{-1} \ ([K_{sn}] \ - \ \omega_r{}^2[M_{sn}]) \ \{\phi_n\}_r$$
$$\text{sx1} \qquad\qquad \text{sxs} \qquad\qquad \text{sxn} \quad \text{nx1} \quad (6.5)$$

$$= \ [S_r] \ \{\phi_n\}_r$$
$$\text{sxn}$$

so:

$$\{\phi\}_r = \begin{Bmatrix} \phi_n \\ .... \\ \phi_s \end{Bmatrix}_r = \begin{bmatrix} \boxed{} \\ ...... \\ [S_r] \end{bmatrix} \{\phi_n\}_r = [T_r] \quad \{\phi_n\}_r$$
$$\quad Nx1 \qquad\qquad\qquad\qquad\qquad Nxn \quad nx1$$

Thus, the orthogonality check

$$\{\phi\}_r{}^T [M] \{\phi\}_q = \delta_{rq} = 1 \quad \text{if } r = q$$
$$= 0 \quad \text{if } r \neq q$$

becomes

$$\{\phi_n\}_r{}^T \ [T_r]^T \ [M] \ [T_q] \ \{\phi_n\}_r = \delta_{rq} \qquad\qquad (6.6)$$
$$\quad nx1 \qquad nxN \quad NxN \quad Nxn$$

and can be computed from the theoretical mass matrix.

6.2.3 Adjustment of Measured Mode Shapes

When we have made such a check on the measured modal properties, and found them to be less than perfect, the question is raised as to what should be done next. If it is decided that the measured data could be in error (although not responsible for all the discrepancies between experiment and theory), then it is possible to derive an improved set of mode shapes by the following procedure. It is necessary to assume that the adjustment to be made is small and thus that the measured mode shapes are already good estimates to the 'true' values. By this assumption we are justified in using first-order terms (in the differences) only and it has been shown in References [22] and [23] that an optimised set of measured mode shapes is given by:

$$[\Phi_x{}'] = [\Phi_x] \ ([\Phi_x]^T [M_p] [\Phi_x])^{1/2} \qquad\qquad (6.7)$$

where $[\Phi_x]$ represents the measured mode shapes and $[M_p]$ the theoretical mass matrix. In this procedure there are two points to note. First, we have NOT assumed that the predicted mode shapes are the correct ones: we have only assumed that the mass matrix part of the theoretical model is correct and have not assigned any validity to the stiffness matrix. The second point is that this procedure again requires us to have complete data on each mode shape included. It is not strictly essential to include all the modes but it IS essential to incorporate all the elements of those which are included.

6.2.4 Adjustment of Theoretical Stiffness Matrix

As a direct sequel to the previous method, we can now offer a rationale for adjusting the theoretical model stiffness matrix (which, after all, is the more likely one to contain errors). This is done on the basis of using the refined measured mode shapes (see 6.2.3) together with the measured natural frequencies, which will be taken as correct. The theory, which is developed in References [22]–[23], is somewhat involved and derives the only stiffness matrix which, together with the theoretical mass matrix, will yield the measured eigenvalues and (adjusted) measured eigenvectors. Thus we can define the adjusted stiffness matrix $[K_p']$ as:

$$[K_p'] = [M_p] \ [\Phi_x'] \ \lceil \omega_x^2 \ \rfloor \ [\Phi_x']^{-1} \ [M_p]$$

$$+ \ [D] \ [K_p] \ [D]^T \ - \ [K_p] \ [D]^T \ - \ [D] \ [K_p]$$

$$+ \ [K_p]$$

$$([D] = [M_p] \ [\Phi_x'] \ [\Phi_x']^T) \qquad\qquad (6.8a)$$
$$\text{NxN}$$

where $\lceil \omega_x^2 \ \rfloor$ is the diagonal matrix of measured natural frequencies. This complex expression reduces in the case that all the modal data are known to:

$$[K_p'] = [M_p] \ [\Phi_x'] \ \lceil \omega_x^2 \ \rfloor \ [\Phi_x']^T \ [M_p] \qquad\qquad (6.8b)$$

6.2.5 System Error Matrices

This section presents another approach to the problem of correlating measured and predicted vibration data in such a way as to produce an improved dynamic model. Here we shall be seeking ways of identifying regions on a structure (specifically regions within the mass and stiffness matrices) which can be shown to be responsible for the discrepancies observed between the two sets of modal properties. Two versions of the approach will be outlined, one which operates on the flexibility (or 'inverse stiffness') and inverse mass matrices and the other which relates to the stiffness and mass matrices directly.

Before describing the two methods, it should be noted that at a theoretical level it is possible to derive a system's mass and stiffness matrices from knowledge of the natural frequencies and mode shapes using the inverted orthogonality equations:

$$[M] = [\Phi]^{-T} \ [\Phi]^{-1}$$

$$[K] = [\Phi]^{-T} \ \lceil \omega_r^2 \ \rfloor \ [\Phi]^{-1} \qquad\qquad (6.9)$$

However, in practice we shall have less than all the modes in a data set obtained by experiment (m<N) and, further, those modes which are included will only be described at some of the many coordinates actually possessed by the model (n<N). This limitation precludes direct use of equation (6.9) in practical situations.

(a) Inverse Mass and Inverse Stiffness Matrices. The first attempt to circumvent this difficulty is to examine the extent to which the properties contained in equation (6.9) can be used. For example, it is clearly possible to make the calculation:

$$\{\phi\}_r \ \{\phi\}_r{}^T = [A_r] \qquad\qquad (6.10a)$$
$$\text{nx1} \quad \text{1xn} \qquad \text{nxn}$$

although the rank of the nxn 'pseudo inverse mass' matrix thus produced, $[A_r]$, is only 1. Also, it is possible to derive a 'pseudo inverse stiffness' matrix $[B_r]$ by a similar equation:

$$\frac{1}{\omega_r{}^2} \ \{\phi\}_r \ \{\phi\}_r{}^T = [B_r] \qquad\qquad (6.10b)$$
$$\text{nxn}$$

Both of these formulae may be extended to include more than one mode so that an overall matrix for each property is given by:

$$[\Phi] \ [\Phi]^T = [A] \equiv [M]^{-1}$$
$$\text{nxm} \quad \text{mxn} \quad \text{nxn}$$

$$[\Phi] \ \lceil \omega_r{}^2 \rfloor^{-1} \ [\Phi]^T = [B] \equiv [K]^{-1} \qquad\qquad (6.11)$$
$$\text{nxm} \qquad\qquad \text{nxn}$$

noting again that the rank of each is limited by the number of modes included (m) and not by the number of coordinates used (n).

The elements in these two new matrices are not readily interpreted in a physical context but they may be used in a comparative way by performing a similar set of calculations for both the experimental and the theoretical data sets. In the latter case, this involves use of less than the complete set of modal properties which are in fact available, but this is necessary in order to ensure compatibility between the two sets of results prior to combining them. Then we may derive error matrices of the form:

$$[E_A] = [A_x] - [A_p]$$

and

$$[E_B] = [B_x] - [B_p] \qquad\qquad (6.12)$$

These may be displayed graphically as shown in Figure 6.4 to give a pictorial representation of those regions in the respective matrices where there is found to be a source of discrepancy. The idea is that such information as may be deduced in this way will be useful in directing efforts to review and revise the theoretical model (see Reference [24]).

(b) Mass and Stiffness Matrices. The main problem with the above procedure is that the end product (inverse pseudo properties) is particularly difficult to interpret and to apply. It would be much more useful if we were able to derive error matrices for the mass and stiffness properties directly, rather than for their inverses. This is not as easy as might at first appear. Although we have derived nxn inverse mass and

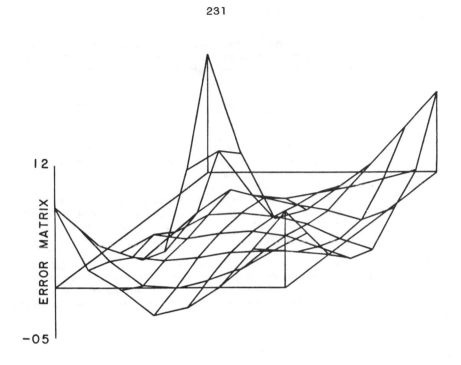

Fig 6.4   Comparison   of   Measured   and   Predicted   Data:
            Pseudo-Flexibility Error Matrix

stiffness matrices (equation (6.11)), we are unable to invert these
because they are singular, a characteristic which derives inevitably from
their inferior rank.   Only if we have used the same number of modes as
there are coordinates can we safely extend the above analysis through the
final step of inversion to produce stiffness and mass matrices from a
modal data set produced by experiment.
An alternative procedure which can be considered for application in cases
where the corrections to be made (usually to the theoretical model) are
relatively small is outlined below.   By defining a stiffness error matrix as:

$$[E_k] = [K_x] - [K_p] \qquad\qquad (6.13)$$

and rearranging, we obtain:

$$[K_x]^{-1} = ([I] + [K_p]^{-1} [E_k])^{-1} [K_p]^{-1} \qquad\qquad (6.14a)$$

This can be expanded in the following series form:

$$[K_x]^{-1} = [K_p]^{-1} - [K_p]^{-1} [E_k] [K_p]^{-1} + ([K_p]^{-1} (E_k))^2 [K_p]^{-1} + \ldots$$

$$(6.14b)$$

In this form the third and higher terms can be neglected under certain conditions which, essentially, are satisfied if the error matrix itself is small. The analysis, given in detail in Reference [25], leads to a final equation:

$$[E_K] \triangleq [K_p{}^R] ([K_p]^{-1} - [K_x]^{-1}) [K_p{}^R] \qquad (6.15)$$
$$\text{nxn} \qquad \text{nxn} \qquad \text{nxn} \qquad \text{nxn} \qquad \text{nxn}$$

where the difference calculation is made on the basis of experimental and predicted pseudo-flexibility matrices, as in the previous technique, but is then converted to stiffness data by using a version of the theoretical stiffness matrix. The matrix which is used here is generally a reduced version of the theoretical stiffness matrix, condensed down to the same coordinate set as is used in the experiments. A similar analysis may be applied to the mass matrix although it is anticipated that most effort will be devoted to the stiffness matrix.

Once again, the results from an error analysis of this type can be presented in graphical form using the same format as before, as shown in Figure 6.5. Here there is an illustration of the identification of a part of the structure where the stiffness properties are particularly poorly defined.

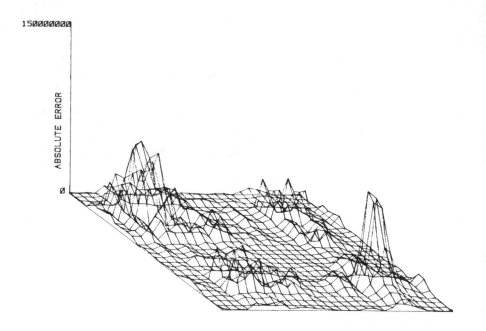

Fig 6.5   Comparison of Measured and Predicted Data: Stiffness Error Matrix

In both the methods outlined in this section we have the advantage that the number of coordinates and modes required is not constrained by the size of the theoretical model. It is generally true that the more complete the description available from the test program, the more likely is the correlation with theory to produce some useful results. However, in these methods we are able to make some progress even with only a small fraction of the total amount of modal data which exists, albeit inaccessible to many test procedures.

6.3   STRUCTURAL MODIFICATION

6.3.1   Basic Method

The preceding sections were all concerned with the task of validating, or obtaining and refining, a mathematical model of a given structure. Once this task is complete, we are in a position to use that model for some further purpose (this is, after all, why it was desired to produce the model in the first place) and the following sections will address a number of applications to which such models may usefully be put.

The first such application we shall consider follows on directly from the process of obtaining and verifying the basic structure's model in that it seeks to predict the effect of making modifications to the structure. These modifications may be imposed by external factors – e.g. design alterations for operational reasons – and in this case it will generally be necessary to determine what changes in dynamic properties will ensue as these might be detrimental, for example by moving closer to a resonance condition than applied before the changes. Another possibility is that it may be required to change the dynamic properties themselves, perhaps to avoid a resonance or to add more damping, and then it is important to know how best to go about modifying the structure so as to bring about the desired changes without at the same time introducing some new unwanted effects. (All too often in the past has a modification been made to move a natural frequency 'by trial and error' only to find that of a different mode moving into prominence at a different frequency.)

In both these cases, a technique which permits the prediction of all the changes in dynamic properties resulting from a given structural modification will be of considerable value. As with many of these application areas, basic concepts such as the one outlined below have been extensively developed and refined and the reader is referred to the specialist literature for discussion of these more advanced aspects. However, we present below the basis of the techniques generally referred to as the 'structural modification method'. We have chosen to present the principles using an undamped system as it is usually the location of the resonance frequencies which is of greatest importance and the inclusion of damping makes little difference in this respect. However, the same approach can be made using the general damped case.

For the general NDOF system, we can write the equations of motion for free vibration in the form:

$$[M] \; \{\ddot{x}\} + [K] \; \{x\} = \{0\}$$
$$\text{NxN}$$

or, using the standard transformation to modal coordinates, as:

$$\lceil \; I \; \rfloor \; \{\ddot{p}\} + \lceil \; \omega_r^2 \; \rfloor \; \{p\} = \{0\} \qquad\qquad (6.16)$$
$$\text{NxN}$$

where

$$\{x\} = [\Phi] \; \{p\}$$

This full set of equations can be reduced in the event that not all the modal data are known to:

$$\lceil \; I \; \rfloor \; \{\ddot{p}\} + \lceil \; \omega_r^2 \; \rfloor \; \{p\} = \{0\}$$
$$\text{mxm}$$

Now suppose that we wish to analyse a modified system, whose differences from the original system are contained in the matrices $[\Delta M]$ and $[\Delta K]$. (Note: it is assumed that the same coordinates are used in both cases: methods for analysing rather more substantial modifications such as adding components will be discussed in the next section.) The equations of motion for the modified system may be written as:

$$[M + \Delta M] \; \{\ddot{x}\} + [K + \Delta K] \; \{x\} = \{0\} \qquad\qquad (6.17a)$$

or, using the original system modal transformation (noting that the eigenvectors and eigenvalues are NOT those of the new system), as:

$$(\lceil \; I \; \rfloor + [\Phi]^T[\Delta M][\Phi]) \; \{\ddot{p}\} + (\lceil \; \omega_r^2 \; \rfloor + [\Phi]^T[\Delta K][\Phi]) \; \{p\} = \{0\} \quad (6.17b)$$

In general, we shall have information about only m ($<$N) modes and these described at only n ($<$N) coordinates. However, using this equation we have established a new equation of motion with a new mass matrix $[M']$ and stiffness matrix $[K']$, both of which can be defined using the modal data available on the original system (such as might be provided by a modal test) together with a description of the changes in mass and stiffness which are to constitute the structural modification:

$$[M'] = \lceil \; I \; \rfloor + [\Phi]^T \; [\Delta M] \; [\Phi]$$
$$\text{mxm} \qquad \text{mxm} \quad \text{mxn} \quad \text{nxn} \quad \text{nxm}$$

$$[K'] = \lceil \; \omega_r^2 \; \rfloor + [\Phi]^T \; [\Delta K] \; [\Phi] \qquad\qquad (6.18)$$

The eigenvalues and eigenvectors of these new mass and stiffness matrices can be determined in the usual way, thereby providing the natural frequencies and mode shapes of the modified structure.

It is worth adding one or two comments concerning the implications of using this technique on real engineering structures. These all stem from the fact that it is much easier to specify changing individual elements in a mass or stiffness matrix than it is to realise such changes in practice. For example, if we wish to add a mass at some point on a structure, it is inevitable that this will change the elements in the mass matrix which relate to the x, y and z directions at the point in question and will also have an effect on the rotational motions since any real mass is likely to have rotatory inertia as well. This means that it is seldom possible or realistic to consider changing elements individually, and also that it may be necessary to include rotational coordinates in the original modal model. This last consideration is seldom made, thanks to the difficulty of measuring rotations, but should be if reliable modification predictions are to be made. Similar comments apply to the stiffness matrix: the attachment of any stiffener, such as a beam or strut, will influence the stiffness in several directions simultaneously, including rotational ones. Lastly, it must be noted that this method, in common with all which rely on a modal data base that may not include all the structure's modes, is vulnerable to errors incurred if the effects of the modes omitted from the modal model are (a) not negligible and (b) ignored. This point will be discussed further in the next section.

6.3.2 Sensitivity Analysis

As suggested above, one of the reasons for using the structural modification method is to bring about a desired change in the structure's dynamic properties, perhaps by moving certain critical natural frequencies. Even on a relatively simple structure, there will be a large number of possible modifications which could be made and it is necessary to determine which of these would be the most effective for the desired change. One way of selecting the parameter(s) to modify is to use a sensitivity analysis based on the modal model of the original structure. Using a form of perturbation theory, valid for small changes, it is possible to determine the rate of change of each natural frequency of the original structure with each of the system parameters. Those with the greatest 'slope' are singled out as the most effective elements for bringing about specific changes and the same information can also be used to assess the secondary effects which will also accrue – i.e. changes in the other natural frequencies – since it is important to avoid removing one problem and introducing a different one.

It should be noted that because of the 'small' differences assumed in the sensitivity analysis, it is not possible to predict accurately the extent of the changes which will result from a specific (non-second order) change in one of the structure's parameters. The analysis will indicate which way the frequencies will change, and will rank them in order of extent of change, but generally will not predict the magnitude of that change reliably.

6.4   COUPLED STRUCTURE ANALYSIS

6.4.1   Rationale of Coupled Structure Analysis

There are many instances in which it is convenient to be able to consider a complex engineering structure as an assembly of simpler components, or substructures.   For example, the theoretical analysis of a large structure can often be made much more efficiently if this is broken down into its component parts, these then analysed separately and the whole assembly reconstituted in terms of the models of each individual component.   The increase in efficiency thus gained derives from the facility of describing a (sub)structure's essential dynamic characteristics very compactly in terms of its modal properties.   Another way of viewing the process, in matrix terms, is to note that the spatial model of a typical large-scale structure would tend to have extensive regions of its mass and stiffness matrices populated by zeros.   In effect, a substructure type of analysis concentrates on submatrices centred on the leading diagonals of the complete system matrices, not involving the remote, null, regions.

One particularly powerful application of the substructure approach is to a range of problems where it is required to combine subsystem or component models derived from different sources – perhaps from quite disparate analyses but often from a mixture of analytical and experimental studies.   Thus we may seek to combine component models from theoretical anlaysis with others from modal tests.

Not surprisingly, there are several different approaches to this concept and it is not appropriate to describe them all in detail here because many have been developed primarily for purely analytical studies, and although these tend to be the more sophisticated and efficient, they are not always immediately applicable to experimentally-derived models.   Thus, we shall select a small number of methods which have the most immediate appeal to the last-mentioned application: that of combining component models where some or all of these have been derived from modal tests.   Within this category there are two main differences of approach, depending on whether the required output for the complete structure model is

    (a)   its response characteristics, or
    (b)   its modal properties.

It is clear from the earlier theoretical sections that either of these results is available from the other (predicted modal properties can be used to calculate response characteristics and vice versa) but it is a question of which are the data of primary interest.   We shall thus describe three methods of analysis which can be used for this application while noting that there are several other variants, many of which are more refined and developed.

In the following illustrative analysis, we shall use two subsystems or components, A and B, which are connected in a prescribed fashion to constitute the assembly, C.   Furthermore, the coordinates used to describe each component and the complete system will be divided into two groups – those at the connection points (x_c) and the others (x_a and x_b).

6.4.2 Impedance Coupling Method

We shall deal first with the method which works in terms of the frequency response properties directly, and which provides as output the frequency response characteristics of the coupled structure.   Having said that, however, it is quite possible that the required FRF data may be obtained from a modal model of the components concerned as that is often the most effective way of storing information on a substructure's dynamic characteristics.

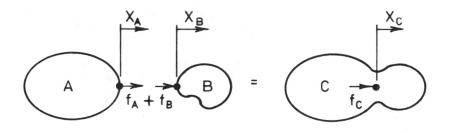

Fig 6.6   *Basic Impedance Coupling Process*

This method is often referred to as the 'impedance coupling method' or the 'stiffness method'.   The basic principle is demonstrated by the simple example shown in Figure 6.6 in which the two components A and B are to be connected by the single coordinate x to form C.   It should   be noted that the number of coordinates used in the coupling process does not restrict the number of degrees of freedom which may be possessed by each component except that this latter number should be at least as great as the former.   Thus, in this case, components A and B may both possess several degrees of freedom each, even though only one coordinate is included for the purpose of coupling the components together.   The implication of the notation and analysis which follows is that the system behaviour is not fully described in the spatial sense. However, those coordinates which are included will exhibit the full range of resonances possessed by the system.

If we consider the dynamics of each component quite independently, we can write the following equation for subsystem A when a harmonic force $f_A e^{i\omega t}$ is applied at the connection coordinate:

$$x_A e^{i\omega t} = \alpha_A(\omega)\ f_A e^{i\omega t}\quad or\quad x_A = \alpha_A\ f_A$$

and similarly for subsystem B:

$$x_B = \alpha_B\ f_B$$

Now, if we consider the two components to be connected to form the coupled system C, and we apply the conditions of compatibility and equilibrium which must exist at the connection point, we find:

$$x_C = x_A = x_B$$

$$f_C = f_A + f_B$$

so

$$\frac{1}{\alpha_C} = \frac{1}{\alpha_A} + \frac{1}{\alpha_B} \qquad or \qquad Z_C = Z_A + Z_B \qquad\qquad (6.19)$$

Thus we obtain the FRF properties of the combined system directly in terms of those of the two components as independent or free subsystems. The equation can be expressed either in terms of the receptance (or mobility) type of FRF, as shown, or rather more conveniently in terms of the inverse version, dynamic stiffness (or impedance). Although it makes little difference in this instance, when we extend the analysis to the more general case where the coupling takes place at several coordinates, and there are also coordinates included which are not involved in the coupling, the impedance formulation is much more straightforward algebraically.

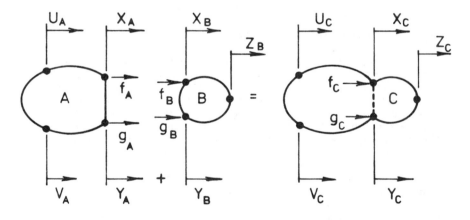

Fig 6.7   *General Impedance Coupling Process*

The above simple analysis can be extended to the more general case illustrated in Figure 6.7. Here it is convenient to note that the receptance FRF properties for component A are contained in a matrix which can be partitioned as shown below, separating those elements which relate to the coupling coordinates (x_c) from those which do not (x_a):

$$[\alpha(\omega)] = \begin{bmatrix} \alpha_A{}^{aa} & \alpha_A{}^{ac} \\ \alpha_A{}^{ca} & \alpha_A{}^{cc} \end{bmatrix}$$

This receptance FRF matrix can be used to determine the corresponding impedance FRF matrix as follows:

$$[Z_A(\omega)] = [\alpha_A(\omega)]^{-1} = \begin{bmatrix} Z_A{}^{aa} & Z_A{}^{ac} \\ Z_A{}^{ca} & Z_A{}^{cc} \end{bmatrix}$$

Similarly, we can write a corresponding impedance FRF matrix for the other component B as:

$$[Z_B(\omega)] = [\alpha_B(\omega)]^{-1} = \begin{bmatrix} Z_B{}^{bb} & Z_B{}^{bc} \\ Z_B{}^{cb} & Z_B{}^{cc} \end{bmatrix}$$

(NOTE: It should be reemphasised here that these FRF properties relate to the components when the connection points, or coordinates, are completely unconnected from any other component or structure, and thus refer to the properties of the component as observed when tested or analysed in isolation.)

By an application of the same equilibrium and compatibility conditions as used before, we can derive an impedance FRF matrix for the coupled structure of the form:

$$[Z_C(\omega)] = [Z_A(\omega)] \oplus [Z_B(\omega)] = \begin{bmatrix} Z_A{}^{aa} & 0 & Z_A{}^{ac} \\ 0 & Z_B{}^{bb} & Z_B{}^{bc} \\ Z_A{}^{ca} & Z_B{}^{cb} & Z_A{}^{cc}+Z_B{}^{cc} \end{bmatrix}$$

(6.20)

Then, it is a simple matter to obtain the (usually-required) receptance-type FRF from:

$$[\alpha_C] = [Z_C]^{-1}$$

This procedure is readily extended to the simultaneous coupling of more than two components, and to cases where several components may be connected at the same coordinates, simply by the correct 'addition' of the component impedance matrices as seen in the above example.

Derivation of the component impedances

There are several ways of providing the FRF data used in this process to analyse coupled structures, including:

(i)   direct computation from mass and stiffness matrices (note that $[Z] = ([K] - \omega^2[M])$);

(ii)   direct analysis of beam-like components for which analytic expressions exist for the required impedance properties;

(iii)   direct measurement of a receptance FRF matrix, and inversion of same;

(iv)   computation of receptance FRF data from a modal model, using the formula:

$$[\alpha] = [\Phi] \lceil (\lambda_r{}^2-\omega^2) \rfloor^{-1} [\Phi]^T$$

(6.21)

In both the third and fourth of these options, it is necessary to invert the receptance FRF matrix originally supplied in order to obtain the impedances necessary for the coupling process and care must be taken to prevent this inversion from becoming ill-conditioned. In the third case, this will be a possibility because of the inevitable small errors contained in the measured data. This can be a particular problem with lightly-damped structures when there is likely to be a 'breakthrough' of component resonances in the coupled structure response characteristics: sometimes there appear spurious spikes on the coupled structure FRF plots in the immediate vicinity of the natural frequencies of one of the separate components. This is less of a problem with less strongly resonant components, such as those with some damping and a relatively high modal density. In this latter case, the direct use of raw measured FRF data may be a more attractive prospect than the alternative of deriving a modal model by curve-fitting what might well be very complex FRF curves.

In the fourth of the above approaches, there is a requirement that the receptance matrix is not rank-deficient so that its inverse does exist. In order for this condition to be satisfied, it is necessary that the number of modes included in the modal model is at least as great as the number of coordinates used to describe that particular component. At the same time, consideration must be given to the possibility that a matrix of residual terms may be required in order to account for the effect of those out-of-range modes not included in the modal model, as discussed in Section 5.3. In many cases, the only way of avoiding the need for obtaining such a residual matrix is by including many more modes in the components' modal models than are contained within the frequency range of interest; e.g. where the final coupled structure properties are required between, say, 40 and 400 Hz, it may be necessary to include all the components' modes in the wider frequency range 0 to 1000 Hz (or even higher).

An example of the application of this method to a practical structure is shown in Figures 6.8 and 6.9. The problem called for a complete system model of the helicopter/carrier/store assembly shown in Figure 6.8a. The essential components or subsystems are illustrated in Figure 6.8b and it was decided to study each by the method felt to be most appropriate in each case: theoretical models for the store and struts plus modal models from modal tests for the airframe (although a model confined to the points of interest on the side of the fuselage) and for the platform. Because of the construction of the system, it was necessary to include several rotation coordinates at the connection points in order to create a truly representative model and where these were required in the experimentally-derived models, the appropriate FRF data were measured using the method described in Section 3.10. An example of a typical measured airframe mobility, together with its regenerated curve based on the SDOF curve-fit method of Section 4.3, is shown in Figure 6.9a. Also, a corresponding result for the platform and store substructure, this time analysed using the lightly-damped structures MDOF modal analysis method of Section 4.6, is shown in Figure 6.9b. One of the set of final results for the complete model, constructed by impedance coupling, is

(a)

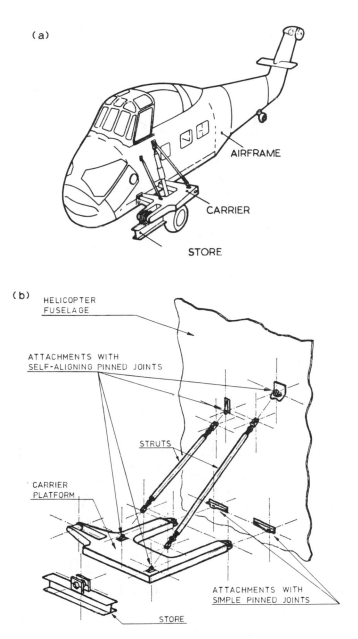

AIRFRAME

CARRIER

STORE

(b)

HELICOPTER
FUSELAGE

ATTACHMENTS WITH
SELF-ALIGNING PINNED JOINTS

STRUTS

CARRIER
PLATFORM

ATTACHMENTS WITH
SIMPLE PINNED JOINTS

STORE

Fig 6.8   Components and Assembly for Coupled Structure Analysis
               (a)   Complete System
               (b)   Components and Connections

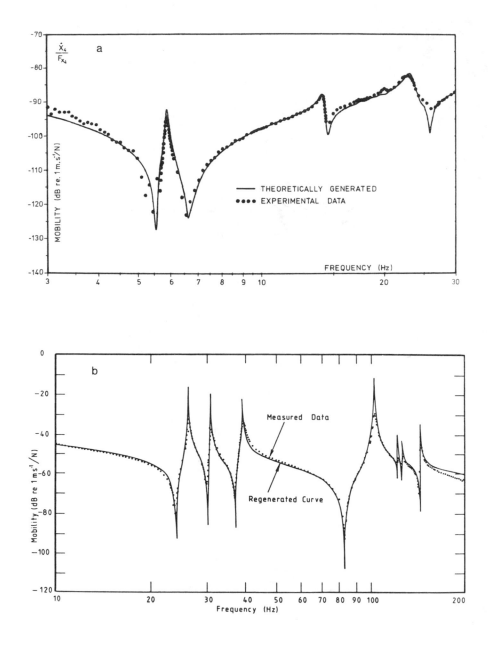

Fig 6.9   *Measured and Regenerated Mobility Data*
(a) Airframe (using SDOF analysis)
(b) Carrier (using MDOF analysis)

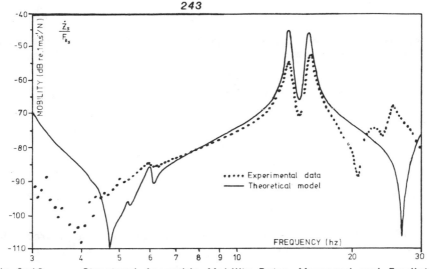

Fig 6.10   *Structural Assembly Mobility Data: Measured and Predicted from Coupled Structure Analysis*

shown in Figure 6.10 together with measurements made on the complete assembled structure – a result not untypical of what can be expected for this type of complex engineering structure, Reference [26].

If it were required to determine the modal properties of the combined assembly, rather than the FRF properties shown here, then it would be necessary to subject these last to some form of modal analysis or to use a different approach to the whole analysis, such as described in the next sections.

One final comment which should be made is to note or to recall that the FRF properties used in this approach must be as accurate as possible. This, in turn, requires that as many of the components' modes as possible should be included in any modal model or data base that is used to regenerate the receptances used in the analysis.   Where it is infeasible to include a near-complete set of modes, then it is necessary to ensure that those excluded are represented by some form of residual terms, as described in Section 4.5, in order to ensure that the regenerated FRF data are accurate away from the component resonances as well as close to them.   The reader is referred back to Section 5.3 for a discussion on the importance of this aspect.

6.4.3 Modal Coupling – Method 1

In the case of a coupled structure analysis in which all the subsystems are described by modal models (so that the necessary impedances are computed from equation (6.21)), it is possible to recast the above impedance coupling equation in a form which leads directly to a solution for the modes of the complete system.   However, it must be observed at the outset that in this formulation it is not easy to accommodate the need for residuals, to account for substructure modes necessarily omitted.

If we return to the basic equation linking the (receptance) FRF properties and the modal model, we can write:

$$[\alpha_A] = [\Phi_A] \; \lceil (\omega_A{}^2-\omega^2) \rfloor^{-1} \; [\Phi_A]^T$$
$$\quad nxn \qquad nxm \qquad\quad mxm \qquad mxn$$

Thus,

$$[\alpha_A]^{-1} = [\Phi_A{}^+]^T \; \lceil (\omega_A{}^2-\omega^2) \rfloor \; [\Phi_A{}^+]$$

where

$$[\Phi_A{}^+] = [\Phi_A]^T \; ([\Phi_A] \, [\Phi_A]^T)^{-1} \qquad\qquad (6.22)$$
$$\quad mxn \qquad\quad mxn \qquad\quad nxn$$

and it is assumed that $n \leqslant m$. Thus we are able to express the impedance matrix in the form

$$[Z_A] = [\alpha_A]^{-1} = ([D_A] - \omega^2 \, [E_A]) \qquad\qquad (6.23)$$

where

$$[D_A] = [\Phi_A{}^+]^T \; \lceil \omega_A{}^2 \rfloor \; [\Phi_A{}^+]$$

and

$$[E_A] = [\Phi_A{}^+]^T \; [\Phi_A]$$

A similar expression may be derived for the second substructure:

$$[Z_B] = ([D_B] - \omega^2 \, [E_B])$$

and when the impedance coupling equation (6.20) is applied, we obtain an expression for the impedance matrix of the complete system which has the form:

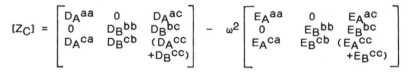

$$[Z_C] = \begin{bmatrix} D_A{}^{aa} & 0 & D_A{}^{ac} \\ 0 & D_B{}^{bb} & D_B{}^{bc} \\ D_A{}^{ca} & D_B{}^{cb} & (D_A{}^{cc}+D_B{}^{cc}) \end{bmatrix} - \omega^2 \begin{bmatrix} E_A{}^{aa} & 0 & E_A{}^{ac} \\ 0 & E_B{}^{bb} & E_B{}^{bc} \\ E_A{}^{ca} & E_B{}^{cb} & (E_A{}^{cc}+E_B{}^{cc}) \end{bmatrix}$$

or

$$[Z_C] = ([D_C] - \omega^2 \, [E_C]) \qquad\qquad (6.24)$$

where $[D_C]$ may be treated as a stiffness matrix and $[E_C]$ as a mass matrix for the coupled system. Although these matrices have limited value as a means of describing the actual distribution of mass and stiffness in the structure, they can be used in a standard eigenvalue type of calculation to determine the natural frequencies and mode shapes of the coupled structure.

It can be seen from the above analysis that the order of the final system model is (a+b+c) which depends on the number of coordinates used to describe the subsystems and not on the number of modes they contain. This feature could present a limitation to the usefulness of the method and it is recommended that a sufficient number of coordinates be included in order to construct a useful model (although not more than the number of modes, as this would violate the basic requirements for nonsingular FRF matrices).

6.4.4 Modal Coupling – Method 2

As mentioned earlier, there are many procedures available for performing the analysis of a coupled structure using the modal properties of the separate components. One of the limitations of the previous method is the constraint imposed on the order of the final system model – being related to the number of coordinates used rather than to the number of modes in each component. In this section we shall present an alternative method which also uses the free or unconstrained modes of the separate components (ie. those which would be obtained by modal tests of individual components or substructures), but which arranges the analysis in such a way that the order of the final system model is dictated by the number of modes included for the various components. The method also differs slightly from the previous cases in that it allows for (indeed, assumes) the existence of a spring and/or dashpot element between each pair of connected subsystems. Thus the basic system is shown in Figure 6.11.

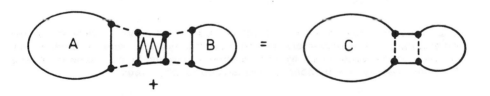

Fig 6.11   Assembled Structure with Connector Component

We shall present the basis of the analysis below, using the same notation as for the earlier methods, but for a more detailed study, with examples, the reader is referred to Reference [27]. The equation of motion for substructure A may be written:

$$[M_A] \{\ddot{x}_A\} + [K_A] \{x_A\} = \{f_A\}$$
$$N_A{\times}N_A$$

where the only forces present are those at the connection points. This equation may be transformed into modal coordinates as:

$$\lceil 1 \rfloor \{\ddot{p}_A\} + \lceil \omega_A^2 \rfloor \{p_A\} = [\Phi_A]^T \{f_A\} \qquad (6.25a)$$
$$m_A{\times}m_A \qquad\qquad m_A{\times}n_A \quad n_A{\times}1$$

where both m_A (the number of modes included) and n_A (the number of connection points) $< N_A$. Similarly, for component B, we can write:

$$\lceil I \rfloor\,\{\ddot{p}_B\} \;+\; \lceil \omega_B^2 \rfloor\,\{p_B\} \;=\; [\Phi_B]^T\,\{f_B\}$$
$$m_B x m_B \qquad\qquad\qquad\qquad m_B x n_B \quad n_B x 1 \qquad\qquad (6.25b)$$

These two equations can be combined to form:

$$\begin{bmatrix} I & 0 \\ 0 & I \end{bmatrix}\begin{Bmatrix} \ddot{p}_A \\ \ddot{p}_B \end{Bmatrix} + \begin{bmatrix} \omega_A^2 & 0 \\ 0 & \omega_B^2 \end{bmatrix}\begin{Bmatrix} p_A \\ p_B \end{Bmatrix} = \begin{bmatrix} \Phi_A^T & 0 \\ 0 & \Phi_B^T \end{bmatrix}\begin{Bmatrix} f_A \\ f_B \end{Bmatrix} \quad (6.26)$$

but through the connection we can also relate the forces and the responses by:

$$\begin{Bmatrix} f_A \\ f_B \end{Bmatrix} = [K_C]\begin{Bmatrix} x_A \\ x_B \end{Bmatrix} \qquad\qquad\qquad (6.27)$$

where $[K_C]$ is the stiffness (and damping, if included) matrix for the connection element and $\{x_A\}$ the geometric coordinates at the connection points. These, in turn, are related to the modal coordinates by:

$$\{x_A\} = [\Phi_A]\,\{p_A\} \qquad\qquad\qquad\qquad (6.28)$$

Thus, if no external forces are applied to the coupled structure, we can derive an equation of motion for the assembly of the form:

$$\lceil I \rfloor\begin{Bmatrix} \ddot{p}_A \\ \ddot{p}_B \end{Bmatrix} + \left(\begin{bmatrix} \Phi_A^T & 0 \\ 0 & \Phi_B^T \end{bmatrix}[K_C]\begin{bmatrix} \Phi_A & 0 \\ 0 & \Phi_B \end{bmatrix} + \begin{bmatrix} \omega_A^2 & 0 \\ 0 & \omega_B^2 \end{bmatrix} \right)\begin{Bmatrix} p_A \\ p_B \end{Bmatrix} = 0 \quad (6.29)$$

This equation may now be solved in the usual way to determine the eigenvalues and eigenvectors of the coupled system, whose number will be seen to be determined by the number of modes in components A and B rather than by the number of spatial coordinates used.

6.5   RESPONSE PREDICTION AND FORCE DETERMINATION

6.5.1   Response Prediction

Another reason for deriving an accurate mathematical model for the dynamics of a structure is to provide the means to predict the response of that structure to more complicated and numerous excitations than can readily be measured directly in laboratory tests. Hence the idea that by performing a set of measurements under relatively simple excitation conditions, and analysing these data appropriately, we can then predict the structure's response to several excitations applied simultaneously.

The basis of this philosophy is itself quite simple and is summarised in the standard equation:

$$\{x\}e^{i\omega t} = [\alpha(\omega)]\,\{f\}e^{i\omega t} \qquad\qquad\qquad (6.30)$$

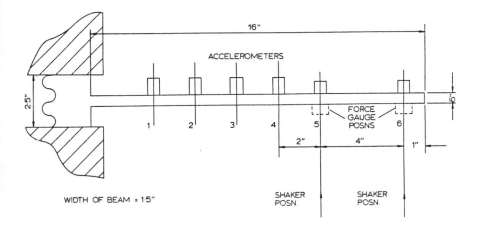

Fig 6.12   Beam Structure Used for Force Determination

where the required elements in the FRF matrix can be derived from the modal model by the familiar formula:

$$[\alpha(\omega)] = [\Phi] \lceil (\lambda_r^2 - \omega^2) \rfloor^{-1} [\Phi]^T$$

A simple example illustrates the concept. Figure 6.12 shows a cantilever beam with six responses of interest and two excitation positions (coinciding with two of the responses). A modal model was formed for the beam referred to the six coordinates shown using standard single-point excitation FRF measurement methods followed by curve-fitting. It was then required to predict the responses at each of the six points to an excitation consisting of two sinusoidal forces applied simultaneously, both having the same frequency but with different magnitudes and phases. Thus the following calculation was performed at each of a number of frequencies in the range of interest (30–2000 Hz):

$$\{x\} \, e^{i\omega t} = [\alpha(\omega)] \, \{f\} \, e^{i\omega t}$$
$$6\times1 \qquad 6\times2 \quad 2\times1$$

The results are compared with actual measurements (made here for the purpose of assessing the validity of the method) and a typical example of these is shown in Figure 6.13, where it can be seen that the predictions are very reliable indeed, even though we are calculating six response quantities from only two excitations.

In general, this prediction method is capable of supplying good results provided sufficient modes are included in the modal model from which the FRF data used are derived.

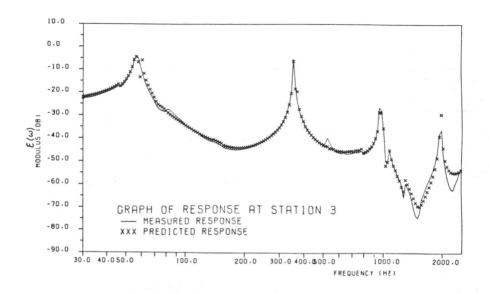

Fig 6.13   Responses Predicted from Measured Forces

6.5.2 Force Determination

Although used less frequently, the inverse calculation procedure to that just described is also a potentially useful application of a modal model. The basic idea of force determination is very close to that of response prediction   except that in this case it is the excitation forces which are predicted or 'determined'.   Here, it is proposed to use n_2 measured responses together with knowledge of the dynamic characteristics of the structure in order to determine what must be the n_1 forces which are causing the observed vibration.

The basic equation is simply the inverse of the previous case and is:

$$\{f\}\ e^{i\omega t} \quad = \quad [\alpha(\omega)]^{-1} \quad \{x\}\ e^{i\omega t}$$
$$n_1 \times 1 \qquad\qquad n_1 \times n_2 \qquad n_2 \times 1 \qquad\qquad\qquad (6.31)$$

However, once again we encounter the difficulty of inverting the rectangular and possibly rank-deficient FRF matrix in order to apply equation (6.31).   To accommodate the former feature, we shall make use of the pseudo−inverse matrix but in order to proceed it is first essential that there be at least as many responses measured as there are forces to be determined ($n_2 \geqslant n_1$).   This is a restriction which does not apply to the response prediction case.   In fact, it transpires that it is advantageous to use several more responses than there are forces to be determined   and   to   use   the   consequent   redundancy   to   obtain   a least−squares optimisation of the determined forces.   Thus we may write our basic equation for finding the excitation forces as:

$$\{f\} = [\alpha(\omega)^+] \{x\}$$
$$n_1 \times 1 \qquad n_1 \times n_2 \quad n_2 \times 1$$

where
$$[\alpha(\omega)^+] = ([\alpha(\omega)]^T [\alpha(\omega)]^T [\alpha(\omega)])^{-1} [\alpha(\omega)]^T \qquad (6.32)$$

(NOTE: when using complex FRF data for damped systems, it is necessary to use the Hermitian transpose in place of the ordinary transpose shown here.)

Once again, we shall use the simple cantilever beam shown in Figure 6.12 as an example, referring first to a series of measured results and then later to a numerical study made to explore the behaviour of what turns out to be a calculation process prone to ill conditioning.

In the first example, the beam is excited simultaneously at two points with sinusoidal forces of the same frequency but differing magnitude and relative phase and we measure these forces and the responses at six points. Using the previously obtained modal model of the beam (see 6.5.1) together with the measured responses in equation (6.32), estimates are made for the two forces and the results are shown in Figure 6.14 alongside the actual measurements of the forces. Close examination of the scales on these plots will show that the prediction of the forces is very poor indeed, especially at lower frequencies; the estimates sometimes being greater than an order of magnitude different from the measured data and of the opposite sign!

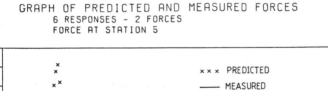

GRAPH OF PREDICTED AND MEASURED FORCES
6 RESPONSES - 2 FORCES
FORCE AT STATION 5

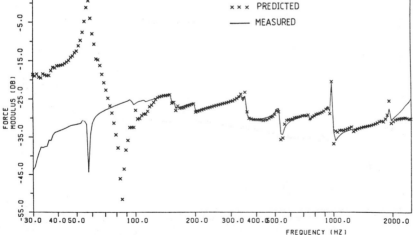

Fig 6.14   Forces Predicted from Measured Acceleration Responses

A numerical study is then undertaken based on the same structure, taking advantage of its simple form to make a closely parallel computer study of the actual experiments. With this model, it is possible to introduce known and controlled discrepancies to simulate experimental errors. Polluting most of the parameters by typically 5% produced only correspondingly small errors in the force predictions with one notable exception: the whole calculation process is found to be extremely sensitive to the accuracy of the mode shape data used in the modal model. Errors of only 5% in individual eigenvector elements result in major discrepancies in the force predictions and of just the same form as those observed in the experiments. A typical result is shown in Figure 6.15 from which the similarity with the results in Figure 6.14 is evident.

It is also observed in the course of this study that if strain gauges were used to measure the response (instead of accelerometers, or displacement transducers), then much better results would be obtained for the force estimates. Figure 6.15 also includes a result using a modal model based on strains instead of displacements but with the same 5% random error in that model's eigenvectors. Returning to the experimental investigation and using strains instead of accelerations, results in the predictions shown in Figure 6.16 which, while not perfect, are a considerable improvement over those derived from acceleration measurements, Figure 6.14. Further details may be found in Reference [28].

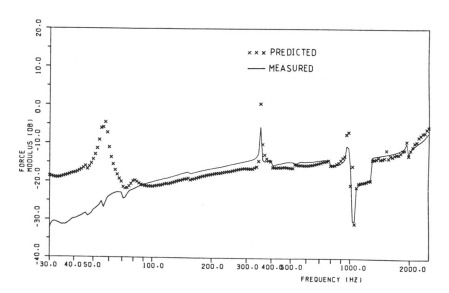

GRAPH OF PREDICTED AND MEASURED FORCES
6 RESPONSES - 2 FORCES
FORCE AT STATION 5

Fig 6.15   Forces Predicted from Measured Strain Responses

Clearly, the determination of forces from response measurements is considerably more difficult an application for a modal model than is the corresponding calculation of responses from given or measured forces.

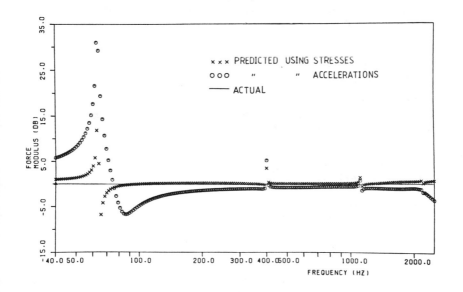

GRAPH OF PREDICTED FORCE AND ACTUAL FORCE
NUMERICAL STUDY - 6 RESPONSES, 2 FORCES
FORCE AT STATION 5

Fig 6.16   Forces Predicted from Given Responses: Numerical Simulation

References

1   KENNEDY, C C and PANCU, C D P
    "Use of Vectors in Vibration Measurement and Analysis"
    J Aero Sci 14(11)   1947

2   BISHOP, R E D and GLADWELL, G M L
    "An Investigation into the Theory of Resonance Testing"
    Proc Roy Soc Phil Trans 255(A)241   1963

3   SALTER, J P
    "Steady State Vibration"
    Kenneth Mason Press   1969

4   ALLEMANG, R J
    "Experimental Modal Analysis Bibliography"
    Proc IMAC2   February 1984

5   MITCHELL, L D and MITCHELL, L D
    "Modal Analysis Bibliography – An Update – 1980–1983"
    Proc IMAC2   February 1984

6   EWINS, D J and GRIFFIN, J
    "A State-of-the-Art Assessment of Mobility Measurement Techniques
    – Results for the Mid-Range Structures"
    J Sound and Vibration 78(2), 197–222   1981

7   COOLEY, J W and TUKEY, J W
    "An Algorithm for the Machine Calculation of Complex Fourier Series"
    Maths of Comput 19(90), 297–301   1965

8   NEWLAND, D E
    "Random Vibrations and Spectral Analysis"
    Longmans Press   1975

9   BENDAT and PIERSOL
    "Random Data: Analysis and Measurement Procedures"
    Wiley-Interscience   1971

10 INTERNATIONAL ORGANISATION FOR STANDARDISATION (ISO)
    "Methods for the Experimental Determination of Mechanical Mobility"
    Part 1   –   Basic definitions
    Part 2   –   Measurements using single-point translation excitation
                   with an attached vibration exciter
    Part 3   –   Measurement of rotational mobility
    Part 4   –   Measurement of the complete mobility matrix using
                   attached exciters
    Part 5   –   Measurements using impact excitation with an exciter
                   which is not attached to the structure

11 WHITE, R G and PINNINGTON, R J
    "Practical Application of the Rapid Frequency Sweep Technique for
    Structural Frequency Response Measurement"
    Journal of Roy Aero Soc   May 1982

12 HALVORSEN, W G and BROWN, D L
    "Impulse Technique for Structural Frequency Response Testing"
    J Sound and Vib, 8-21   November 1977

13 SIMON, M and TOMLINSON, G R
    "Application of the Hilbert Transforms in the Modal Analysis of
    Non-Linear Systems"
    J Sound and Vib, 96(3)   1984

14 GAUKROGER, D R and SKINGLE, C W and HERON, K H
    "Numerical Analysis of Vector Response Loci"
    J Sound and Vib 29(3), 341-353   1973

15 COPLEY, J C
    "Numerical Analysis of Vector Responses"
    Roy Aircraft Est Tech Rept 80135   1980

16 EWINS, D J and GLEESON, P T
    "A Method for Modal Identification of Lightly Damped Structures"
    J Sound and Vibration 84(1), 57-79   1982

17 BROWN, D L, ALLEMANG, R J, ZIMMERMAN, R and MERGEAY, M
    "Parameter Estimation Techniques for Modal Analysis"
    SAE Congress and Exposition, Detroit   1979

18 PAPPA, R S and IBRAHIM, S R
    "A Parametric Study of the Ibrahim Time Domain Modal Identification
    Algorithm"
    Shock and Vib Bull 51(3)   1981

19 GOYDER, H G D
    "Methods and Application of Structural Modelling from Measured
    Structural Frequency Response Data"
    J Sound and Vib 68(2), 209-230   1980

20 VOLD, H, KUNDRAT, J, ROCKLIN, G T and RUSSELL, R
    "A Multi-Input Modal Estimation Algorithm for Mini-Computers"
    SAE Int Congress and Exposition, Detroit   February 1982

21 BERMAN, A and WEI, F S
    "Automated Dynamic Analytical Model Improvement"
    NASA Contract Report 3452   1981

22 TARGOFF, W P
    "Orthogonal Check and Correction of Measured Modes"
    AIAA Journal, Vol 14   February 1976

23   BARUCH, M
     "Proportional Optimal Orthogonalisation of Measured Modes"
     AIAA Journal, Vol 18 No 7   July 1980

24   DOBSON, B J
     "Modification of Finite Element Models Using Experimental Modal
     Analysis"
     Proc IMAC2   February 1984

25   EWINS, D J and SIDHU, J
     "Correlation of Finite Element and Modal Test Studies of a Practical
     Structure"
     Proc IMAC2   February 1984

26   EWINS, D J, SILVA, J M M and MALECI, G
     "Vibration Analysis of a Helicopter with an Externally-Attached Carrier
     Structure"
     Shock & Vibration Bulletin 50, Part 2, pp 155-171   September 1980

27   GHLAIM, K H and MARTIN, K F
     "Reduced Component Modes in a Damped System"
     Proc IMAC2   February 1984

28   HILLARY, B and EWINS, D J
     "The Use of Strain Gauges in Force Determination and Frequency
     Response Function Measurements"
     Proc IMAC2   February 1984

29   ZAVERI, K
     "Modal Analysis of Large Structures - Multiple Exciter Systems"
     Bruel and Kjaer Publication

General Notation

$_rA_{jk}$	modal constant (mode r, FRF jk)
$A(\omega)$	accelerance or inertance
$_rB_{jk}$	residual term FRF approximation near ω_r
$[C]$	viscous damping matrix
$_rD_{jk}$	diameter of modal circle
$[H]$	hysteretic damping matrix
$\lceil I \rfloor$	unit matrix
$[K]$	stiffness matrix
$[M]$	mass matrix
N	number of DOF in MDOF system
$[Y(\omega)]$, $Y_{jk}(\omega)$	mobility FRF matrix, function
$a(t)$, a	acceleration response
b	coefficients
c_{jk}	viscous damping coefficient
c_o	critical damping ratio $(2\sqrt{km})$
d	coefficients
$f(t)$, f	force
h_{jk}	hysteretic damping coefficient
k_{jk}	stiffness coefficient
j, k	coordinates
m_{jk}	mass coefficient
m	number of modes in FRF series
n	number of coordinates included in model
q, r, s	mode number

s	complex variable
$v(t)$, v	velocity response
$x(t)$, x	displacement response
$\alpha_{jk}(\omega)$, $[\alpha(\omega)]$	receptance FRF, matrix
β	constant
$\{\psi\}_r$	eigenvector/mode shape for r^{th} mode
	$(_r\psi_j = j^{th}$ element)
$\{\phi\}_r$	mass-normalised mode shape for r^{th} mode
	$(_r\phi_j = j^{th}$ element)
$[\Psi]$, $[\Phi]$	eigenvector/mode shape matrices
ζ_r	critical viscous damping ratio for mode r $(= c_r/c_{r,o})$
η_r	hysteretic damping loss factor for mode r
ω	frequency of vibration
$\bar{\omega}_r$	undamped system natural frequency
$\omega_r{'}$	damped system 'free' natural frequency $\quad\rbrace$ see Chap
ω_r	damped system 'forced' natural frequency $\quad\rbrace$ 2
Ω_i	specific value of frequency, ω

Appendix 1

USE OF COMPLEX ALGEBRA FOR HARMONIC VIBRATION

If $x(t) = x_0 \cos(\omega t + \phi)$

we can write this as

$$x(t) = \text{Re}(xe^{i\omega t}) \quad \text{or, usually:} \quad x(t) = xe^{i\omega t}$$

where x is a COMPLEX AMPLITUDE (independent of time) containing information on MAGNITUDE and PHASE

$x = x_0 e^{i\phi}$ (where x_0 is REAL and is the magnitude of the sine wave and ϕ is its phase relative to a chosen datum).

Thus $x(t) = \text{Re}(x_0 e^{i(\omega t + \phi)})$

$$= \text{Re}(x_0 \cos(\omega t + \phi) + i x_0 \sin(\omega t + \phi))$$

$$= x_0 \cos(\omega t + \phi)$$

Time derivatives are easy:

$$v(t) = \dot{x}(t) \qquad = \text{Re}(d/dt(xe^{i\omega t}))$$

$$= \text{Re}(i\omega xe^{i\omega t}) \quad = \quad \text{Re}(i\omega x_0 e^{(i\omega t + \phi)})$$

$$= \text{Re}(i\omega x_0 \cos(\omega t + \phi) - \omega x_0 \sin(\omega t + \phi))$$

Thus: $\dot{x}(t) \qquad = -\omega x_0 \sin(\omega t + \phi)$

and, also; $\ddot{x}(t) \qquad = -\omega^2 x_0 \cos(\omega t + \phi)$

Appendix 2

REVIEW OF MATRIX NOTATION AND PROPERTIES

(i) NOTATION AND DEFINITIONS

COLUMN VECTOR

(N rows x 1 column)

$$\{x\}_{Nx1} = \begin{pmatrix} x_1 \\ x_2 \\ . \\ . \\ x_N \end{pmatrix}$$

ROW VECTOR

(1 row x N columns)

$$\{x\}^T_{1xN} = \{x_1 \ x_2 \ . \ . \ . \ x_N\}$$

RECTANGULAR MATRIX

$$[B]_{NxM} = \begin{bmatrix} b_{11} & b_{12} & . & . & . & b_{1M} \\ b_{21} & b_{22} & . & . & . & b_{2M} \\ . \\ . \\ b_{N1} & b_{N2} & . & . & . & b_{NM} \end{bmatrix}$$

SQUARE MATRIX

$$[A]_{NxN} = \begin{bmatrix} a_{11} & a_{12} & . & . & . & a_{1N} \\ a_{21} & a_{22} & . & . & . & a_{2N} \\ . \\ . \\ a_{N1} & a_{N2} & . & . & . & a_{NN} \end{bmatrix}$$

element $a_{ij} = i^{th}$ row, j^{th} column

DIAGONAL MATRIX

$$\lceil \lambda \rfloor_{NxN} = \begin{bmatrix} 1 & 0 & 0 & . & 0 \\ 0 & 2 & 0 & . & 0 \\ . \\ . \\ 0 & 0 & . & . & N \end{bmatrix}$$

TRANSPOSED MATRIX

$$[B]^T_{MxN} \qquad b^T_{ij} = b_{ji}$$

(ii) PROPERTIES OF SQUARE MATRICES

SYMMETRIC MATRIX

$$[A]^T_{NxN} = [A]_{NxN}$$

$$a_{ij} = a_{ji}$$

INVERSE $\qquad$ $[A]^{-1}$ $[A]$ = $\lceil \mathsf{I} \rfloor$

'UNIT MATRIX'

(iii) **MATRIX PRODUCTS**

Matrices must conform for multiplication:

$$[A] \quad [B] \quad = \quad [C]$$
$$NxM \quad MxP \quad \qquad NxP$$

Generally,

$$[A] \quad [B] \quad \neq \quad [B] \quad [A]$$

except for

$$[A]^{-1} \quad [A] \quad = \quad [A] \quad [A]^{-1} \quad = \quad \lceil \mathsf{I} \rfloor$$

SYMMETRY $\qquad$ $[A] \quad [B] \quad = \quad [C]$
$\qquad$ NxN $\quad$ NxN $\qquad$ NxN
$\qquad$ SYMMETRIC $\qquad$ NOT SYMMETRIC

But

$$[B]^{T} \quad [A] \quad [B] \quad = \quad [D]$$
$$\qquad SYMMETRIC \qquad SYMMETRIC$$

Also:

$$([A] [B])^{-1} \quad = \quad [B]^{-1} \quad [A]^{-1}$$

and

$$([A] [B])^{T} \quad = \quad [B]^{T} \quad [A]^{T}$$

(iv) **MATRIX RANK**

The product $\quad \{\phi\} \quad \{\phi\}^{T} \quad = \quad [A]$
$\qquad$ Nx1 $\quad$ 1xN $\qquad$ NxN

$$[A] \quad = \begin{bmatrix} \phi_1^2 & \phi_1\phi_2 & \cdots & \phi_1\phi_N \\ \phi_2\phi_1 & \phi_2^2 & \cdots & \phi_2\phi_N \\ \cdot & & & \\ \cdot & & & \\ \phi_N\phi_1 & \phi_N\phi_2 & \cdots & \phi_N^2 \end{bmatrix}$$

where [A] has ORDER N but RANK 1.

(v) PSEUDO-INVERSE

Given equations

$$\{x\} \quad = \quad [A] \quad \{y\}$$
$$\text{Nx1} \qquad \text{NxN} \quad \text{Nx1}$$

We can solve for $\{y\}$ by:

$$\{y\} \quad = \quad [A]^{-1} \{x\}$$

However, sometimes equations are OVERDEFINED by redundant data. Then, we have

$$\{x\} \quad = \quad [A] \quad \{y\}$$
$$\text{Nx1} \qquad \text{NxM} \quad \text{Mx1}$$

where $N > M$ and we

cannot solve directly (since $[A]^{-1}$ does not exist) so:

$$[A]^T \quad \{x\} \quad = \quad [A]^T \quad [A] \quad \{y\}$$
$$\text{MxN} \quad \text{Nx1} \qquad \text{MxN} \quad \text{NxM} \quad \text{Mx1}$$

from which

$$\{y\} \quad = \quad ([A]^T [A])^{-1} \quad [A]^T \quad \{x\}$$
$$\text{Mx1} \qquad \text{MxM} \qquad \text{MxN} \quad \text{Nx1}$$

or

$$\{y\} \quad = \quad [A]^+ \quad \{x\}$$
$$\text{Mx1} \qquad \text{MxN} \quad \text{Nx1}$$

$[A]^+$ is the PSEUDO-INVERSE of $[A]$ and gives a LEAST-SQUARES solution of the redundant equations

$$[A]^+ \quad = \quad ([A]^T [A])^{-1} \quad [A]^T$$

Appendix 3

FOURIER ANALYSIS

In this appendix we list some of the more important features of Fourier Analysis, as required for most modal testing applications. These will be summarised in three categories:

(i)   Fourier Series
(ii) Fourier Transform
(iii) Discrete Fourier Series (or Transform)

All share the common feature of being the means of describing a time-varying quantity in terms of a set of sinusoids and, conversely, of reconstituting a time history from a set of frequency components.

Only a summary will be included here. For a more detailed treatment, refer to a specialist text such as Bendat and Piersol (Reference 9) or Newland (Reference 8). However, it must be noted that there exist slight differences in definition and terminology which can make cross referencing from one source to the other somewhat confusing!

(i)   FOURIER SERIES

A function $x(t)$ which is periodic in time T can be represented as an infinite series of sinusoids:

$$x(t) = a_0 + \sum_{n=1}^{\infty} (a_n \cos \omega_n t + b_n \sin \omega_n t)$$

where $\omega_n = 2\pi n / T$

in which the coefficients are given by

$$a_0 = \frac{1}{T} \int_0^T x(t) \, dt$$

$$a_n = \frac{2}{T} \int_0^T x(t) \cos \omega_n t \, dt; \qquad b_n = \frac{2}{T} \int_0^T x(t) \sin \omega_n t \, dt$$

Alternative Forms

(a) $$x(t) = c_0 + \sum_{n=1}^{\infty} c_n \cos (\omega_n t + \phi_n)$$

where

$$c_n = \sqrt{a_n^2 + b_n^2} \; ; \quad \phi_n = \tan^{-1} (-b_n / a_n)$$

(b) $\quad x(t) = \sum\limits_{-\infty}^{\infty} X_n e^{i\omega_n t}$

where

$$X_n = \frac{1}{T} \int\limits_{0}^{T} x(t) e^{-i\omega_n t} \, dt$$

NOTE: $X_{-n} = X_n{}^*$; $\quad Re(X_n) = a_n/2$
$\qquad\qquad\qquad\quad\ I_m(X_n) = -b_n/2$
$\qquad\qquad\qquad\quad\ |X_n| = c_n/2$

(ii) FOURIER TRANSFORM

A non-periodic function $x(t)$ which satisfies the condition $\int\limits_{-\infty}^{\infty} |x(t)| \, dt < \infty$ can be represented by the integral:

$$x(t) = \int\limits_{-\infty}^{\infty} (A(\omega) \cos \omega t + B(\omega) \sin \omega t) \, d\omega$$

where

$$A(\omega) = \frac{1}{\pi} \int\limits_{-\infty}^{\infty} x(t) \cos \omega t \, dt; \qquad B(\omega) = \frac{1}{\pi} \int\limits_{-\infty}^{\infty} x(t) \sin \omega t \, dt$$

Alternative Form

The alternative complex form is more convenient, and familiar as:

$$x(t) = \int\limits_{-\infty}^{\infty} X(\omega) e^{i\omega t} \, d\omega$$

where

$$X(\omega) = \frac{1}{2\pi} \int\limits_{-\infty}^{\infty} x(t) e^{-i\omega t} \, dt$$

NOTES

$\quad Re(X(\omega)) = A(\omega)/2$
$\quad Im(X(\omega)) = B(\omega)/2$

also

$\quad X(-\omega) = X^*(\omega)$

(iii) DISCRETE FOURIER SERIES/TRANSFORM (DFT)

A function which is defined ONLY at N discrete points (at $t = t_k$, $k = 1, N$) can be represented by a FINITE series:

$$x(t_k) \; (= x_k) = a_0 + \sum_{n=1}^{\frac{N}{2} \; \text{or} \; \frac{(N-1)}{2}} \left(a_n \cos 2\pi nk/N + b_n \sin 2\pi nk/N \right)$$

where

$$a_0 = \frac{1}{N} \sum_{k=1}^{N} x_k; \quad a_n = \frac{1}{N} \sum_{k=1}^{N} x_k \cos \frac{2\pi nk}{N}; \quad b_n = \frac{1}{N} \sum_{k=1}^{N} x_k \sin \frac{2\pi nk}{N}$$

Alternative Form

$$x(t_k) \; (= x_k) = \sum_{n=0}^{N-1} X_n e^{2\pi ink/N}$$

where

$$X_n = \frac{1}{N} \sum_{k=1}^{N} x_k e^{-2\pi ink/N} \qquad\qquad n = 1, \; N$$

NOTE

$$X_{N-r} = X_r{}^*$$

NOTES ON THE DISCRETE FOURIER TRANSFORM

(a)   This is the form of Fourier Analysis most commonly used on digital spectrum analysers.

(b)   The DFT necessarily assumes that the funtion $x(t)$ is periodic.

(c)   The DFT representation is only valid for the specific values x_k ($x(t)$ at $t = t_k$) used in the discretised description of $x(t)$.

(d)   It is important to realise that in the DFT, there are just a discrete number of items of data in either form: there are just N values x_k and, correspondingly, the Fourier Series is described by just N values.

Example   let N = 10

In the time domain, we have $x_1, x_2, \ldots x_{10}$

In the frequency domain, we have $a_0, a_1, a_2, a_3, a_4, a_5, b_1, b_2, b_3, b_4$

OR

X_0(=Real), $Re(X_1)$, $Im(X_1)$, $RE(X_2)$, $I_m(X_2)$

$Re(X_3)$, $Im(X_3)$, $Re(X_4)$, $Im(X_4)$, X_5(=Real)

(NOTE X_5 = Real because X_{10-5} $(=X_5)$ = $X_5{}^*$).

Index